FALSE FRONT

Chicago Studies in American Politics

A series edited by Susan Herbst, Lawrence R. Jacobs, Adam J. Berinsky, and Frances Lee; Benjamin I. Page, editor emeritus

Kenneth Lowande

FALSE FRONT

The Failed Promise of Presidential
Power in a Polarized Age

The University of Chicago Press · Chicago and London

The University of Chicago Press, Chicago 60637
The University of Chicago Press, Ltd., London
© 2024 by The University of Chicago

Published 2024

33 32 31 30 29 28 27 26 25 24   1 2 3 4 5

ISBN-13:978- 0-226-83723-9 (cloth)
ISBN-13:978- 0-226-83725-3 (paper)
ISBN-13:978- 0-226-83724-6 (e-book)
DOI: https://doi.org/10.7208/chicago/
9780226837246.001.0001

Library of Congress Cataloging-in-Publication Data

Names: Lowande, Kenneth, author.
Title: False front : the failed promise of presidential
    power in a polarized age / Kenneth Lowande.
Other titles: Chicago studies in American politics.
Description: Chicago : The University of Chicago
    Press, 2024. | Series: Chicago studies in American
    politics | Includes bibliographical references and
    index.
Identifiers: LCCN 2024011758 | ISBN 9780226837239
    (cloth) | ISBN 9780226837253 (paperback) |
    ISBN 9780226837246 (ebook)
Subjects: LCSH: Executive power—United States. |
    Presidents—United States. | United States—
    Politics and government—21st century.
Classification: LCC JK516 .L885 2024 |
    DDC 352.23/50973—dc23/eng/20240402
LC record available at https://lccn.loc.gov/
    2024011758

For Claire

CONTENTS

1: PRESIDENTIAL POWER IN A POLARIZED AGE

When presidents sign orders, they put on a show. They invite cameras to ceremonies and issue press releases. They pose for photos with activists, politicians, and special interests. Today, these "executive actions" are normal in the United States and most of the rest of the world. Import taxes, the legal status of nearly one million immigrants, the public funding of abortion, carbon emissions, bailouts for farmers, border-wall construction, and other life-altering policies all seem to be at the whims of the president. That fact is missing from what we teach kids about democracy. You will not find the appropriate scope of executive actions in the text of the Constitution, and remarkably little about how they happen enumerated by any law. So what explains these actions, and what do they tell us about the American presidency, or American democracy, in general?

This book is my answer. Start with two facts. First, despite relentless fighting among the major political parties in the United States, executive action is increasingly embraced by both. Democrats and Republicans alike—politicians, pundits, and voters—all tend to think presidents should act alone if Congress is in the way or not doing its job (whatever that means). For people who want to be president, this is the literal promise of their oath of office: to change policy to the extent of their ability—not to the extent of their power.[1]

It is no surprise, then, scholars are interested in this "unilateral" presidential power. They have counted it, said it is more important than ever, and jumped to explain it. Next to the rise of political polarization and the decrease in Congress's productivity, their explanations confirm current folk wisdom: Congress is broken, so the president steps in to get things done. This is the first fact. It is well-known: executive action is on the rise, and it is more important than ever.

The second fact is less well-known. After some of these actions, *almost nothing happens*. No policies change. No status quo is challenged. Commissions are formed, nonbinding and inconsequential reports issued. Bureaucrats make minor changes to what they had planned to do, but even those might be superficial or symbolic. In stunning contrast to the flurry of news coverage and the Oval Office photo op, the government (and everyone else) goes on doing what they were doing before the order—leaving whatever problem the order was supposed to solve unaddressed.

Our politics hides this fact, but it is obvious once you start looking. President Barack Obama, for example, signed an order to fund research on gun violence. Almost no research was funded.[2] He also signed orders to close the prison at Guantanamo Bay. Before the ink was dry, most of the prisoners held there had already been transferred or released, and over a decade later it is still open. President Donald Trump signed an order to release military equipment to police departments around the country. Almost none of it was given out. President George H. W. Bush signed an order protecting giant sequoias. Logging continued. Examples are everywhere. I brought these up because presidents are supposed to have authority over grants, terrorism, military hardware, and public land. They are exactly the kind of case that fit the stories we tell about presidents and their power to act alone. They should have been wins—and they were, only of a different kind. The moment they were signed, they were *political* wins, even if the *policy* win they proposed never materialized.

What made them *policy* losses, then? If you asked people who study this, they would tell you a few stories. Perhaps these actions failed because they required Congress to fund them. Maybe a judge stepped in to overturn them. Most frequently overlooked is that presidents have to get bureaucrats to cooperate, a massive task that vexes the best managers. All of this can stop real change in its tracks. Each of these obstructions is the conventional wisdom saying failure is an error or an exception—not the rule.

This book argues something different, based on a fundamental, frequently overlooked idea. Often, no change happens because the action itself had symbolic, political value. It was packaged and enacted to be symbolically effective, not substantive. The president did not order anyone to do anything. He asked for advice, set out broad goals, created unfunded suggestions, or implied that he would like something done, without the real authority to do it. Or he guaranteed his order would be challenged, watered down, or moderated. But, beyond any failure to change the way government operated, there was a different kind of success. The president made his position clear. He showed some special interest or voting bloc that he cared. Or, in his own mind, he made history—the president who went first, who set the stage, who laid the groundwork for a sea change yet unknown.

Presidents go it alone more than ever, and their action is apparently indispensable. Despite that, many of their actions fail, are totally empty, or are otherwise ineffectual. This book is about how both those things can be true.

I show evidence both that executive action is prominent in modern politics and that it often has little substance behind it. More important, I show it is no accident. Presidents' incentives and strategies led us here. Presidents are not fakes or hucksters who set out to fool the American public for fun. They are politicians who respond to incentives. These have led to a new era of presidential politics, one in which the office is increasingly designed to help its occupant *appear* to govern. Executive action is the critical work product.

Presidents take action—even when it does nothing to affect policy—because our political system is not designed to let presidents solve major policy problems. But it lays these problems at their doorstep. There is no elected official on Earth better equipped to attract attention by appearing to govern. For the purposes of their relationship with a public focused elsewhere, and with interest groups concerned with their continued survival, appearances are often enough.

Unilateral action helps presidents take credit. It gives the impression of action but carries little risk of blame if the results are less than advertised. That is because the public does not hold them responsible for those results. The public does not pay attention to most policy change or retain information about who was responsible for the change. This is not their fault. Both news organizations and even the opposition party give presidents credit for actions—even those that do nothing. Finding out whether an action was impactful is hard. It is difficult for everyone, even experts, to know whether a symbolic win is a real, policy win. I do not know most of the time, and I am writing a book about it.

This is why presidential power is a *false front*. The power to credit-claim, to get attention by acting alone, is the best way to understand what the office of the presidency gives the politician who holds it. Presidents are still policymakers who push the boundaries of their power and build institutions that help them do it. But sometimes they create what amounts to a facade, one that suits their political goals. Those goals are served by appearing to do something, by placating favored interests, and by generally playing into modern Americans' expectations that a president can and should solve huge problems in American life.

If you care about having a well-functioning democracy, it is important to know that presidents spend a lot of time creating the impression of policy impact. If you share a few basic values—such as "politicians should spend time on substance, not showmanship," and "it is better to live in a democracy than an autocracy"—false-front actions are damaging. Presidents have limited time and resources. Because of their incentives, they spend their energy on things that may have little impact. And the trade-off is often zero-sum. Their efforts are wasted because potential accomplishments are left on the table. In other words, they miss out on net improvements in areas where they do have the authority and opportunity to act. Most often, these are tasks that are complicated, boring, and difficult to turn into a public-relations win.

But there are worse nightmares than underperformance. Presidents' actions have a more long-term and corrosive effect on democracy. By over-promising and failing to deliver, presidents serve short-term goals while further undermining public trust in government, and reinforcing norms of governing common in present-day China, Russia, or Venezuela. Playing a dictator for short-term political gain has consequences.

Watchers of American politics have always worried about what presidents do alone. The antifederalists, today's opposition-party politicians, states'-righters, and some political conservatives, all lament the rise of executive power generally and see the concentration of power in the president as problematic. The argument in this book implies that we should also be concerned with what presidents have *not* done, how they have failed on their own lofty terms, and what this might enable their predecessors to do in the future.

Claims like these should not be taken seriously unless accompanied by logical arguments and credible evidence. Most of this book is dedicated to that: laying out an argument, then documenting presidents' political environment and how they behave. Though the argument itself is agnostic about whether this is a good way for presidents to spend their time, it is impossible to ignore its normative implications. I take them up at the end of the book.

Not everyone will buy this argument. But if nothing else, it will draw attention to something in American politics that is hiding in plain sight: presidents are both symbolic and substantive policymakers. Their symbolic behavior is largely ignored or thought of as unimportant. But the symbolic demands our attention, because it is key to understanding presidential power and the democracy it is supposed to serve.

1.1 Easy as Shouting

Ju Hong had an idea of what he was going to do when the president came out. Shortly after college at Berkeley, the twenty-four-year-old immigrant from South Korea started attending protests. He had already been arrested twice—once for sitting in an intersection near San Bernardino Valley College, the other time earlier that year for jumping a barrier to stop Janet Napolitano from becoming head of the University of California. The day of the president's speech, he could see Napolitano in the audience. She was now two months into a term that would last almost seven years.

Hong and Napolitano had similar reasons for being there. Hong was part of an emerging community of young immigrants in California opposed to federal immigration policy. The White House had invited him to hear President Obama speak, and when one of the event organizers offered him a spot on the rafters behind the president himself, he took it.

While Hong was new to politics, Napolitano was reaching her peak. Once the attorney general and then governor of Arizona, politicos talked about her as a potential candidate for president. But after the Obama administration sought out her border-state expertise and nominated her to head the Department of Homeland Security, the prospect dimmed. Managing the huge, multimission department—more than five times the size of Arizona's state government—led Napolitano into inevitable controversy.

It came from both sides. A department report offended veterans when it suggested they would be attracted to right-wing extremist groups. Male employees of the department passed over for promotions sued her, alleging sex discrimination. But the harshest criticism came over immigration. During her time in office, deportations hit record figures. The department would remove over 600,000 people in her last year. Activists like Hong called the president the "deporter in chief," and it was all those raids and deportations that helped fill the room during the University of California Regents vote. Five years in, when the UC system needed a new boss, she left national politics and returned west.

For the president, the trip west was briefer and more ceremonial. He emerged to raucous applause and was flanked by the state flag of California and the Stars and Stripes. He shook hands with the front row of a standing audience. He wore no jacket, and his shirt sleeves were rolled up. He was there to work, or at least to talk about it. This was the first year of his second term as president. There would be no more elections with his name on the ballot. In the fifth year of his presidency, he still had a lot of unfinished business.

He put that business front and center when he started speaking. He thanked local officials—including Napolitano—and then announced a win in progress. After long negotiations, a deal had been reached to stop Iran from getting a nuclear weapon: "Key parts of the program will be rolled back. International inspectors will have unprecedented access to Iran's nuclear-related facilities. [. . .] And over the coming months, we're going to continue our diplomacy." Republicans in Congress would vote overwhelmingly against the deal but fail to stop it, months after also voting to make stopping the deal require a supermajority. The next president, a Republican, would walk away two years into the agreement, which would last less time than it took to negotiate.

This was the kind of combat the president could expect as he negotiated the more vexing issue, decades in the making—his main reason for speaking that day. Business interests, law enforcement, populists, and human rights advocates all called the immigration system broken. The Senate had passed a bipartisan package, but it appeared to be dead or dying in the House. Reform may have been a national good, but for these members, the opposition of their smaller, vocal voting base was their primary concern. This was not lost on Obama: "Look, let's be honest, some folks automatically think, well, if Obama's for it, then I've got to be against it."

So, when he spoke, he painted a picture of America's past and present, reminding his audience that ours was a nation with millions of immigration stories, that this was not just a story of the U.S.-Mexico border. This was the theme for the day, and everyone was part of it. He was the first president to speak in Chinatown. The gym set up for this purpose was at the Betty Ann Ong center, named for the American woman of Chinese descent who first notified authorities a plane had been hijacked on September 11, 2001. Hong had been invited because he highlighted Asian Americans, whom the immigration system had deeply impacted. He stood on the rafters with dozens of others, all with different ancestry, an American flag from floor to ceiling hanging behind, as President Obama told stories of Asian immigrants and their journeys to America. It was the week of Thanksgiving.

For all the careful symbolism of the day, the place, and the people there, it was not enough for Hong. He had good reasons. His mother had brought him to the United States when he was eleven years old, and remained here for decades unlawfully. His sister was still here unlawfully. Earlier that month, Hong's grandmother died without seeing his mother since their move to the United States from Korea. The opportunity to confront the president fed his convictions, and he spent the speech working up the nerve to do something. Finally, the president's speechwriter unwittingly gave him a last push: "We're going to make our country more secure; we'll strengthen our families. . . ."

Hong started shouting. At the mention of family, he cupped his hands around his mouth and shouted, "I need help! Mr. Obama! My family has been separated for 19 months now! I've not seen my family. Our families are separated. I need your help. . . ." Obama continued speaking, until the crosstalk and heckling from the rest of the audience threw him off the prompter. He waved off the security detail preparing to remove Hong and listened.

"Mr. President, please use your executive order to halt deportations for all 11.5 million undocumented immigrations in this country right now. We need to pass comprehensive immigration reform at the same time . . . you have a power to stop deportation for all undocumented immigrants in this country." But on hearing this claim, the president interrupted: "Actually, I don't. And that's why we're here."

The president had given him reason to think otherwise. Midway through the president's reelection campaign, the administration announced its

Deferred Action for Childhood Arrivals (DACA) program. Once a rare designation that prevented deportation on a case-by-case basis, it became a national program covering almost a million immigrants. They were called "dreamers"—students without criminal records, brought to the United States as children. Check those boxes, pay a fee, and the protected status could be theirs.

Hong and Napolitano knew this well. DACA had shielded Hong himself from deportation and allowed him to visit his ailing grandmother before her death. Napolitano built the program before leaving government. But Hong wanted more. One million is not eleven million, and like Hong, those one million had family members—parents, grandparents, siblings—who could also be deported. Legal counsel said the administration could likely go no further, and this is what the president explained.

"We're also a nation of laws. That's part of our tradition. And so the easy way out is to try to yell and pretend like I can do something by violating our laws. And what I'm proposing is the harder path, which is to use our democratic processes to achieve the same goal that you want to achieve. But it won't be as easy as just shouting."

Almost a year later to the day, the president did what Hong was shouting for, what legal counsel had said he could not. His administration announced a program for parents of lawful residents that would shield another 3.7 million people from deportation. It failed after conservative attorneys general sued. The immigration system would see no significant legislative reform for the rest of the president's term. The gaping problems would be picked up by Donald Trump, who would use immigration as the central issue of his presidential campaign.

Hong, Obama, and Napolitano pushed the limits of what they could do under the circumstances, with no guarantee of breakthrough. Hong was called a "heckler" by the national newswire, but he manifested the demands of activists, the kind with the energy that put Obama in the White House, who expected the president to fix a problem that had frustrated Congress for decades. Time only made the problem worse. Deportations hit record levels under Napolitano because illegal immigration skyrocketed—not because of some intentional crackdown. Obama invented a new means-tested program that benefited hundreds of thousands and would survive legal challenge, but it could never touch the core problems. He needed help from Congress.

There were glimmers of that he might get it, but they did not turn into votes. Representative John Boehner, the House Speaker, stood in front of cameras and said, "We are ready to be led," the day after the president's reelection, as pundits credited Obama's support among Latino voters for that reelection. But Boehner would not allow a bill from the Senate to get to the

House floor. It would mean too many hard votes for members of his caucus and an apparent win for the president. Defeat of the bill was the safer bet. It kept the contrast between Republicans and Democrats clear for voters.

The unresolved issue aside, Hong, Obama, and Napolitano would each do fine. After the speech, Hong was interviewed by national news outlets and celebrated in South Korea. Local news outlets profiled him the following year when the president acted, falsely attributing the new program to his outburst. Napolitano had a successful career as president of the University of California, which included removing barriers for students with DACA status. Approval of the president was evenly divided at the time of the speech, but Obama left office with polls better than those of both his predecessor and his successor. He did his best with what he had been given, and he was more popular than ever.

1.2 Unilateral Action in a Polarized Age

It is not often that a constituent literally shouts from the rafters, asking the president to sign an executive order. But there is no better allegory for the situation recent presidents find themselves in. Polarization, along with parallel developments in Congress and the legal profession, have helped redefine their office. That office demands action, for presidents to leverage what is in their immediate reach. Their action has become a promise, a potential answer to the seemingly intractable problems America has governing itself.

Throughout this book, I call this action "unilateral" or "executive" action. All it means is that the president directs subordinates to carry out some new policy within the executive branch. I will go into more detail in a later chapter. But for now, it is most important to distinguish executive action from other things presidents do. It is not giving speeches or attending events. It is not purely rhetorical. Obama speaking in Chinatown was not in itself executive action. Executive action is also not wholly lobbying about or taking a position on what goes on in Congress—although, as I argue later, it can serve a similar purpose. Presidents send all kinds of written and verbal messages to members of Congress about pending legislation.

Executive action is distinct because it does not require the action of other branches of government to make new policy. This was certainly the case for DACA—and for the administration's attempt at an expansion, known as Deferred Action for Parents of Americans (DAPA). If the Obama administration had been left alone to do its work, unimpeded by lawsuits or oversight, a new policy would be in place today—no Congress needed, no judicial go-ahead. In this way, executive action is the president acting alone.

But presidents never really act alone. Even when endowed with legal authority and resources, their orders are just that—orders—and orders are only as good as the people who carry them out. President Clinton once compared his people to corpses in a cemetery.[3] It frustrates many presidents. Obama could order Napolitano to sign the DACA memo, but the details determined whether it actually worked. He had to do things like pick standards, create an application, train people to review it, and organize processing centers. He had to ensure that the people they wanted to have DACA status would get it, and to make it easy enough that many would apply. He had to find a way to pay for it. This is another important theme of the book. Executive action—the real, substantive kind that makes a difference—is *hard*. It requires effort and coordination, it ties up time and energy while introducing a slew of agency problems, and it can expose presidents to legal entanglements and political attacks. So it is worth asking why anyone would find this route politically appealing. The answer helps illustrate how executive action fits into a popular narrative about American government.

Polarization can make even the most frustrating road seem tenable. This term has become a catchall for the ills of politics. When I say "polarization," I am referring to stark differences between the two major parties on policy issues, or what political scientists often call "elite polarization." But polarization in our era is more than that, because it comes during a period in American history when the two major parties are roughly equal in national strength. They both have a decent shot at winning the presidency and taking control of one or more chambers of Congress. Frances E. Lee (2016) argues that this generates incentives for partisan team play. Now major policy reforms in Congress are more difficult to come by, while the norm is to use the institution as a platform for messaging and political combat.

None of these phenomena are new. With 250 years of history, hardly anything in American government is. But the present is different from the situation other presidents have faced. When Richard Nixon took office in 1969, Democrats in Congress could work with him knowing Republicans had not come close to controlling Capitol Hill in decades. The year before, Republicans could do the same knowing that whatever minor legislative wins they achieved alongside President Lyndon Johnson would not jeopardize their prospects for party control. The days of a president like Johnson presiding over supermajorities in both chambers are dead and gone. It prompts the question: how, then, will the federal government address persistent problems like immigration, gun violence, or climate change?

Executive action has been an answer. It is not a new tool. There are examples from almost every president since Washington. But today it is different. It is normal—even professionalized. In the last several decades, for example, a group of legal scholars have advanced the theory of the unitary executive. Proponents of this theory make up legal justifications for presidents controlling the executive branch and placing it above the other two branches. They provide an academic backdrop for the idea that, as the one popularly elected, national office, the president ought to be unimpeded as head of the executive branch. They say this will make government more effective, responsive, and transparent.

The theory is controversial, but it is received wisdom that we now live in an era in which presidents are less impeded in their control of the executive branch, relative to past periods in American history. One often-cited law-review piece declares, "We live today in an era of presidential administration." The author goes on: "Faced for most of his time in office with a hostile Congress but eager to show progress on domestic issues, Clinton and his White House staff turned to the bureaucracy to achieve, to the extent it could, the full panoply of his domestic policy goals." Later, the author writes: "I argue that a statutory delegation to an executive agency official [. . .] usually should be read as allowing the President to assert directive authority, as Clinton did, over the exercise of the delegated discretion." A hostile political situation induces presidents to make policy on their own, and Congress empowers the president to do exactly that when it writes laws. Normally it is tempting to discount what law professors write for law reviews edited by law students. But the person who wrote these words is Elena Kagan, who worked in the White House and now has a job for life on the Supreme Court (Kagan 2001, 2246, 2248, and 2251).

The judiciary is not the only place these ideas live. Lawyers are everywhere in government. In addition to writing a good deal of the actual legalese that makes up official marching orders to bureaucrats, they advise everyone from food inspectors to AC-130 gunners. They are also overrepresented in Congress and at almost every other level of government (Bonica 2020; Bonica and Sen 2021). This does not mean that all (or even most) lawyers subscribe to unitary executive theory, or that there is agreement on what it means. The point is that the legal profession fosters the ideas, training, and work practices for pushing the boundaries. It exists alongside the precedents presidents have set and the contemporary problems of Congress. Unilateral action turns political questions into legal ones, to be argued and invoiced about by lawyers.

Presidential candidates and their advisors know the narrative appeal of unilateral action. They build it into campaign promises. Vote for Donald Trump and he will make murdering a police officer a capital offense, ban Muslims from entering the United States, and make it easier to sue people who defame the famous. Vote for Hillary Clinton and she will end a tax loophole for hedge-fund managers. Vote for Elizabeth Warren and she will stop Arctic drilling and forgive all student debt. Vote for Newt Gingrich and he will stop foreign aid from funding abortions. Vote for Barack Obama and he will close the prison at Guantanamo Bay. All of them will do these things on January 20—"day 1."

Promises like these are almost mandatory now, but they go back at least sixty years. It was then-Senator John F. Kennedy who said that "many things can be done by a stroke of the Presidential pen," then promised his would address civil rights and raise tariffs on wheat.[4] Jimmy Carter promised to pardon those who evaded the Vietnam draft. Politicians are good at what they do because they sense political demands when they exist. They do not need a constituent to shout. Even President Obama knew this, since years earlier he did something similar to what Ju Hong asked for. In recent political history, unilateral action, and the narrative it constructs, tap that demand.

Journalists also pick up on this narrative and the template it provides. There is a whole chapter in this book dedicated to how they help reinforce the narrative and inform recent presidents' incentives. Since the presidency of Barack Obama, national news outlets have carefully tracked executive action by presidents. The *Washington Post* dedicated a web page and a podcast to the actions Trump took to "undo" Obama's legacy.[5] In advance of his transition to power, numerous articles speculated about the avalanche of executive orders President Joe Biden would sign.[6] In these and other examples, a similar story is told: Congress has been stuck on an issue, and the president is now stepping in.

Executive actions now fill lists of presidential accomplishments. Data journalists make companion graphics that allow the reader to take stock of the current president relative to his predecessors. Regardless of the meaning of such figures, it is obvious executive action is one of only a handful of countable diagnostics for a presidency in progress. It is easy news and valuable source material. In 2007 Charlie Savage won the Pulitzer Prize for writing about the unilateral actions of President George W. Bush. It did not matter that the titular assertion of his work—that Bush had "changed hundreds of laws"—was mostly false.[7]

Presidents go it alone, and they might as well, since Congress is so polarized and dysfunctional these days. This is the prevailing narrative, and the public, candidates, presidents, their administrators, and the news media contribute to and mutually reinforce it. On its face, what could be more boring than a president signing a memo that asks a bureaucrat to do something? But not so—not anymore. Unilateral action in our polarized age is an essential story about how government works.

Of course, the stories about unilateral action are just that: narratives, collections of loved facts with characters and a plot. Whether such narratives *explain* anything is an entirely different question. It could be that cases like DACA are exceptionally rare, or that the sequence of events implied by the narrative is wrong. Sorting these possibilities out is not the job of constituents, journalists, or politicians. It is usually the work of scholars, and of those who study political institutions in particular. In that sense, this book is very late to the party. Not counting related disciplines such as law or economics, political science offers hundreds of books and articles about executive action. These have a lot to teach readers. But the questions they leave unanswered are what motivate this book.

1.3 Unilateral Action and the Separation of Powers

Why did DACA, or any other executive action, happen? We can answer that by abstracting away from most stories. The rules and institutions of American government tell us why we saw the outcome we did and what would have occurred if the rules had been different. The U.S. Constitution divides power among three branches. That same Constitution, in combination with Congress's internal rules of debate, sets up supermajoritarian thresholds for reacting to a president who takes executive action. That, of course, also points to another important idea: that the president has the authority to do it. Armed with these points, it is easy to explain how DACA occurred.

The president had the discretion to change existing policy—in this case, who was and was not subject to deportation. That policy started out conservative, meaning more could be deported. But Obama preferred a more liberal policy. So he acted alone in 2012 to shield more undocumented immigrants. Many in Congress, perhaps even a majority, did not like this. But that majority was too small. If they passed a bill overturning the policy, the president would veto it, and then Congress would be unable to come up with the two-thirds vote to override the veto. The explanation comes from the rules and preferences of the people playing by them.

What would have stopped DACA in its tracks? Any of the following: a president who liked the status quo, a Congress with enough Republicans to override a veto, a Supreme Court with more conservative preferences, or a U.S. Code that omitted "deferred action," robbing the president of the necessary legal authority. There was no DACA when George W. Bush was president, or before John Lennon overstayed his visa and helped invent the legal concept, and there might not have been a DACA if the Court had been nothing but clones of Antonin Scalia.[8] The theory tells us why.

The scholars most responsible for putting this theory together are William Howell and Terry Moe. I have condensed and simplified what they write in their article "The Presidential Power of Unilateral Action" and what Howell writes in his book *Power without Persuasion* (Moe and Howell 1999; Howell 2003). It is no exaggeration to say that for two decades most of the scholarship on this subject—and to a certain degree on the American presidency in general—responded to their work. Reducing it to a few paragraphs understates how different it is from research on the topic in the decades before. It reset the way scholars think about presidential power.

That thinking had mostly come from Richard Neustadt, whose book *Presidential Power and the Modern Presidents* is still the most-read thing ever written about the office (Neustadt 1960). Others before Neustadt had obsessed over the president's formal powers. But if you really want to judge presidents, he claimed, you have to understand that they are formally weak: "In form all Presidents are leaders nowadays. In fact this guarantees they will be no more than clerks" (7). Their power is partly a function of their ability to bargain and persuade others. Presidents are powerful because, being at the top of the government, they are in the best position to bargain.

After asserting this for the first time, Neustadt launches into a narrative about the officials who made the Marshall Plan happen, despite the institutional weakness of the Truman administration. On Neustadt's reading, people like General George C. Marshall made the plan a reality because President Truman offered his personal support in exchange for advancing the program. Extend this analysis to DACA. We might argue that the go-ahead came only because of bargaining between the president and his agent, Secretary Napolitano. The success of the action depended on Obama's ability to convince her to risk her career to accept an unprecedented and difficult challenge. Presidents are powerful because they manage to convince others to go along.

Howell and Moe did not disagree with something so plainly true, but this explanation also missed something. Neustadt downplayed the fact that presidents order subordinates to do things without much persuasion or bargaining. After all, Truman desegregated the military,[9] and Dwight Eisenhower deployed the National Guard for school integration.[10] The pattern goes back to the earliest presidents. One-fourth of the continental United States was bought on the fly without prior approval from anyone but Thomas Jefferson. Presidents act alone all the time, and this is too important to dismiss. Presidential power, then, is a function of the constraints placed on executive action. In this case, the main constraint was the separation of powers. The Constitution puts presidents in a position to propose policy, forcing the issue for Congress, courts, and anyone else who might stand in the way.

With the terms of debate set, subsequent scholarship refined this perspective by redefining what "Congress," and "propose" meant. For Howell, Congress is a collective decision-making body with supermajoritarian voting thresholds, and presidential proposals were only limited by their legal discretion. Fang-Yi Chiou and Lawrence Rothenberg (2014) showed the specific voting and proposal rules determine how advantageous unilateral action is. Congress is made up of members, yes, but it is run by political parties. Republicans and Democrats set their own rules, concentrate power in their leaders, and help members mitigate some of Congress's disadvantage. Executive action is more constrained, and presidential power is more contingent than is apparent from actions like DACA.

But Congress is also more than parties or voting thresholds. It can do more than vote. It holds hearings and issues subpoenas. Its weapons are paper and sunlight, wielded by thousands of support staff—including investigators, accountants, researchers, and lawyers. The effectiveness of these weapons is determined in large part by the people who do the job and whether they have all the resources they need. Empower Congress as an organization and its check against the president strengthens. These are the insights of Alexander Bolton and Sharece Thrower (2021), who show that executive action, and presidential power more broadly, is contingent on the capacity of Congress to be the check the founders designed it to be.

While Bolton and Thrower highlight the importance of the people supporting Congress, Andrew Rudalevige (2012, 2015, 2021) does the same for people under the president. Rudalevige is motivated by an overlooked fact: presidents are not the authors of executive action. In fact, fewer than one out of every five executive orders is even written by the president's direct agents. Most come from outside the White House. Executive action is an expression of *bureaucratic* will, along with presidential will. There are even times presidents would like to sign something but do not because of pushback from the rest of the executive branch. Presidents are less free to choose than they appear, because the executive action we observe is censored by massive bureaucracies with minds of their own.

In each of these refinements, of course, the focus is on the elites with authority to do something about a unilateral actions. These counterweights seem insufficient to check aggressive presidents, but presidents are clearly not dictators. The "true puzzle" of unilateral action, Dino Christenson and Douglas Kriner write, is that it is rare (2020, 6). According to Christenson and Kriner, as well as Andrew Reeves and Jon Rogowski (2021), it is the public that prevents presidents from taking full advantage of their strategic position. Presidents care about their public image, which can be damaged by overstepping their boundaries or by picking policies that a majority of the public dislikes. Their president lives in fear of opinion polls.

I could go on summarizing scholarship, but the ideas about presidential power would be the same. These works, along with many others I exclude, have much to teach about the president and American politics. But they all retain the way of thinking that Howell and Moe advance. Bureaucrats, parties, the public, and capacity—these were added to a list of constraints within the separation of powers, each of which tells us when presidents are powerful. This basic conception is not that far removed from the public narrative of candidates, pundits, and legal theorists. They all tell stories about presidents overcoming obstacles to make policy alone. Theory and evidence have arrived at an idea about presidential power that few could disagree with. But like any theory, it does not explain a lot of things that are in plain sight.

We can start with the threads left by President Obama and deportation protections. The theory of unilateral action provides a good account of DACA, but a stunningly poor one of DAPA. The president should have anticipated the legal failure of DAPA and stuck with the status quo. He did, initially, and said as much in his answer to Ju Hong: "We're [. . .] a nation of laws." Expanding protections would mean "violating our laws." He did not make a mistake, he changed his mind—and perhaps not even about its legality. Years later I asked Jeh Johnson, who was Obama's Secretary of Homeland Security at the time, about this. He wrote those DAPA memos himself, using his own laptop. What did he think their chances were? "I knew it would be a close call, and it would depend upon the judges we drew." He also knew conservatives would bring a lawsuit in Texas, where they would draw a conservative judge. The deck was stacked.[11]

So the administration knew the odds were long, but it sank time and money into DAPA anyway. Why? And, more important, why then? The separation of powers alone says almost nothing about the precise timing and sequence of events, or about what presidents get out of failure. It is not meant to. In the same way unilateral-action theory pivots away from Neustadt's bargaining president, these are questions outside the theory, and they are raised by many more examples than DAPA.

Some actions are categorically ineffectual. For decades presidents have assembled advisory commissions made up of expert volunteers. President Biden did so when he announced the establishment of the Presidential Commission on the Supreme Court of the United States, which was tasked with reviewing potential reforms.[12] The conservative majority on the Court provoked calls to pack the court with liberal judges. The esteemed panel delivered its final report, and no such reforms have been seriously considered.

The report joins dozens of others ordered by presidents that led to nothing. Is this unilateral action? And, if so, what is its purpose?

Then there are cases, like DAPA, that direct the action of government and appear to be big policy moves. But on further inspection, they fall well short of the headlines they grab. In 2015 President Obama announced new restrictions on the use of military weapons and vehicles by local police departments. After the killing of Michael Brown in Ferguson, Missouri, police responding to riots were photographed in military gear obtained from the Department of Defense. The president's co-partisans in Congress and public supporters called for a response. But that response omitted 95 percent of the police departments that used the program, and left over 99 percent of the equipment untouched. Most of the equipment returned by police departments had never been used, anyway (Lowande 2021a). But who could have known this at the time, or after the fact?

At the outset of the SARS-CoV-2 pandemic, President Trump met with CEOs and announced partnerships with pharmacy chains and Google. He said that soon Americans would be able to report their symptoms on a streamlined website and then visit one of thousands of drive-through testing facilities.[13] But the website worked in only sixteen states, and fewer than one hundred testing centers ever emerged.[14] The announcement by the White House pandemic task force was empty on its own terms. Even the term "partnership" is generous. Both of these ideas were under way well before the president's speech. This example is extreme, but it has the same flavor as other stories of presidents co-opting and branding the work others were already doing.

Some of these actions may even foreshadow policy change. President Trump ordered construction of a wall on the U.S.-Mexico border his first month in office. But this order did nothing to get it built. It was only years later that the declaration of a national emergency and the reprogramming of military construction funds allowed them to break ground. This took far more effort than the initial order, which was reported on by national news outlets, but totally ineffectual. Even something as apparently efficacious as protecting public lands can be superficial. After all, since the Clinton administration, presidents have designated millions of acres national monuments under the Antiquities Act. Less well-known is that often the land designated is already protected under the Bureau of Land Management's wilderness study area program, which confers similar protections on natural areas. The difference is symbolic—just the president's signature and a name.

Articles occasionally appear in the popular press about this apparent sleight of hand with executive action, and many were published during the Trump administration. But they are disconnected—just a collection of curious anecdotes. Nothing is made of them other than the implication that Trump was either particularly incompetent or worried about appearances. Every theory has cases like these. Most social science deals in averages. The problem comes when patterns do not align with predictions of the theory. As it turns out, the central tendencies of executive action are sometimes difficult to line up with the theory meant to explain it.

In this case, theory is built to explain policy change, which is far easier to narrate than quantify. Presidential directives like executive orders, on the other hand, can be counted. So there is a gap: the theory tells us when policy becomes more liberal or conservative, but we just observe how many times the president acts. That means that directly testing the theory is out. Instead, studies guess how many policies are politically suited for change, given the limits imposed by the separation of powers. They then weigh these circumstances against how productive presidents have been. What determines that productivity depends on what study you read. Does, for example, divided control of Congress and the presidency encourage or discourage executive action? Some studies find the former, some the latter, and others argue that it depends (Lowande and Rogowski 2021).

Trying to move beyond the simple patterns over time raises more questions. One way to get closer to studying policy change is to take stock of how conservative or liberal policy is just as the president is taking office. Project VoteSmart has done this for decades by asking congressional candidates whether the government is spending enough on agriculture, defense, education, and a host of other issues. If you know where these candidates stand, along with whether they think policy is too liberal, too conservative, or just right, you can get an educated guess about where the status quo is. Unilateral-action theory tells us whether that status quo should be moved. But the argument does not pass this test, mostly because presidents appear to be acting when the theory says the separation of powers should stop them (Lowande 2021b). That last point is an important clue. Why are presidents acting *more* often than the separation of powers should, in theory, allow?

Something is missing. A good place to look for an explanation is the common oddities of the border wall, military surplus, the pandemic, national monuments, and many other cases. Few could dispute that there were upfront, symbolic benefits for the presidents who chose to take executive action. Executive action itself, regardless of its outcome—or its efficacy—has symbolic value for presidents. It often looks good to be doing something, and that is different than its substantive effect on what the government actually does.

Every politician knows this. In fact, the conventional understanding of members of the U.S. Congress is that facilitating this appearance—what is called "credit-claiming"—is standard and necessary (Mayhew 1974). They issue press releases to tell voters they secured some grant or project. They grandstand in hearings (Park 2021). This behavior is almost universally acknowledged as important, and it is necessary to explain why people in Congress behave the way they do. The imperative extends beyond the United States. Officials in China sometimes take actions to placate public criticism, even when those actions have no discernible effect on the underlying problem (Ding 2020).

U.S. presidents are not special. To understand executive action, we must start with the fact that it fulfills a symbolic function well before its policy implications are realized—if they ever are. This changes the dominant narrative. If an executive action has symbolic value, presidents may take actions they expect will fail or spend time on things they know *can't* fail. Congress will not sink its own limited time and resources into undoing a symbolic action. Courts cannot invalidate something with no material implications for litigants. And sometimes the symbolic benefits might motivate presidents to take costly action they expect to fail, as DAPA seems to have done. As I elaborate in the next chapters, this implies a distinctive way of thinking about presidential power.

Presidential power is not just the exercise of policymaking authority despite obstacles. Presidents use their unique position as head of the executive branch to serve electoral and other goals. Every politician credit-claims, presidents just have the loudest megaphone. Their first and most direct power is over the appearance of governing, not governing itself.

1.4 The Library

"They were already starting to form mold by the time we got them." Neil Troppman led a TV crew past rows of hand-cranked stacks, down halls lined from floor to ceiling with cardboard boxes. The tour is now normal. Over the previous decade, Troppman had given it to the attorney general, local news, investigative reporters, and documentary filmmakers. This time, the crew of FOX 45 had traveled four hundred miles, from Dayton, Ohio, for the story Troppman explained to politicians, high-ranking officials, and journalists.

They all traveled to Martinsburg, West Virginia, to the National Tracing Center run by the Bureau of Alcohol, Tobacco, Firearms and Explosives (ATF). Martinsburg is a town of less than twenty thousand people at the northern tip of the Shenandoah Valley. In 1999 the Internal Revenue Service moved out and handed down the building, which the ATF picked for its location. Martinsburg is closer to Washington, DC, Baltimore, and Philadelphia than it is to the capitol of West Virginia. From any of those origins, a scenic drive terminates at a gated facility with an armed guard, surrounded by a barbed-wire fence.

FOX 45 made the drive just before Halloween in 2017 for the same reason as the others. Earlier that month, at a country-music festival in Las Vegas, a sixty-four-year old man fired into the crowd from a thirty-second-floor window of the Mandalay Bay Hotel. There were 928 casualties, including 58 killed, in ten minutes. This is the worst body count in history, surpassing many others that triggered similar media trips—among them, ISIS-inspired attacks like the fourteen people killed at a San Bernadino disability benefits center in 2015, and the forty-nine people killed at an Orlando nightclub in 2014. The attacks led to large, public-facing investigations. Meeting Troppman meant each journalist had pulled the same thread, the obscure process behind a simple question: How did the shooters get their guns?

Troppman runs the only place where this can be answered. This is by design. So, too, are the movable stacks, cardboard boxes, and chronically undersized staff. Their work is tracing weapons over the phone with firearm producers, wholesalers, and gun stores. They fish answers out of records that are often decades old. About a thousand times a day, police call with a request and a serial number, which sends an investigator on the hunt for a chain of custody—from manufacturer to retailer to buyer, and any middlemen in between. In the early 2010s the process took about three to five business days and involved more than phone calls.

When any link in the chain can no longer be telephoned, more entries pile up at the Center. Concerned that the closing of firearm businesses would lead to gaps in provenance, Congress mandates that all must mail their purchase records, in full, to Martinsburg. It has said nothing, however, about their condition or form. There are almost sixty thousand gun stores in the United States, more than all Walmart, Starbucks, and McDonald's locations combined. So the records come, millions a month, stored within password-protected hard drives, handwritten in spiral-bound notebooks, or scribbled on napkins. They come burned, ripped, waterlogged, or moldy. They come packed in boxes with garbage or soiled laundry and wait their turn to be digitized by two scanners who pull double shifts every working day of the year.

The words "scan" and "digitize" imply that the process transforms them into some database where a trace can be run in seconds or minutes. Not so—again, by design. Since 1986 it has been illegal to create a national list of gun owners and gun ownership. So the records are not scanned or read by computers. They are photographed, then carefully filed in a complex directory organized by location and time. Much is stored on microfilm. If the records in question still await the scanners, the search for a buyer means searching the sides of boxes labeled with felt-tip marker, then flipping page by page.

Even afterward, the pages cannot be encoded and searched. They must, by law, be clicked and scrolled through, one at a time, until the right bill of sale is found.

Troppman is one of several who steward the team answering these calls. A former Army brat who grew up in nearby in Maryland, at the time of this most recent visit, he had been at the ATF for eighteen years. Work for this particular employer can be thankless. The agency is a strong contender for most hated in the federal government. Like all such contenders, its successes are invisible to the public, while its failures have self-annotating names. For the ATF, these names are "Waco," "Ruby Ridge," and "gunwalking." Its gravest political sin, however, is that it is tasked with regulating guns. Much of the work is necessary for police everywhere, which stops opponents from axing it entirely. But its mission guarantees it will be underfunded, handicapped by rules, and often headless. From 2007 to 2021 it had one Senate-confirmed director, who served only two years before leaving for more lucrative work as a senior vice president at the National Football League.

For Troppman, there have been no similar escape hatches. He is one of thousands who work every day with the political realities of his employer as a backdrop. He manages a large unit that houses a collection unlike any other, carefully organized to keep manual reading to a minimum, and to avoid breaking the law. In movies and television, he would be invented by some screenwriter. He would oversee a database updated in real time, held on secure servers, returning answers in seconds. He would be a technologist or a chief information officer. Politics has made him a librarian.

This did not go unnoticed. After another mass shooting in December of 2012, Democrats in Congress and the Obama White House recognized a target of opportunity. They hoped the moment would generate sufficient resolve. Twenty first-graders and six staff had been murdered in Newtown, Connecticut. If this did not lead to new gun-control measures, they said, what could? Proponents of reform demanded action through television advertisements, press conferences, and opinion columns. Congress would not reconvene until the new year. A task force met at the White House and drew up proposals. The president had to do something, now.

What they did made headlines. The president announced twenty-three executive actions exactly a month after Newtown, and families who had lost children in the shooting watched as he added his signature. The White House urged the new Congress to write new laws, but the president was not waiting. The moves were widely celebrated by proponents and maligned by opponents. Mark Glaze, the head of an organization that pressured the president with ads, celebrated one of the moves as a "sea change." Marco Rubio, a Republican senator with presidential ambitions, said that the president was "abusing his power by imposing his policies via executive fiat instead of allowing them to be debated in Congress."

Among the twenty-three was a clear order for the National Tracing Center in Martinsburg. Tracing a recovered firearm had been voluntary, left to the investigating detective. Hundreds or maybe thousands of firearms a year, it was thought, were not traced, leaving an incomplete picture of which guns were used to commit crimes and where they came from: "The effectiveness of firearms tracing [. . .] depends on the quantity and quality of information and trace requests." By not submitting requests, police were "depriving all Federal, State, and local agencies the value of complete information for aggregate analyses."

The president had no power over the thousands of state and local police departments. But as head of the federal government, with a hundred thousand police working beneath him, he could act. He required all federal police to request traces for recovered guns and asked the ATF to teach them how. In the order's long preamble, the president touted the work of the Center and extolled the virtues of tracing. The federal government would set an example for the rest of the law enforcement community. With the example set, the hope was that Congress would infuse the Center with new resources to do its work.

From this point onward, that workload increased. The new rule meant many more requests from federal agencies. At events around the country, the ATF promoted their online request system to police outside the president's legal reach. At the same time, guns in circulation and gun crimes rose. Gun stores around the country mounted framed photographs of the president above the title "Salesman of the Year." In the last year of his presidency, there would be 27.5 million new purchases, up 115 percent from the last year of the Bush administration. But for the National Tracing Center, no new money or tech came, and no statutes were changed. These facts converged. Requests went from under a thousand a day to more than 1,700 by 2021 as the total number of purchase records to search through approached one billion. Typical wait times went from under five days to over ten days. The Center could fast-track high-profile cases, but it could never catch up. After one official left the Center, he called the program "pathetic." Year after year, Troppman explained the situation to each film crew that showed up in Martinsburg.

Promotion of the program had been one action out of twenty-three in an executive-action portfolio that showed the president was doing everything he could and that pressured Congress to take complementary action on the core issue. The signing ceremonies were held, but no legislative help came. The straightforward rule imposed by the order, along with its symbolic value, had only added to the weight of the responsibility in the hands of Troppman and others. It had been written and developed in under a month after a brief visit from the attorney general. No one in Martinsburg, Troppman or otherwise, was consulted. But its spirit mirrored hundreds of others. The political goals of presidents leave their most direct imprint not on the statutes and laws of the United States, but on the operating procedures of the federal government.

In the final year of his presidency, the president summed up his 2013 action portfolio without meaning to. As his time in office ran out and after Republicans won back Congress, he took regulatory action on background checks. This was immediately challenged in court. Announcing the moves, the president said the public could believe these newer actions really had teeth: "I'm not on the ballot again. I'm not looking to score some points." Whatever points had been scored after Newtown, one side effect was to increase the strain on the agency charged with solving the problem the president wanted to address.

The last stop on the tour is always the same. Troppman leads the crew to the parking lot, where there are rows of rented shipping containers. He removes a padlock and unlatches the door of one, revealing a makeshift hallway of boxes that sun-bakes in the Shenandoah Valley's humid summers. They started with five containers, but by 2021 there would be twenty-six. Troppman explains why. It is not that the Center has run out of floor space. The weight of their special collection became a safety concern for him and his staff. The floors were buckling.

1.5 The Symbolic Value of Unilateral Action

Try to explain the story of Neil Troppman and Obama's executive action on firearm tracing. If you reach for the dominant narrative, it will make a few basic points. Why wasn't the president able to unilaterally "fix" firearms tracing—or any other gun reform—in the United States? He did not have the legal discretion. If he had, he would have used it. Then Democrats in Congress would have been sufficiently numerous to thwart serious challenge. Case closed. We now have an explanation that is neither wrong, nor satisfying.

For one thing, it does not say much about why the president acted when he did, or why he acted at all. President Obama had both the legal authority and sufficient co-partisans in Congress to do exactly what he did for his full first term. It does not take a PhD to know that absent Newtown, no gun-control directives would have been signed on January 16, 2013. So perhaps this event changed the opinions of the relevant players. Not likely, given the inaction on gun control by the 113th Congress. This shock seemed to have no meaningful impact on the preferences of the relevant officials there, or in the courts.

Newtown was not a shock to the separation of powers, it was a shock to the political agenda. It was a push factor, a demand for action—one the president was in the best position to tap.

The existing narrative also says little about what the president actually did. Obama did not simply exercise what little discretion he had to move the dial ever so slightly. In this case, he took action on a *different* policy, one on which he did have legal discretion. Yet, there is little question this procedural non sequitur was the president trying move gun control to the political Left. It was ideologically clear. The majority of the words of the directive discuss firearm tracing requested by state and local police.[15] It is so broad that if you read only the first few paragraphs, you could be forgiven for thinking the president was about to mandate that all police everywhere trace guns. Moreover, it was part of a broader portfolio of actions and accompanied proposals he and others hoped Congress would pass.

Failing to shed light on these questions does not mean the existing perspectives are wrong. They are incomplete. They place policy change and the separation of powers at the center, and this defines what they can explain. There is nothing in these arguments about credit-claiming, agenda-setting, or the political benefits of symbolic action. Yet, cases like these leave little doubt that these things matter. They have sway over the presidents' behavior in office. To understand the American presidency, we need the full story, one about how the separation of powers conditions real policy change—and about credit-claiming and symbolic governance. When we teach kids in civics classes, should we tell them about DACA and Ju Hong, or gun tracing and Neil Troppman? Can we paint an accurate picture without both stories?

The American presidency is not just powerful when it takes action without others stopping it. Often it is beleaguered by demands it cannot meet. The only honest, human response, which is "I cannot deal with this," is politically forbidden. There are a few presidents in history who have taken this tack, and it is hard to argue that it served them well.[16] DAPA and attempts at significant gun control during the Obama administration, which mostly failed, illustrate that presidents are well aware of this fact. But these actions illustrate one of the office's key powers: to act, and to reap the political benefits of public effort. There is no other office where politicians have similar opportunities. No other office could assemble activists, politicians, and victims in one room and sign something that carried the force of law. Whether this force addressed the problem—or even exacerbated it—can be immaterial. The action is self-contained and serves its own purpose. This is a core idea in this book.

In other words, there was political value to acting. That value can have something to do with its impact on policy, but the connection between the two is not as tight as people think. In fact, as many scholars have pointed out, the political value of action can undermine its quality. When observers have less information than a president and cannot independently verify the quality of a policy, the president often has incentive to pick policies that make the public worse off. For example, presidents might pander to public opinion, knowing full well they chose a suboptimal policy, as Canes-Wrone, Herron, and Shotts (2001) demonstrate. Or, as Gleason Judd (2017) explains, presidents might "show off" by replacing a good policy with a bad one just to demonstrate that they're a skilled policymaker as an election approaches.

Presidents take advantage of being seen. The actions themselves were designed for various audiences. Most important, they were for activists and members of Congress. Moreover, in this case, when that action did nothing, or even hurt, the president paid no serious cost. No one thinks of President Obama as adding to the problem or blames him for failing to fix the gun-tracing program. Even if reporters had full information and were inclined to assign such blame, how could they? The political and societal forces—the legal environment, the circulation of firearms, the recalcitrance of Congress—are daunting and practically immovable.

This emphasis on the value of announcements, alongside the real results, is consistent with a different kind of political behavior, one usually reserved for discussions of members of Congress: credit-claiming. This property is important for understanding when and how presidents act unilaterally, in addition to the standard stories about separation of powers and policy change. The next chapter describes the particulars, but for now the Troppman case is useful for addressing a few potential objections to this way of thinking.

First, symbolism and substance are not mutually exclusive. The executive action on gun tracing had some impact on what the government did. Some actions with a similar flavor do not. In fact, there were other actions within the set of twenty-three that were regarded as purely symbolic or advisory at the time and at least one that was not symbolic but was nonetheless never implemented. As with most things, the differences are a matter of degree. Some actions are more impactful than others. The point is that the efficacy of an action is not the same as its ideological content. This means the important strategic questions are also matters of degree. When will the president take action, and when will that action be more or less efficacious?

Second, the gun-control case helps head off another important objection. When I say that presidents are taking actions that have symbolic value, it inevitably leads to discussions of intentions, even personal character. Is this argument simply a way of saying that presidents are cheats and liars who intentionally deceive the American people? Is American politics nihilistic to its core, a mere showcase of smoke and mirrors designed to propel some and not others into positions of power? Sometimes it feels that way.

But my argument does not say that, and the Troppman case helps illustrate why. Whatever your political disposition, most reasonable people agree that Barack Obama is "a decent family man," as Senator John McCain famously said during the 2008 campaign. Obama publicly wept after recalling the Newtown shooting because he was a father having a normal, human reaction to evil. He sincerely wanted to move the ball on gun violence. At issue is whether the political system would allow him to do that, and whether the same system incentivized him to make symbolic moves part of his portfolio. My argument is that it does, and you can think of presidents as good people while agreeing with me.

This does not mean presidents are off the hook. There are circumstances in which their political incentives make their behavior pernicious. Every executive action, no matter how small or ineffectual, absorbs the time and resources of personnel inside and outside the White House. There is no avoiding it. One question is whether these resources would have been better spent on something else. Would the public at large be better off with a president that assigned people to different tasks? Relatedly, would they be better off if the president had not been motivated by the demand for action? I don't know.

But we can imagine alternatives. It might have been better to wait until the National Tracing Center's funding came through before increasing their workload. Presidents can hire temporary appointees. It might have been better to place some of these officials in Martinsburg. What would have happened to the NTC funding proposals if the administration had led with them when he had majorities in Congress back in 2009? These counterfactuals are debatable. Obama officials will argue vehemently that they did their best. But there may still be daylight between the administration's best response, given its moment-to-moment incentives, and the best thing for the public welfare. I leave these issues for a longer discussion at the end of the book.

Finally, this kind of executive action is different from rhetoric. Presidents often "go public," using speeches to frame issues. Scholars like Samuel Kernell (2006) describe this as an attempt to persuade Congress. Others, most notably Brandice Canes-Wrone (2006), think it puts an issue on the agenda, compelling Congress to adopt a popular stance. But the executive action in this book is different. Even when it does not have an impact, it requires costly action by the government. Signing an order requires more work than giving a speech. More important, executive action creates the impression the president has accomplished something. Only speechwriters think speeches change the world. If speeches are not persuasive or agenda-setting, there's little point in giving them. But presidents have incentives to take executive action when it will have neither effect because of the signal sent to audiences.

1.6 Learning about the Presidency

The historian Jeremy Suri describes the American presidency as "the most talked about and least understood office in the world" (Suri 2017, xviii). There are good reasons for that. Because of presidents' role in American life and America's position in the world over the last century, almost no one is more famous. Opinions about presidents and the presidency are never in short supply. But because of the basic features of the office, knowledge is. The Constitution creates a presidency with a single occupant. As of this writing, there have been forty-six presidents, forty-seven presidential administrations, and 60.94 presidential terms. Setting aside the veto, pardon power, and vague references to the State of the Union, the Constitution provides remarkably little detail about what the president actually does. That leaves presidents to fill in the gaps, and each does so differently. This makes the American presidency difficult to study systematically relative to other institutions.

It helps to contrast this with the U.S. Congress. Since 1929 Congress has had 535 voting members. They serve at the same time. The details of Congress's day-to-day activities are not prescribed in the Constitution itself but are explicitly laid out in rules adopted at the beginning of each term. Though Congress has informal norms, it is two chambers built on a pile of rules. That means the behavior of legislators is structured and easy to catalog—with trackable outputs such as hearings, reports, and bills. The result is that since the digitization of these outputs in the mid-1980s, the scientific study of Congress has made a lot of progress. There are rigorous theories of voting, productivity, committee assignments, and party control. New ideas and assertions can be put to the test using data generated by a relatively structured environment.

The American presidency is not amenable to systematic study. Because presidents serve sequentially, we have to compare any given president to other presidents who may have served in very different historical contexts. The fact that there have only been a couple of dozen administrations means that any prediction at the level of the administration is very unreliable. Suppose, for example, you wanted to test the reasonable hypothesis that presidents with combat experience would be less likely to send soldiers to war. Gary King (1993) pointed out that under reasonable assumptions, you would need to wait hundreds of years before the test statistic addressing your theory was reliable. An entire category of claims is out of bounds.

For these reasons, the study of the presidency has always been dominated by historians, journalists, and people who once worked in the White House. When there are so few cases, it makes sense to learn about them in detail. Much of what goes on in a presidency happens behind closed doors, leaving those with inside information to fill in the story. Much of this is fun to read because these other professionals are typically better writers than social scientists. So knowledge about the presidency usually means a combination of public documents, contemporaneous reporting, interviews, and personal experiences, all woven together to produce an overarching descriptive narrative.

This book takes a different approach, even though it also includes similar historical narratives. I present an argument that explains the use and effectiveness of unilateral action by American presidents. I then describe how well that argument matches up with data. What distinguishes this approach from most presidency books—especially those of journalists and practitioners—is not its reliance on arguments or data. Everyone has those, whether they make them explicit or not. This book is different because of sunlight. I present the assumptions and logic of my argument as clearly as I can. This argument is not merely descriptive or primarily normative—it tries to explain and predict presidential behavior, rather than describe or make judgments about whether it is "good" or "bad." It starts with the presumption that presidents are, in general, strategic thinkers who respond to incentives. I then collect data and tell readers how so that they can look under the hood to see how I came to my conclusions. In fact, if I have done my job, at this very moment, you should be able to go to the hyperlink in this endnote and download my data.[17]

I was taught this approach by the generation of scholars who first applied it to the presidency decades ago.[18] I have referenced some of their work already. If you read (or have already read) their research, you will notice that they often write about how far behind the scientific study of the presidency is. Since then, there has been what Terry Moe called a "revolution" in presidential studies, with a lot of research adopting the approach I have described.[19] How much progress has been made is debatable, but it is clear this approach is better than the alternatives.

This book uses many kinds of data. I rely on descriptive and experimental evidence from surveys, text from news reports, government records of presidents' actions, and, occasionally, firsthand accounts from interviews. There are some benefits to pulling together different kinds of evidence. Learning about the presidency is not like learning whether a new drug produces positive health benefits. There is no critical test that can answer all the important questions, and even if there were, the randomized, controlled trial that would be needed would be impossible. Given that, the best option is to rely on different types of evidence to determine whether they generally support a coherent explanation. All data have limits, and this guards against being misled by the weaknesses of any single type.

Here is where the book is headed. This chapter used examples to motivate questions about presidential power and showed that existing arguments provide incomplete answers. The next chapter is my attempt to fill in the gaps with a new theory. The key piece of that theory is that policy has both substantive and symbolic components, and there are circumstances in which a president would act knowing their action may have little substantive effect. In brief, I argue that their central goals—to make policy, get reelected, and be remembered—sometimes motivate presidents to substitute their normal policymaking agenda for symbolic actions.

The next five chapters deal in evidence. Chapters 3 and 4 deal with the implications of this way of thinking about the presidency. In particular, chapter 3 presents data on executive actions and reveals patterns that suggest presidents incorporate the symbolic value of actions in their strategy. In chapter 4 I show that the set of actions that have minimal direct effects—that is, orders that do not direct government agents to change some policy in the immediate term—are concentrated in areas of policy where the president has less discretion. I also show these same orders tend to be issued close to presidential elections, then drop off in the lame-duck period. This suggests presidents are conscious both of their capacity constraints and of the fact that what they do is likely to have short-term political benefits, best reaped as they approach election day.

A key objection to this argument is that the public and the media would never let presidents get away with it. How could they? After all, the public may dislike executive action. They may hold the president responsible for everything. They may punish presidents who take action that is symbolic and not substantive. The media are a bunch of muckraking idealists exposing cracks in governance. Chapters 5 and 6 address these possibilities. I show that the public generally thinks of executive action as effectual and has little inherent aversion to it. I then show that the media, in general, do remarkably little reporting about the consequences of these actions. Each of these stylized facts supports the assumptions of my argument—namely, that executive action is an effective credit-claiming device, even when its consequences fall well short of its stated goals.

Chapter 7 looks at these actions from a different angle. I consider the implications of my argument for the way presidents organize their presidencies. It is normal to think of presidents as institution builders. The White House is supposed to be a counterweight to the vast federal bureaucracy. But if presidents also care about the symbolic values of their actions, they have other needs. They need to facilitate their own credit-claiming activities. Mirroring recent developments in the U.S. Congress, they invest in the capacity to produce symbolic political wins. This means investments in communication and political strategy, which are distinct from strategies of law and bureaucratic control. Chapter 8, then, is my conclusion. I explain what this new understanding of the presidency means for American democracy. In addition, I describe what we still do not know about the presidency, and where an argument like mine is likely to generalize beyond the presidency.

All this legwork pays off for understanding the presidency and American democracy. The president is the only nationally elected politician—perhaps the most famous politician in the world. Today the presidency is so big and important that any single story told about it must ignore things in plain sight. Presidents are policymakers and institution builders, yes. But presidents are also vague, showy, and given to puffery, and they seem to invest their time in ways that could never help them change the status quo. Executive action often fails to be effective on its own terms. This book recasts both sets of facts as central to understanding the presidency and the political system it sits at the center of.

2: THE PRESIDENCY FOR REALISTS

Every year around the last Thursday in November, the president gathers supporters, staff, and press to pardon a Thanksgiving turkey. This use of presidential power for holiday cheer became a tradition after the Reagan administration and has created good press ever since. Most people do not know these turkeys are bred to be slaughtered. They have terminal health conditions because of their enormous size. All die within months of being pardoned.[1]

We like to think presidents care most about what the government they lead actually accomplishes. This is central to most scholarship on the American presidency. In the words of William Howell (2013), presidents want the ability to "alter the doings of government," because they want to be reelected and to leave a legacy (13). People expect them to solve huge problems in American life. But the system mostly ties their hands, so they struggle. They leverage all their authority (and then some) to get done what they can. This is how scholars teach us to think about presidential power. Presidents are policymakers.

But that is not all they are. Alongside substantive moves to change the status quo, there are symbolic moves that do not. There are both DACAs and National Tracing Centers, new emissions rules and blue-ribbon commissions. Sometimes presidents are dynamic policymakers with undeniable effects on the world. Other times they are little more than showmen. How can we reconcile these two kinds of president?

Presidents hold an office uniquely suited to symbolism. They are the most famous politicians in the world. Their ability to change the subject, set the agenda, and attract press coverage is second to none. Even their typos are headline news.[2] Actions they take—whether they change what the government does, impact some real-world outcome, or do nothing at all—can create the impression of success and clarify their position for audiences. This helps make them popular. It serves their electoral interests and helps them build their legacy.

When faced with all their expectations and challenges, they can fight the good fight—risk time, people, and money on difficult and uncertain routes to changing the status quo. But they can also eschew the hard task of governing in favor of inch-deep actions that leave the status quo untouched. Form feckless blue-ribbon commissions. Declare waterways protected that remain vulnerable. Close detention camps that remain open. Pose with noncontiguous border walls. Pardon damned turkeys.

But why would any president do that kind of thing? After all, some say, the public holds them accountable for everything. People know when something is empty. If it is not obvious, the media and the opposition magnify flaws and make them known. And even if there were no one to do any of that, presidents themselves care about doing a good job. They "play to the ages," as Howell and Moe (2020) write (161). They are intrinsically motivated to make the most impact. It may not be obvious at first, but symbolic policymaking can be the president's best strategy, even if all of the above is true.

Presidents who play to the ages, have sincere policy preferences, and want to get things done still have incentives to engage in symbolic policymaking. You do not need to assume much to understand why. First, symbolic policy can precede real change down the line. Few would argue against this. History looks at plenty of executive actions which were symbolic at the time as catalysts of eventual sea changes. There is always some chance any action by a president, no matter how legally or administratively vacuous, could be the first in a chain of events that mark real change. This is a crucial story people tell. When the impacts of policy are not clear, the possibility that they are efficacious can make them politically rewarding.

Presidents care about those political rewards. For presidents to get things done, they have to be reelected, see that someone like them succeeds them, and give their co-partisans coattails to ride. But elections are imperfect referendums on how well the incumbent has done (Caplan 2008; Achen and Bartels 2016). When people go to the polls, they are thinking as much about where the president stands as about what he has done. This is because the effects of what presidents have done are difficult for anyone to judge, let alone the typical voter. When they see presidents make policy, they get a clearer sense of what presidents care about and where presidents stand, not the substantive impact of those policies. Presidents are not duping the public—or anyone else, for that matter. The link between "objective" performance and the ballot box is weak because the former is the kind of thing that needs scare quotes. What stands in for it is the general impression of competence and the degree to which the president holds certain views.

The same applies to special interests, albeit to a lesser degree. They are more informed than the typical voter, but that information only buys them so much. Sometimes their leaders have incentives to portray symbolic moves as substantive. The president exploits a basic problem for all nonprofits. Their leaders must show supporters results, and supporters are not in the best position to judge those results. Other times, simply knowing where the president stands is valuable enough to earn special-interest support.

Still, if that were all, it would not be enough to explain the mix of presidential actions we see. Suppose America elects a lying huckster, a cheating charlatan who knows nothing about policy or government, someone who only cares about remaining in office and how he looks to a public that was not in a position to know better: a nihilist. According to what we have assumed so far, that person will fill up their docket with nothing but symbolic policymaking. All turkey-pardoning and commission-creating with a smattering of regulations that stand no chance of ever being finalized. What prevents the president from adopting this strategy? In a word: unraveling. For symbolic policymaking to be effective politically, there has to be *some* policymaking that is substantive. The nihilistic strategy would eventually reveal all policymaking to be empty. People would gradually learn to ignore that new thing the president is doing, elites would speak up about it, or both.

Now suppose the reverse. America has elected a purehearted dreamer, a policy wonk who wants to earn their place alongside the other sixty-foot heads carved into the Black Hills of South Dakota. Again, according to what we have assumed so far, that person would be all substantive, all the time. He knows he can get away with symbolic action, but substantive ones can serve the same symbolic purpose, so he sticks to fighting the good fight, day and night. What makes this strategy unattractive, even for policy dreamers? There are diminishing political returns to going that costly, substantive route. To serve the president's longer-term interests, those resources would be better spent on symbolic moves. It might make the president more impactful to invest more of their present energy in substantive moves. But the added effort will not make him much more popular in the moment.

These are boundary conditions, and the rest of this chapter explains them and others in more detail. But they enclose whichever type of person voters elect to be president. The rules of the game turn all presidents—nihilists, dreamers, and everyone in between—into politicians. In a way, there should be nothing surprising about this. What could be more normal?

But there is another side to this. I am arguing that presidents sometimes forgo doing a good job because it is politically expedient. To go along with that argument means, in effect, taking seriously the possibility that the American political system does not always incentivize effective and durable policymaking on the part of the president. Some people will have a problem with that idea, so it needs to be explained.

Presidents make different choices because they know they will be judged by how their actions appear, relative to what they would do if their objective performance could be judged. They sign different directives, delegate to different subordinates, foster different bureaucracies, and shift scarce time and resources. This fact has real-world consequences. It implies presidents may leave some policy change on the table in pursuit of actions that are purely symbolic. The institutions that structure their symbolic actions also differ. Substantive actions have a long list of potential legal and administrative obstacles. Veto players like Congress and the judiciary may halt the president's initiatives. Alternatively, bureaucrats may simply fail to carry out the directives.

But the institutional constraints on symbolic policymaking are different. Actions that do not result in changes to the status quo typically will not be stopped in court because no party can demonstrate injury. Challenges to these actions from Congress will also be rhetorical or symbolic. Career civil servants may ignore (or humor) the president for his remaining time in office. The standard explanation for inaction from these other political players is that they face collective-action problems or are concerned about enforcement. It is a supposed to be a sign of their weakness. But the lack of formal response can also show that what the president did was weak.

This chapter explains how presidents behave when you start with different ideas about how certain policymaking strategies serve presidents' goals. In the remainder of this book, I demonstrate that these ideas are often consistent with the structure of the presidency and the behavior of recent presidents.

2.1 What Presidents Want

Presidents care about policy. Few will argue with this. Scholarship on the presidency since around 1990 could be called the study of presidents "picking a preferred policy among relevant alternatives" (Beckmann 2010). Analyses of presidents' legislative agenda, vetoes, unilateral directives, political appointments, judicial nominations, and more proceed from the same essential foundation. The president cares "about policy outcomes" (Lewis 2008). This is a simplification for analytical convenience, but it tells you what to think about presidential power. Chiou and Rothenberg (2017) define presidential power as "the ability to move policy toward one's own preference regardless of whether other political actors are opposed, indifferent, or supportive" (23). A glut of examples motivates this view. Presidents care about public policies as diverse as greenhouse gas regulation, immigration reform, health-care subsidies, drone strikes, extraordinary rendition, and almost anything else.

There are other reasons presidents pursue substantive policymaking, independent of their own wants. They have to win elections: "Unlike legislators, presidents are held responsible by the public for virtually every aspect of national performance. When the economy declines, an agency falters, or a social problem goes unaddressed, it is the president who gets the blame, and whose popularity and historical legacy are on the line" (Moe and Wilson 1994, 11). This is an accountability link, one recent books by Reeves and Rogowski (2021) and Christenson and Kriner (2020) look into by examining public opinion regarding unilateral action. Christenson and Kriner argue that presidents "rationally defer taking executive action [. . .] if they believe that the long-term political costs of pursuing an unpopular policy exceed the benefits" (2020, 7). Reeves and Rogowski write, "Americans hold presidents accountable not only for what they accomplish but also for how they wield power" (2021, 21). In short, even if presidents did not care about policy, they would have to pursue it because they are rewarded and punished over it. Elections mean they have to care about their rolling popularity, even when their name is not on the ballot. The fate of their agenda is linked with whether politicians like them get elected to lower offices.

But presidents also care about their long-term popularity, or what is often called a "legacy." This is best articulated by Howell and Moe (2020): "To their core, presidents care about their legacies. They play to the ages. And because of this they are predisposed to seek coherent, durable policy solutions that will succeed in addressing the nations key problems and enhancing social welfare. [. . .] More than anything else, presidents ultimately want to be regarded as great leaders. They want future generations to exalt them [. . .] they seek to marshal the capacity of government to make their mark and leave policy achievements that succeed and endure" (161–62). Presidents do play to the ages. If you read presidents' memoirs, this is what they and their ghostwriters try to sell you on.

Presidents want to make good policy, to win elections, and to be remembered. So far, so good—as far as the rest of scholarship on the presidency is concerned. But there is a potential implication of these motivations, which I have purposely clipped from some of the quotes you just read.

Given these underlying motivations, scholars argue that presidents are "predisposed to seek coherent, durable policy solutions that will succeed in addressing the nations key problems and enhancing social welfare" (Howell and Moe 2020, 161). Again, according to Moe and Wilson (1994), presidents pursue those goals "by trying to build an institutional capacity for effective governance" (11). This is the leap I cannot take. There is nothing wrong with these implications as a starting point. But the pursuit of substantive policy is not the *only* implication of those three goals. It is not the only strategy that helps presidents reach them. Symbolic and *ineffective* policymaking can help the president toward those goals. Under certain conditions, which I lay out in the next sections, both kinds of policymaking can be more suitable than effective policies.

2.2 Substantive and Symbolic Policymaking

Presidents do not always fight the good fight. To understand why, we need better definitions of their strategies, the costs and benefits of each strategy, and the political circumstances that influence them. Presidents' key decisions are to allocate effort and resources on two dimensions: a *symbolic* dimension, which is defined as the degree to which an action clarifies the position of the president, and a *substantive* one, which is the degree to which an action alters the doings of government.

I am not the first to write about symbolic politics. But when I say something is "symbolic," I do *not* mean that it is not substantive, or that it is "performative." This distinguishes me from other writers. Murray Edelman (1964) wrote that "the most conspicuously democratic institutions are largely symbolic and expressive in function" (19). For Edelman, political actors are motivated to give people a sense meaning. Among sociologists like Jeffrey C. Alexander (2010, 2011), "performative" governance is a way of describing the behavior of politicians. According to him, presidents succeed or fail based on their ability to become "collective representations" of the public by putting on "compelling performances of civil competence to citizen audiences" (2010, 9).

These accounts are interpretive. They assign aesthetic labels to things presidents do, but they do not address important questions. Why do these performances work? What leads presidents to become more symbolic and less substantive? Why be symbolic at all? Alexander (2010) also sees symbolic actions in media relations, rhetoric, and advertisements. Executive actions—and most other policymaking—are left out. There are scholars who explain symbolic governance, but their area of expertise will be ominous to democratic citizens: authoritarian rule in China (Gilley 2008; Zhao 2009; Zhu 2011). The political scientist Iza Ding (2022) argues that performative governance helps bureaucrats maintain regime legitimacy when their actual capacity to address problems is low. She defines this as the "theatrical deployment of language, symbols, and gestures to foster an impression of good governance among citizens" (529–30). A key distinction between their argument and mine is, I argue that *all* policy has a symbolic component, even if it is substantively impactful.

I am also not the first to write about things presidents do that have little substantive heft. There are books and articles about the "rhetorical" presidency, about the so-called bully pulpit, and public appeals (Tulis 1987; Edwards 2003; Canes-Wrone 2006; Kernell 2006). Presidents these days spend hundreds of hours giving speeches, appealing to audiences to support their initiatives. Scholars sometimes view this instrumentally: presidents are attempting either to persuade or to browbeat Congress into acting on behalf of the majority. The speeches influence policy, but they aren't policies themselves. That makes them different from executive action.

The two dimensions, symbolic and substantive, give us different kinds of strategies. There are actions that are both highly symbolic and highly substantive. DACA changed the way government operated and made it clear where Obama stood. Of course, its substantive and symbolic dimensions are inseparable. The fact that DACA had the potential to protect almost one million immigrants from deportation made it clear what Obama thought about that topic. The substance and symbolism of policy are often complementary.

At the other end, there are actions low on both. Presidents routinely enact pay raises for the whole government. But those are prescribed by Congress annually. They curate theme weeks and give government employees half days off before Thanksgiving. These kinds of directives do not help the president with their political brand, nor do they alter the status quo in a way you can describe with a straight face. These are clerkship orders. The theme-week orders also make clear that when I say "symbolic," I also do not meant "ceremonial." Presidents do all kinds of things as the ceremonial head of state. My point is that none of those things help the president claim credit for anything.

Then there are substantively important orders without much symbolic content. Modern presidents enact technical changes to the tariff schedule, sign off on nuclear energy cooperation agreements, and approve requests for disaster declarations. Some of these are not so routine. Under the Bush administration, the Office of Management and Budget (OMB) launched an ambitious rating system for federal programs. The Obama administration followed with a transparency initiative, which resulted in mountains of data being made publicly accessible for the first time. Each successive president has revised government preparedness plans for responding to threats to critical infrastructure. All of these changed the doings of government. Something was different, money was spent, technology was shared, taxes were collected—all on the president's say-so. But even if people were told about this (and they mostly are not), it would not help them define the incumbent.

This brings into focus actions that are symbolic but not particularly substantive. In terms of presidents' own policy ambitions, they are ineffective. These are the orders that go nowhere, the blue-ribbon commissions, the advisory decisions, the summary reports, and the vague instructions for bureaucrats to do everything within their power to stop the climate from changing, fix the broken immigration system, and end mass shootings. This encompasses a lot, so we need more descriptions of the kinds of actions that qualify. In general, it is helpful to group them into three kinds of actions:

THINK PIECES.   Suppose you are president. You have a goal but do not know how to achieve it. Maybe the goal is too lofty, or the things you would need to do are not within the bounds of your authority. Maybe there is not enough time to work out the details needed to get things done. Whatever the reason, your position on the issue is still important to get out there. Saying nothing would be bad. It will leave people wondering what you think, or you might miss some opportunity to declare your position on some issue before Congress or the Supreme Court takes it up. Worse still, doing nothing will leave key interest groups and party activists with little to occupy their time.

What you might reach for is a "think piece," an executive action that orders the development of policies and guidelines, usually through the creation of some new and special commission, working group, or task force. Every president in the modern era issues these now. They help solve the president's predicament. Asking for advice is well within the boundaries of the president's legal powers. Convening people who work for the federal government is usually simple enough. The ask can be tailored to make clear what presidents think. The preamble will contain the goal, and the name of the group will be branded with it. Interest groups and activists will be named to it or invited to appear before it. With luck, news articles will be written about the action and make it real.

This kind of symbolic action is the easiest to track. It involves the least subjective judgment for a researcher, because it is straightforward to show that an order requests a policy or guidance, rather than imposes one. This is what I do in chapter 4: I identify executive actions that have minimal direct effects on policy and then look for evidence of the implications I discuss later in this chapter. For now, it is simple enough to state the obvious. On their own, these orders do not do much to alter the doings of government. At best, they start a longer process that may do so, someday. But who knows if that day will ever come. Meanwhile, the president has declared that he cares about the issue and is doing something about it.

NON SEQUITURS. Punting the details of how you intend to achieve your goal may not be the only option. Given how deferential the U.S. Code is to the president these days, there often is some authority, somewhere, to be leveraged. But the thing to be done might miss the mark in a key way. It does not actually address the problem or achieve the stated goal. It is a policy non sequitur.

Presidents issue these all the time, sometimes in their role as managers of the federal bureaucracy. The memo that required federal agencies to trace all recovered firearms was a policy non sequitur. It had almost nothing to do with mass shootings and very little to do with addressing the causes of gun violence. It did order administrators to change what they were doing, and by all accounts, they did. But we cannot miss that what they ended up doing was obviously counterproductive. It made one key outcome the president probably cared about—how long it takes to trace a firearm—worse.

These policy non sequiturs are not always counterproductive, of course. They might just not do much. The American Heritage Rivers Initiative, which I talk more about in chapter 6, falls into this category. It was benign enough but toothless on its own terms. Its goal was to improve the ecological health and commercial outlook for river communities nationwide. At the same time, it was designed to demonstrate that the administration was dedicated to conservation at a critical moment in President Clinton's political career. There are other examples from that same administration. In July of 1995, after criticism from religious organizations demanding formal protections of prayer in schools, President Clinton signed a directive ordering the attorney general and the secretary of education to outline guidelines for such protections (Clinton 1995). Though the memorandum was published in the *New York Times* and received considerable press coverage, the guidelines themselves did not change any policy (e.g., Holmes 1995). During the 2004 presidential election, President Bush signed an order requiring emergency preparedness plans to incorporate the needs of individuals with disabilities. The first such government-wide plan issued following the election ignored them (Waterstone and Stein 2006).

Unlike think pieces, these non sequitur actions will be harder to track. We cannot simply rely, for example, on orders that ask the bureaucracy to change some standard operating procedure. That would be far too broad. It would cover a lot of things that are substantive and not particularly symbolic. Worse still, these require more subjective judgment to identify. Someone has to decide whether the thing done addresses the problem described. Let me warn you now: I will not do that at scale in this book.

BASKET BETS. Suppose the president does not want to procrastinate on details or pivot to some minor thing he does have control over. He wants his stand to be clear, public, and in the news, and to address the concerns of activists head-on. The way to do it is to take an immense risk: do something you think will fail, something with long odds, and go down for the sake of appearances.

I use words like "initiative," "goal," "proposal," and "action" because the symbolic dimension of these initiatives is not defined by the *outcome* they achieve. That is, something does not become symbolic because it failed in court or was mismanaged. But there is a fine line. An action can be nonsubstantive if the president knows it has very little chance of success. Suppose, for example, that President Trump had signed an executive order on the first day of his presidency that made the death penalty mandatory for people convicted of killing police officers. It would have been the fulfillment of a campaign promise, a clear signal about where Trump stood. If successful, it would mean a unilateral change to state and federal sentencing laws. But that would never happen, because murder is a state charge and presidents cannot change criminal sentences. It would die as fast as legal aides type.

This is a silly example, but it has some things in common with DAPA. The president and others stated publicly that they knew the president did not have the authority to expand DACA protections. They knew they would be sued, and the case would be brought in a district where the odds were good it would be decided by a conservative judge. They knew this and acted anyway. That is the point. Stepping far outside the boundaries of one's authority can be symbolically powerful. Presidents know this. President Trump signed an executive order just before the 2020 presidential election banning TikTok from operating in the United States unless it severed ties with its Chinese owners. After the announcement of a deal, the administration repeatedly delayed its enforcement until time ran out, and it was reversed by President Biden (Elegant 2021). There was always some chance there would be a ban. If the point of the order was to get one, the administration behaved oddly. What is clear, however, is that it made Trump look tough on China and alienated a voting bloc (i.e., young people) he was going to lose anyway. As of this writing, a video of a person pretending to fly on a broom has been viewed two billion times and counting by U.S. users.[3]

These orders are not just difficult to track. Most of them are probably unknowable, almost by definition. I can guess that when President Biden attempted to forgive $400 billion in student debt, using the coronavirus pandemic as a justification, he suspected it would fail and went willingly into it anyway. After all, the week after issuing that directive, he declared the pandemic to be over.[4] But we do not know his mind, or what his legal counsel advised. We can only learn later, if ever. DAPA is rare in that we have statements on the record beforehand about what the president and his advisors thought about the odds of success. Moreover, some of these will succeed. DACA succeeded. Did lawyers think the odds were as long as those of DAPA before the president signed off?

Think pieces, non sequiturs, and basket bets—these are shorthand for the kinds of actions that tend to be more symbolic than they are substantive. They are also not mutually exclusive. Suppose, for example, the president creates a working group that develops a set of policies. Some are non sequiturs, others are doomed to failure. The point is that all of these actions have the same basic properties and follow a similar data-generating process. They all serve the same basic purpose. They send a signal about the position or commitments of the president, while not doing much to change the status quo directly. To get to the all-important question—when do presidents go substantive versus symbolic—we need to understand the costs and benefits of each dimension.

It is easy to think through the costs of substantive policymaking, thanks to decades of research on American politics. As president, what do you face if you want to change the status quo? A long list of obstacles. Bureaucrats may drift or fail to carry out your orders. States and interest groups may sue you. The present or future Congress may review, oversee, or defund your actions.

In recent years Congress has been set up to engage in this kind of sabotage. Contemporary research describes the decline in the institution's capacity to legislate positively (see, e.g., Clarke 2020; LaPira, Drutman, and Kosar 2021; Crosson, Furnas, LaPira, and Burgat 2021). This trend has numerous symptoms. Congressional staff tend to be younger, less experienced, and poorly paid, and they have a quick turnover (Fong, Lowande, and Raugh, forthcoming). The nonpartisan instrumentalities of Congress lack resources. Its members are inexperienced and know less about policy than their predecessors (Hansen and Treul 2019). Corry Bliss, an advisor to Senator Rob Portman, recently provided an apt summary of the modern Congress: "If you want to spend all your time going on Fox [. . .] be[ing] an asshole, there's never been a better time to serve. [. . .] But if you want to spend all your time being thoughtful and getting shit done, there's never been a worse time to serve" (quoted in Kraushaar 2021). It is no surprise the Congresses of the modern era—with some notable exceptions (e.g., Rothenberg 2018)—do not address major policy questions (Howell and Moe 2016). This has two important consequences. First, it sets up the expectation that the president will solve the problems that Congress won't. Second, because legislative and executive power are complementary, it decreases presidents' own capacity to govern (McCarty 2020). Congress is set up to highlight and amplify the distinctions between the majority and the minority party. As the de facto leader of one faction, the president is the biggest target.

Even if Congress posed no obstacle, the president would still face a much bigger challenge. He heads a federal bureaucracy that spans the globe, employs millions, spends trillions, and does everything from financing sheep farms to maintaining nuclear warheads. Imagine running two hundred different organizations, remotely, from a white mansion surrounded by reporters. It seems impossible because it is.

This challenge animates a vast academic literature on presidential control of the bureaucracy. It says that given the scale of the problem, trade-offs are inevitable. If the president wants to find people loyal to their political goals, he will probably have to be satisfied with having someone less competent (see, e.g., Krause and O'Connell 2015). If the president goes too far down this road, it will make agencies function worse (see, e.g., Krause, Lewis, and Douglas 2006; Lewis 2008; Lowande 2019). If the president wants people to develop expertise, he is probably going to have to settle for ideologues insulated from firing (see, e.g., Gailmard and Patty 2007, 2013). If presidents want to bring everything in-house, or "centralize" the decision-making for one process, they're going to have to pay less attention to some other area of policy (Rudalevige 2015; Lowande 2018).

There is no free lunch in presidential management. Bureaucrats have their own incentives, their own ideas about good policy—and other masters. They worry about Congress and the courts as much as, or maybe more than, the president. Bureaucrats' time and energy go to die in court. Public officials are sensitive to the fact that virtually everything they do may be subject to litigation (e.g., Canes-Wrone 2003; Farhang 2010). In today's judicial system, a single judge in Texas or California can issue an injunction that abruptly halts a nationwide initiative.

What does all this add up to? Substantive policymaking ties up time and resources. It starts a longer process that may lead to a change in the status quo. But it is a hard road. Announcing the policy is only an inflection point. Before the announcement there is internal debate about what to do, with draft after draft of marching orders. After the announcement, the obstacles present themselves, and if presidents are serious about scaling those obstacles, it will cost them.

In short, the more substantive a policy proposal is, the greater the expense of effort to make it so. The upside, of course, is that this proposal might actually do something. It may change a policy the president cares deeply about. That success might reinforce the symbolic value of the action by keeping it in the news and presenting yet another credit-claiming opportunity. But whether it fails or succeeds, the effort is sunk. There is no getting back that most precious resource: agenda time.

This does not mean that symbolic and less substantive actions are either effortless or costless. They are less effort, but also a different kind of effort. Making something a symbolic success requires skill. Subordinates have to have a sense of timing, have to prepare press releases, leak information to reporters, craft the preamble of orders, convene meetings, issue talking points, and more. The people fit for this kind of work are usually not also masters at maneuvering the administrative state. This fact is a helpful marker of their motives, because as I go on to argue, it implicates how presidents organize the White House and the Executive Office of the President (EOP).

The costs of symbolic policy have more to do with the dilemmas any politician faces when picking a policy. Policy choices are often zero-sum. To favor one interest group means alienating another. The president cannot take all positions. He cannot take symbolic action that is both pro– and anti–gun control, both supportive of and antagonistic toward transgender soldiers, both protective of undocumented immigrants while working to deport them. If he tried, it would muddy, not clarify, his position. An affirmative stance on something activates supporters and opponents.

Think back to when President Obama signed gun-violence directives in response to mass shootings. The reaction from the opposition was not, "So what—these are toothless and symbolic." Instead, then-prominent Republicans like Rick Perry said that the Second Amendment "cannot be [. . .] abridged by the executive power of this or any other president."[5] Others used the opportunity to criticize how often Obama issued executive orders.[6] The same concerns followed the Biden administration. Less than two weeks passed before Senator Marco Rubio argued that the new president was "governing from the radical left" by executive "fiat."[7]

These criticisms reinforce the president's credit-claiming. The president must have made a difference, because the opposition is upset. The other party has a shared interest in the partisan combat induced by the president's actions. It helps keep the choice clear for voters. But this is also no free lunch: planting a flag means upsetting some constituency. When used well, the symbolic content of an action should bolster the president's popularity on net.

Now suppose the president does decide to act. When and how does that action pay off? It depends on the kind of reward. There are two key distinctions between symbolic and substantive: the president feels their benefits at different times, and they serve different goals.

The symbolic content of an action mostly impacts the president's popularity. This brings up two related questions. For whom is the president is trying to be popular? Many audiences. A few actions are targeted at the mass public, but most will be geared toward particular constituencies and interest groups who care. They are the ones paying the most attention. Another attentive audience is Congress. This poses a potential complication, which is that presidents use executive action differently depending on the audience they're trying to reach. These audiences have different information, along with different tools with which to sanction the president. We can still make generalizations, however, because presidents have to think about all these audiences at once. They sign hundreds of orders, not one. The forces I talk about in the next few pages shape their portfolio in the aggregate.

The other big question is how symbolism impacts presidents' popularity. Remember that any audience will have trouble understanding the substantive consequences of presidential decisions. Often the consequences may be unclear or just unobservable. Even specialists find the implications of presidential policymaking difficult to recognize. In September of 2020, for example, the Trump administration ostensibly banned diversity training among government employees and federal contractors (Trump 2020). Though met with lawsuits from consultants that developed the training, the vague prohibition also led to confusion (Safdar and Weber 2020). What effect did it have on the presence of diversity training among federal contractors? It would take a dissertation's worth of data collection and analysis to get the faintest idea.

Take another example. For forty years, every change in partisan control of the presidency has resulted in a reversal of whether foreign aid can be given to organizations that provide abortions. Yet, public health researchers claim prohibiting abortion funding actually *increased* the number of abortions in the impacted countries (Brooks, Bendavid, and Miller 2019; Kavakli and Rotondi 2022). Put differently, when I say that audiences cannot observe the substantive effects of policy, it does not mean they are being duped. This is just a fundamental fact about policy. We are all uncertain about the president's impact.

But executive action can still give people useful information. It tells people where the president stands—that they are pro-life or pro-choice, that they are pro-DEI or anti-DEI. It is more powerful than a speech because it creates the impression of action. Like members of Congress, presidents help these audiences learn about what they stand for (Grimmer, Westwood, and Messing 2014). That's what symbolism is. Executive action is just a more credible signal of influence, because examples like DACA, Japanese internment, are accessible. That does not mean that all are equally informative, or that they last forever. The effect on the president's popularity is typically immediate. It comes at announcement, during the credit-claiming opportunity itself. It is also typically short-lived. Public assessments of politicians' performance are subject to severe recency bias (Huber, Hill, and Lenz 2012; Achen and Bartels 2016).

For more credit-claiming opportunities to come, there needs to be some other newsworthy event—a court case, a finalized rule, or some other payoff that occurs while the administration tries to make the policy a substantive success. Take, for example, the Obama administration's Race to the Top initiative. There was the announcement and initial press about what the president planned to do. But there were also rounds of competition between states for grants and waivers, followed by announcements about winners. The path that carried the policy from a piece of paper to an implemented program generated additional opportunities for the president to declare victory. In practice, very few actions follow this symbolic pattern. In fact, Race to the Top is *the* outlier in this respect. As I show in chapter 6, for the most part, executive actions are announced, covered, then disappear off the political radar.

Another critical point is symbolic benefits serve the presidents' goals differently. A symbolic win impacts popularity. So a symbolic win can only serve the president's policy preferences *through* its effects on popularity. In other words, an action can make the president more popular, which may allow them to secure reelection, which may allow them to pursue more substantive wins. Alternatively, an action might make the president more popular, which might allow them to pitch a substantive change to Congress, which might later be enacted. The reward of popularity is immediate, but getting more of what the president wants in terms of policy is delayed and up in the air.

The payoff for substance is different. Having a real impact on the status quo demands more than announcement. It is a process. It usually requires overcoming some combination of hurdles. Then there may be delay between the implementation of a policy and the outcomes the president wants to achieve. Even something as simple as declaring a national monument involves some delayed gratification. Days before leaving office in 2001, Clinton enlarged a national monument near the U.S. Virgin Islands to protect a coral reef.[8] Presidents do this all the time under a law written before my grandfather was born. In this case, the regulations to protect the reef were not finalized until May of 2003 and not enforced until 2005. There were disputes over whether the federal government actually "controlled" or "owned" the land protected by the order, accompanied by a Government Accountability Office (GAO) report and a congressional hearing. So it took over four years—stretching into his successor's second term—for Clinton to ensure that vacationers in St. Croix would have better snorkeling.

To make a real difference and see its benefits, presidents typically have to wait. This kind of payout serves all of the presidents goals. President Clinton himself preferred that the reef be protected. Protecting the reef would forever stamp his name in the history books, even if only for the island of St. Croix. Perhaps the conservation effort would even impact the support for his co-partisan successors. But he had to act on the expectation that those things might occur at some later date. If you saw the proclamation and showed up with a snorkel and flippers the next day, you would have been disappointed. All the president had on January 18, 2001 was a symbolic, political payout and the expectation that one day there would be a substantive one.

2.3 Implications

Presidents want to be popular—now and in the history books—and they have things they want to accomplish, policies they care about. They can pursue those goals with executive actions. Those actions have a symbolic component, something that helps clarify their position and claim credit for acting, in order to bolster their popularity in the moment. Acting unilaterally also has a substantive component. It can change what the government does. But that involves a longer-term process that, in general, requires more effort for uncertain gain. So when will they exert that effort? What determines the kind of executive action they take?

A few implications follow from these assumptions. We can start with the simplest, which began this chapter.

Some executive actions will fail to move policy, while creating the impression that it does.

The president's portfolio of executive actions will be neither entirely symbolic nor entirely substantive. These are simple boundary conditions, which began the chapter and hold under a few basic conditions. As long as presidents place some value on policy change, policy change improves their popularity and helps them retain office. Alternatively, if substantive policy is needed to legitimize nonsubstantive (i.e., to prevent "unraveling"), then a strategy of nothing but symbolic governance is out.

But what about the reverse—a strategy of nothing but substantive policy, all the time? Again, it too is out, as long as the president wants to be popular, and as long as nonsubstantive action improves their popularity and helps them retain office. Action that is mostly symbolic needs to get the president something *over and above* what he would get merely by being substantive all the time. The rest of this section lays out when that will happen. There are political conditions—related to how much authority the president has, how strong the opposition party is, and when the next election is—all of which generate situations that make mostly symbolic moves the best strategy.

But there are other reasons to think the mixed strategy is a better use of the presidents' resources. Often, trying to control the executive branch produces diminishing returns. I have already said these investments are all about trade-offs. When these benefits start to tail off, what should the president do with resources that would not yield as much as those earlier investments? This is where investments in mostly symbolic policy become additive and superior. Those additional personnel hours might be put toward lower-effort actions that generate opportunities for credit-claiming. In essence, by diverting efforts that would only marginally increase their control over policy, presidents can appear to accomplish more and make themselves more popular.

One related implication is that presidents should organize their administrations with this fact in mind. To this point, this argument has been about executive actions that presidents take. But their management choices can be powerful indicators of their motives. They have a lot of say over the White House and the EOP. The people they hire, systems they endorse, and offices they create can teach us about how they see their needs. This is what chapter 7 is about.

We can be more specific about when the president will be less substantive—or more "purely" symbolic. The first thing to consider is discretion. When I write that presidents have discretion, I mean they have "the authority to decide whether or not to take policy action, and if so, which action or policy to choose" (Lowande and Shipan, 2022, 2). If presidents act to change policy in ways that press the boundaries of their discretion, those actions are more likely to fail. Relatedly, when people opposed to the policy attempt to sabotage a change, that sabotage is more likely to be successful.

For presidents, this kind of failure is costly. The time and energy sunk on the initiative is gone. There is some chance that failure itself will generate bad press, undermining the original claim of accomplishment. This implies a straightforward substitution effect, because it means the substantive payout for the president is more uncertain as discretion goes down.

As the president's discretion decreases, their actions should become less
*   substantive and more symbolic.*

We should expect presidents to launch ineffective initiatives in policy areas where their authority is weak. Likewise, retracting or expanding the president's authority in some area—gun control, trade, immigration, abortion—should have an impact on how substantive presidents' policy initiatives become.

This relationship is straightforward enough, but it is very different from existing ideas about presidents, unilateral action, and discretion. In the conventional view, if there is no discretion, then there is no action. That's true here, in a sense. Presidents with little discretion do not do much to change policy. But that does not mean that they do nothing. It is best that they *pretend* to do something. Moreover, there are always what I've called "basket bets"—moves that have really low odds of success but signal the presidents' positions in a way that is useful to them. The theory accounts for failures like these.

Opposition strength is another limiting factor that raises the downsides of acting substantively. I am conflating a lot of underlying factors that impact the potency of sabotage—most immediately, the raw count of legislators caucusing with the opposition party and the material resources of impacted interests. These factors are important because they impact a president's estimation of the risks of governing effectively. When presidents face majority opposition, for example, they can expect that Congress's tools of oversight and legislation will change the odds that their initiatives will succeed. Those initiatives can be defunded, and the agents implementing them can be hauled before Congress.

As the president's opposition increases, their actions should become less substantive, and more symbolic.

A slight digression into existing research is warranted. There is a dispute over how to interpret an important correlation. Is there an empirical association (or lack thereof) between the frequency of executive action and the opposition party's control of Congress? Some say "yes," some "no," others "sometimes" (see Lowande and Rogowski 2021). Each perspective thinks of presidents as policymakers. The first is the evasion hypothesis, which states that when opposition in Congress is strong, presidents turn to executive action to get things done (e.g., Mayer 1999, 2009). This is the folk narrative with which this book began. The second suggests precisely the opposite: when the opposition party is weak, presidents get away with the most (e.g., Howell 2003). To resolve this debate, some studies have introduced moderating variables such as congressional capacity (Bolton and Thrower 2016) or classifying directives into types (Fine and Warber 2012). We need to know which is more correct, because one seems worse for democracy than the other.

But understanding that some actions are intentionally ineffectual can help reconcile the two arguments. Presidents do evade, because their incentives to be symbolic are greatest when opposition in Congress strongest. However, because that opposition is able to disrupt and defund meaningful actions that change the status quo, these actions tend to be nonsubstantive. As Christenson and Kriner (2020) and Reeves and Rogowski (2021) show, the unilateral-politics narrative typically resonates best with respondents when it is justified on the basis of congressional gridlock. This makes unilateral action more attractive.

But congressional tools for disrupting executive action are nontrivial. These include congressional oversight and appropriations riders, which typically evade the president's veto threats. Moreover, congressional inaction usually implies some corresponding limit in executive-branch capacity. Without some statute that requires the government to take the necessary action, the prospects for policy change are usually not good. This leads to the production of mostly symbolic and nonsubstantive policy and suggests an alternative interpretation of evasion-related actions. Evasion is most likely precisely when it is the most ineffectual.

Discretion and political opposition set up the circumstances under which presidents' actions are more symbolic than substantive, but they are distinct from questions about timing. There is a long history of writing about the presidency that breaks presidential terms into "stages," with many discussions of beginnings and endings. Chiou and Rothenberg (2017), for example, point to the first two years of a term following a change in the party that controls the office. They say the previous administration will have left behind many policies that are now politically feasible to overturn. Others, such as Mayer (2001), argue that presidents rush to lock in policies in the last month of their term. To sort some these things out, consider the risks and benefits of different kinds of executive action and when these risks and benefits are felt. How does the president's strategy change over the course of their term?

The logical place to start is at the end: the day the president leaves office. In this moment, their authority to govern ceases. But in an important sense, this is an illusion. The president's successor does not start with a clean slate. What is left behind continues to matter years or decades later. Though some executive orders are nothing more than pieces of paper, the vast majority of them are still on the books (Lowande and Poznansky 2024). The satisfaction presidents get from real policy accomplishments can be with them even if they are no longer in office. They might also dedicate themselves totally to pleasing the eyes of history. By the day of the transition of power, a successor has already been decided. So presidents' final months should be more substantive relative to the remainder of their term.

The president's lame-duck period will be more substantive relative to the rest of their term.

Another way to put this is that the weight presidents place on present popularity goes down during this period. They do not have to worry about the election. The polls have no say over their policy influence past January 20.

Election days are the other critical moments. Elections with their name on the ballot matter most, followed by ones with their potential successor, and then those of their co-partisans in Congress. These are days presidents cash in whatever popularity they have managed to maintain. This means elections make present popularity more important for presidents, relative to the importance they place on substantive accomplishments. This fits the conventional wisdom of people who actually work in the White House. Presidents can be rousing successes at governing, but if they cannot sell these accomplishments, they can still fail at the ballot box.

This makes actions that are more symbolic and less substantive attractive. Symbolic moves give the president near-term political benefits and minimal risk of negative headlines. There are also fewer obstacles to their enactment within the time frame required. Presidents approaching reelection might huddle with advisors, inventory what they have accomplished, and realize there is some gap in their résumé. They promised to move the dial but had few talking points to demonstrate they followed through. Less substantive moves become viable alternatives. They do not have time to go bigger.

As election day approaches, executive action should become less substantive and   more symbolic.

Examples of this kind of behavior are easy to come by. One is the "We Can't Wait" campaign by the Obama administration, which included dozens of public events describing executive actions and ended rather abruptly after the 2012 presidential election (Lowande and Milkis 2014). Similarly, in 2000 the Clinton administration signed numerous toothless executive orders related to the environment. It was a key theme in the sitting vice president's presidential campaign, an issue he expected would distinguish him from the Bush campaign. In each case, the question was not whether the president would act at all. It was *how* he would act—how he would invest scarce resources and strategically adapt to the political realities in the face of a finite end date when his present popularity mattered most.

You could think of the president's problem the way people think of a financial portfolio. It holds different kinds of assets. In the simplest case there are two: a risky, high-return asset and a less risky, low-return one. The young and far from retirement take more risk, knowing that it pays off over the longer term. As you age, you move toward safer bets. This is what presidents do. Elections give them the date they know they will use their political support. Because that support has only partly to do with policy substance, and with limited time left, symbolic actions are the safest investment in the moment.

In principle, the election-day and lame-duck difference should be present for any date on which present popularity becomes particularly important relative to longer-term policy accomplishments. I have used the term "audience" mostly in connection with the electorate. But again, the term is generic. Presidents have many audiences. In foreign affairs, audiences are nation-state allies and enemies. Beyond the electorate, audiences might be special interests in the president's base.

But Congress itself is also an audience. Congress generates critical moments that, unlike elections and presidential terms, are not fixed in the calendar. Congress sets its own legislative calendar, with bills presidents have a stake in. When Congress votes, it partly signals political support for the president. These votes become moments that, like elections, clearly demonstrate the success or failure of the occupant of the White House. The question, then, is how presidents respond to these moments to enhance that support. The answer is consistent with the elections analogy.

In the lead-up to considering legislative initiatives that are mainstays of the president's agenda, executive action on that issue should become more symbolic and less substantive.

Again, the reason is that the symbolic aspects of policy attract short-lived media attention. They keep the issue under consideration in the news for the moment. They show off the president's position and describe what the president would like done. But when those moments pass, so does the need to declare their position. Like presidents in lame-duck periods, they shift their attention to substance. This holds whatever the outcome of the vote. In victory, they begin administrative processes that implement the new law. In defeat, they focus on what they can get with their existing authority.

Discretion, opposition, and timing jointly describe when presidents are likely to be more symbolic and less substantive. These are explicit hypotheses. This is one potential use of theory. It attempts to organize patterns in data, patterns I describe in chapter 4. But, again, this way of thinking about executive action and presidential power has other uses. One of those is to interpret the historical development of the office. The original purpose of the expansion of the White House Office and the EOP was to provide the president with a set of neutral, competent bureaucrats with the kind of experience necessary for guiding the implementation of presidential initiatives (Dickinson 2005).

It quickly went another direction and instead became a bastion of presidential loyalists who would remain on message. Not surprisingly, these trends mirror Congress's investment in public relations. Notably, the growth of congressional staff in the first half of the twentieth century preceded the growth of the EOP (Heclo 1977). Scholars of Congress have rightly identified this as an observable implication of members' incentives. Members shifted their priorities away from legislating and toward messaging. But because presidency scholars tend to adopt the idea that presidents pursue policy change above all else, this institutional development has been seen as trading competence for loyalty. I view things differently. Presidents are allocating resources toward activities that help serve their interests. If the pursuit of competently executed policy did that, the White House and the EOP would look very different today. I return to this in chapter 7.

2.4 Policy, Symbols, and Presidential Power

In modern American politics, there are two political dynamics seemingly at odds. Presidents are dramatic first-movers who challenge the status quo while being cheered on by co-partisans and the public. But at the same time, they do things that have little to do with changing policy. They invest limited time and resources in signaling to audiences—voters, interest groups, Congress—that they are in charge, that they care about problems and are addressing them.

This state of affairs is not absurd or random. It is also not new or unique to any particular president. It is the result of a political system that does not always incentivize presidents to pursue policy accomplishment. This is because policy accomplishment itself is not the only thing that matters for president's electoral prospects or the eyes of history. There are benefits to engaging in acts of symbolic governance.

This is a relatively broad view of presidential power. People see presidents as powerful when they achieve a policy change that is at odds with the preferences of other political actors. But presidents are also powerful because they can create opportunities for credit-claiming. The levers of government help them promote their goals in ways no judge, bureaucrat, or member of Congress can.

The important question is, of course, whether this view explains any patterns in the real world. This is what the next five chapters investigate. Since the implications of this theory all have to do with patterns in executive action, I start by indexing it in chapter 3. In chapter 4 I test the implications set in italics in the previous section using these data. I then back up to examine key assumptions of the theory. Because it rests on the idea that symbolic moves make the president more popular in the moment, I have to examine public opinion and media coverage of those moves, which I do in chapters 5 and 6. Finally, in chapter 7 I examine the historical development of the presidential branch to provide more evidence of presidents' motivations.

3: COUNTING ON ACTION

Every presidency gets people counting. During President Obama's second term, the administration was annoyed by Republican talking points about the president's use of executive orders. So when he spoke to a friendly audience at the Paramount Theatre in Austin, Texas, he made the criticism the butt of a joke. "There are a number of Republicans, including a number in the Texas delegation, who are mad at me for taking these actions. They actually plan to sue me." The crowd laughed. "The truth is, even with all the actions I've taken this year, I'm issuing executive orders at the lowest rate in more than 100 years."[1] The low ebb he referred to was the first term of Grover Cleveland.

Now, it was a fact that the president was churning out fewer executive orders per year than any president since the likes of Chester Arthur, James Garfield, and Rutherford B. Hayes—men we routinely forget were president, and none of whom would come up in a discussion of presidents who might have been tyrants. But whether it is true that Obama's use of executive action was Garfieldesque, and whether the number of executive orders says anything about the use of executive power, are both something else. President Obama signed many other kinds of directives, some of which look a lot like executive orders, and one could reasonably argue that these innocuous-sounding "memoranda" were at least as impactful as the executive orders of his predecessors.

This was reflected in the front page of *USA Today* that December (Korte 2014). When questioned in the White House briefing room the next day, the press secretary granted the point: "I would readily concede that this President has, using executive orders and presidential memoranda, used his executive authority to try to move the country forward as much as he possibly can."[2] The president's detractors, on the other hand, picked up the story, recirculating it on conservative outlets such as Fox News and Breitbart. The opposition cried "executive overreach." The president's staff countered with numbers. The opposition countered with different numbers. Discussions like these go nowhere unless they are disciplined with more clarity and better accounting. They are not even discussions, they are dueling talking points.

If we want to know whether President Obama used his executive power more than previous presidents, we have to understand how executive power is typically used. We have to know what to count. Executive action takes many forms. Sometimes it is the signing of a directive, such as an executive order or memorandum, other times the president signs nothing at all. This raises a couple of more important questions: Does the number of these initiatives, if they can be counted at all, say anything about the use of executive power? How did these orders actually impact what the government did?

These difficult questions are the business of this chapter. Executive action takes many forms, and cataloguing them is not easy. Measuring their impact is even harder. I leave that for a separate discussion in chapter 4. But that is what is required if we want to take stock of presidents' behavior and assess the accuracy of the argument laid out in the previous chapter. Thus far, there has been nothing but accessible anecdotes and useful stories. But those can be easily cherry-picked or manipulated. Is the use of executive action, in general, consistent with the idea that presidents use symbolic governance to suit their political needs?

Answering that question requires laying out the nuts and bolts of executive action and introducing data the rest of the book uses. This data, a list of executive actions, has a few features that make it different from a lot of past research. First, it covers George H. W. Bush, Bill Clinton, George W. Bush, Barack Obama, and Donald Trump. That does not mean the rest will be ignored. But the problems of measuring executive action necessitate a narrower scope, and much can be learned by focusing on recent history.

Second, it includes executive actions of all kinds. The list contains public directives with the president's signature, such as executive orders, presidential memoranda, pardons, and proclamations, along with secret ones such as national security directives. It also includes things that did not require the president to sign a directive, such as major changes in enforcement, regulation, drone strikes, and decisions to switch sides in lawsuits. All of these satisfy the basic definition with which I began. Executive actions are, at their core, commands to administrators.

This tedious effort pays off. It demonstrates a few basic points about executive action that go unrecognized. First and foremost, executive action is not one thing. It is dozens of different kinds of actions, many of which involve creative maneuvers and legal artistry. Pick any one of these opaque administrative instruments to count and you will get a skewed picture of what presidents have actually done. It is like picking one asset in a diversified portfolio and expecting it to be a good gauge of total wealth.

The sheer diversity of these tools highlights another important fact: presidents are innovators. Because there is very little in the U.S. Code (and even less in the Constitution) describing the rules and procedures of executive action, what we observe is a product of historical precedent, concerted innovation, and the peculiarities of the individuals who occupy the White House. Simple figures about how executive action has changed over time illustrate this fact.

Importantly, once we take stock of the many tools available to presidents, we find that *executive action is not going up over time* (at least in raw frequency). It is simply not the case that each successive president issues more executive actions than their predecessor. But you could be forgiven for being surprised by this fact, and a closer examination of these actions reveals why. Executive action may not be on the rise, but it is certainly changing. The orders signed by presidents in the last ten years contain long preambles filled with rhetorical justifications that link executive actions to items on the president's domestic agenda. They read like brochures, and they look a lot more like pieces of legislation and even campaign speeches than they once did. If you set them beside anything signed by Theodore Roosevelt, let alone Grover Cleveland, they are virtually unrecognizable. It is obvious that presidents and their staff are aware that these documents will be immediately read by observers. Presidents have changed executive action so that it better serves their political needs.

These simple facts are evidence that presidents are strategically attuned to the symbolic value of their action. They know we are counting. They know that if they sign a directive, it stands a good shot at grabbing the attention of a waiting press and changing the narrative, if only for a short time. In other words, they design their directives to be symbolic. If they were opaque, bureaucratic documents intended only for administrators, they might not send the political signals I say they do. But they seem increasingly designed to do just that.

3.1 Reduction in Force

Captain Jennifer Peace woke on a Wednesday morning to an order that by that time had been read by millions. The thirty-two-year-old Army intelligence officer and mother of three was on vacation. In the thirteen years that led to her current station—this time as a company commander at Joint Base Lewis-McChord near Seattle, Washington—she had enlisted out of high school and made it through officer candidate school. She deployed overseas five times and changed roles seven times. She earned commendations and now served in a position typically reserved for majors. So it was not out of the ordinary for Peace to suddenly get word her station would soon change. But this particular order was different. It was stored in a million-square-foot server farm operated by Twitter Inc. and piped directly to the screens of the public in seconds. It said that Peace's military career was over.

Though only sixty-two total words, it gave the impression of finality: "[P]lease be advised that the United States Government will not accept or allow Transgender individuals to serve in any capacity in the U.S. Military." Peace spent the first ten years of her career being identified as a man. For most of the time since her medical transition, the military enforced the men's rule that her hair not fall below her ears and required subordinates to call her "sir." These indignities aside, the soldiers around her had been supportive. She was hopeful when the military, prodded by President Obama, began the slow process of working groups, third-party research, and new regulations that would overhaul its rules about sex and gender. "I think by this time next year, we'll be talking about how well the implementation has gone," she said at the outset of the process, just over eighteen months before. As she read the posts, Peace said she wondered why she continued to wear her uniform.

Another vacationing soldier read the tweets with similar distress. James Mattis, then secretary of defense, retired from a forty-four-year career in the Marine Corps in 2013 and remained mostly stateside until confirmed to President Trump's cabinet. In his first six months in the cabinet he had made six major international trips, visiting nineteen countries. The sixty-seven-year-old's brief July rest was spent close to his childhood home in Richland, Washington, where his own father had made a living mining the plutonium that went into the bomb dropped on Nagasaki. But Mattis's vacation was now over. An abrupt proclamation from the commander in chief, delivered over social media, upended a process Mattis had been quietly shepherding since January. He was appalled.

He did not say in public why he was upset, but he had plenty of reasons to be. By that time the military was near the end of a plodding sea change in how it handled transgender troops. It had commissioned a study by the RAND Corporation to weigh the costs of allowing transgender personnel to serve openly. Health-care expenses and "undeployable" periods, which had been advanced as reasons for bans on transgender service, were deemed minor relative to medical conditions the military already paid for routinely, like pregnancies and breast reductions.

Whatever their personal views about gender fluidity, leaders of the branches engaged in the long process in good faith and prepared to adapt the military to accommodate the needs of an estimated 0.2 percent of their professional fighting force. Generals had little interest in making the military a battleground for America's culture wars. At Trump's behest they began another extensive review of the subject, along with a reassessment of a policy that had yet to take effect. But the slated deadline for the Obama changes approached, which would allow members to continue to serve openly and to take advantage of health care.

The political timing could not have been worse. The Trump administration and an emboldened conservative faction in Congress were then working toward passage of the president's first defense spending bill. Thirty members of the Freedom Caucus, led by Vicky Hartzler of Missouri, brought an amendment to the House floor prohibiting Tricare from funding medical transitions under any circumstances. Hartzler, a lifelong farmer and former high-school home-economics teacher, would not allow the military to be a mule for the Left's "social experiments"—the phrase used by her cosponsors. Taxpayer dollars should not be used, she argued, to encourage thousands of hormonal injections and surgical procedures to make soldiers' bodies approximate their self-perception.

Hartzler's move, however, was unexpectedly repulsed when twenty-four moderate Republicans crossed party lines to defeat the amendment. The faction next asked Speaker Paul Ryan to include the amendment in the complete spending bill anyway and force the conference into an uncomfortable take-it-or-leave-it: fund the military with the ban, or fund nothing at all. Unwilling to alienate his caucus's fragile center, Ryan refused. Hartzler then tried to reach Mattis, the one person with formal authority to upend the progress of the Obama-era changes.

Through early July Hartzler's calls went unanswered. Finally, Mattis returned them, but only to ask the congresswoman to withdraw her amendment in order to give the military time to work on the issue. He had lobbied Republicans against her measure, and he saw no need for haste. Hartzler felt different about it. She was well aware that either control of the chamber or the entrenchment of the policy could prove irreversible. After all, as sputtering as social changes in the military had been, after officially accepting Black men, women, and gay and lesbian service members, there was no precedent for backtracking. With three attempts and three failures behind them, she and her cosponsors tried a strategy repeated by dozens of others in that administration: they went directly to the White House.

There they found an audience more receptive to their arguments. Astounded by the $250,000 price tag for gender-reassignment surgeries (a figure opponents inflated by a factor of five for effect), and by the idea that soldiers were getting "clipped" on the government's dime, President Trump quickly adopted Hartzler's impatience. But six months into the term, his chief of staff, Reince Priebus, was adapting. He tried to structure Trump's unique way of making decisions.

Priebus's plan was simple enough. He would walk the president through four options, with a team and a prepared briefing: (1) do nothing and leave the Obama policy free and clear, (2) defer to Mattis entirely, (3) ban transgender enlistments but grandfather in those already serving, or (4) ban transgender service entirely. He would explain that the odds of legal trouble increased the closer you got to the last option. He would further prepare the president in advance for this carefully constructed set of choices over the phone, before the president arrived for work that morning.

This last feature of the plan undid the rest. Before President Trump descended the staircase that morning from the White House residence en route to the Oval Office, the option had been chosen and announced: number 4. The decision memo and briefing were scrapped. The deliberation had already happened, between the president's ears. The only discussion would happen after the fact, beginning with the question the president asked Priebus later: "What'd you think of my tweet?"

Plenty of people besides Priebus had an answer. Hartzler was elated, getting by presidential decree more than what her original amendment sought, along with the sudden, dramatic flare-up of media attention to both the issue and her role in fighting for it. Others were more hesitant to take credit for an outright ban on transgender service members. All they wanted were rules about military health-care spending. Proponents of the Obama policies were apoplectic. They said the decision was a "cruel" shell game, calling the president's ongoing scandals the real motive for a policy change by "tweet-fiat."

But that raised a question. By merely thumbing his iPhone, had the president upended the previous administration's policies and banned transgender soldiers from serving? This was in dispute for hours. If answered in the affirmative, the order would be a first in several ways. Technically, the order was not one tweet, but three, to evade the platform's character limits at the time. Nontrivial time elapsed between parts, with the key line "Transgender individuals to serve in any capacity" delivered eight minutes and forty-one seconds after the first part, and three minutes and forty-two seconds before the last. Lawyers were quick to weigh in on the trifurcated decree.

But they too were somewhat divided. Some argued the tweets counted as a bona fide directive. The first lawsuits were in the strange position of affirming the legality of the order so they would have standing in court. If the tweet was just speech, it could not be contested. On the other hand, Jeannie Suk Gerson, a professor at Harvard Law School, used a piece in the *New Yorker* to slam the door shut: "A tweet by a President is neither a law nor an executive order." Russell Spivak, a Harvard law student writing for *Foreign Policy*, concurred: the tweets were not "in force yet. But it's close."

The issue would ultimately be settled the next day, though not by anyone from that Boston-area country club.

General Joseph Dunford, chairman of the Joint Chiefs of Staff, signed a formal notice stating that there would be "no modifications to the current policy until the president's direction has been received by the secretary of defense and the secretary has issued implementation guidelines." There was the rub. The tweets ordered nothing of anyone. The president had no authority to declare that transgender persons could not serve in the military. As commander in chief he could issue orders to subordinates, who would then issue more orders to their subordinates, and so on—down the chain of command so sacred to a professionalized military. Dunford had given the White House the ball again and let those around him paint his reaction for the press: "We're scratching our heads and asking where the hell this came from." The anonymous subordinate continued, "I hope our commander in chief understands that we don't transmit orders via Twitter, and that he can't, either." What he could do was set Priebus and others to work on a presidential memorandum, to be hastily signed and published just under a month later.

That directive, issued on August 25, gave Mattis some leeway. In the month before, his aide had reached out to the White House. Mattis could not "stand by this transgender decision. This is just not right." The president's representative replied that Mattis had to "take one for the team." Though apparently insufficient to stop the order, Mattis's appeal also was not so alarming to the White House that it attempted to tie his hands. So Mattis quickly declared that no transgender persons currently serving openly would be separated. That November the first active-duty service member had sex-reassignment surgery paid for by taxpayers. The following February, the first openly transgender recruit enlisted.

But shortly thereafter, Mattis finally heeded the White House's request and recommended what Trump had asked for. This time, the recommendation came after a dozen working-group meetings and a direct refutation of the RAND study. With this procedural ammunition, the president signed another memorandum directing Mattis and others to enforce the ban. The policy stalled in court for another fourteen months, until the Supreme Court finally cleared the path for it to go into effect in April of 2019.

But even as those legal roadblocks were cleared, the "ban" looked different from the sixty-two plainly stated words Trump had typed two years earlier. A diagnosis of gender dysphoria could only disqualify service members if it came after the effective date—meaning thousands who had come out between the Obama decision and then could continue to serve openly. Captain Peace would not be pushed out of the Army—she had made major by that April, in fact. Nor would the defense department discourage transgender enlistment. "If you are a transgender individual, you are welcome to serve," one spokesperson said years later. Instead, the military would treat gender dysphoria as a preexisting medical condition, which it would not pay for. The only documented cases of persons removed from the military on the basis of their gender identity occurred before the Trump administration, though legal battles continued on the basis of that legitimate possibility.

None of this mattered as far as the president's mass audience was concerned. It was a ban, typed out by the president himself. Administrative minutiae dulled its intent, but the impression that the president was anti-trans had staying power. It settled the questions about his stance on LGBTQ causes. Whatever its material impact on the lives of transgender persons who served their country, its message had been received the minute the president tweeted.

3.2 Defined by Action

Sometimes the most important thing about executive action is not what it forces the government to do. Politically speaking, the most important thing about Trump's tweets was that they taught America something about him as an incumbent. For years his position on LGBTQ issues was unclear. Not anymore. His actions had a symbolic component, which cannot be divorced from his strategy as president.

The action was also substantive: it changed what the government did, and it mattered to transgender people in the military, their families, and potential enlistees. On the books, though, there was (and is) no ban on transgender military service—only rules about health-care coverage and leave. These differed from the ones the Obama administration would have issued, so they are a change in the status quo. But most people probably still believe Trump imposed an outright ban. Can you blame them? He said so in plain English. That set up the questions pollsters had asked for years and reset the fault line between Republicans and Democrats. A supermajority of the American public disagreed with a ban. It was costly in terms of time and effort for the Trump administration to go this route, but the most significant costs had more to do with alienating that majority. The administration did not have to write any briefing memos, enter any courtrooms, or change any rules to do that. The case helps us pull apart the substantive and symbolic components of executive actions and shows that each has its own costs and benefits. When presidents sign executive actions, the symbolic component is most prominent, and it can be loosely connected to what the government ends up doing. After the transgender military policy was finalized in 2019, no one moderated their beliefs about Trump's position.

President Trump's tweets of July 26, 2017 were not themselves executive actions, but they explain what is. They also bring up data and measurement issues encountered by anyone trying to track executive action. If you are uninterested in those thorny issues about definitions and indexing, you can safely skip to section 3.4. Executive actions are orders from the president, usually directed at administrators, to carry out some new policy using the executive branch. Already, the transgender military tweets do not qualify. They did not technically order anyone to do anything. They proclaimed, without force or effect, that transgender people were not allowed to serve.[3]

But, of course, the tweets were only the loudest part of this particular story. The president signed not one but two official directives. Both of them satisfy the minimum requirement. The first ordered the secretary of defense to stop implementing the Obama-driven changes that would have allowed transgender persons to serve openly, and to submit a plan for putting the old policies back in place.[4] The second gave the secretary complete discretion to carry out his own recommendations.[5] The document trail can be followed further down, to the memorandums outlining official policy, and even the PowerPoint presentations that briefed the rank and file.[6]

This brings up an important point about executive action. It is not these latter steps—the implementation—that define executive action as such. Suppose, for example, the Supreme Court did not allow the new policy to go into effect in 2019. It still counts as an executive action. It failed, but the failure is worth studying in its own right, and excluding cases like these will distort the picture. As straightforward as this sounds, it still means drawing a line in a gray area. Suppose, instead, that President Trump's White House had flatly refused even to draft the presidential memorandum. That would be a similar kind of failure—so would the tweets count as executive action, then? It is best to say "no," because if the tweets do count, any rhetorical flourish in a speech or anywhere else could count as executive action. Before the official orders to subordinates, the tweets were not executive actions. They were political speech.

There is another important boundary to this definition, which is that executive action is just that: "executive," or "presidential." This references both the source and the way it is carried out. They are distinct from actions that merely carry out functions required by law. It must be a change from whatever the government had been doing before. The impetus for the action cannot be the legislature. Plenty of congressional statutes ask the president carry out very specific duties. For example, presidents make annual adjustments to the rates of pay for public employees, including active-duty military personnel. Though presidents can propose a pay raise above or below the one that is indexed to private-sector wage growth, these are only recommendations, and the final figures are legislated by Congress. In other words, for executive action to count, presidents cannot be acting as Congress's clerk. This is not to say that presidents have no say in legislative negotiations. They certainly do. But executive action is distinct from attempts to change policy this way—that is, by lobbying for or against legislation, vetoing legislation, or communicating positions on pending legislation. Again, without drawing that line, the term becomes so inclusive that it is meaningless.

The tweets on transgender military service members also bring up important points about the way executive actions occur. There is nothing in my definition that excludes tweets as a publication format for executive action. Again, suppose the president transmitted the August 2017 memorandum via Twitter in a long tweet thread. This would be nontraditional and inefficient. But it would be executive action, according to the way I define it. If the president had signed no directive but instead convinced Mattis to issue a new policy first, without the official prod from the White House, this too would count as executive action. This is why I prefer the term "executive action," because it is inclusive of all the ways policy is carried out and is, ultimately, less misleading. The term "unilateral action," which is sometimes used by researchers, implies that presidents carry out the action alone, which is not true. Another term, "directive," is sometimes not applicable because the policy change cannot be traced to one signed by the president. DACA, for example, was clearly initiated by the Obama White House. But the paper trail begins with Janet Napolitano. President Trump's policy on transgender military service members could have been done this way. In fact, this is the way the Obama changes occurred in 2016. This makes executive action difficult to count. If your list of executive actions was only a list of presidential memoranda (or any other list of documents the president signed), you would miss the Obama action but count the Trump action.

Executive action takes many forms. Measuring it accurately requires accounting for each. This leads to another issue about counting in general. Not only would you miss Obama's action and count Trump's—you would count Trump's action *twice*. Yet, that second memorandum could hardly be considered a separate executive action. It is simply another document in a collection that changes the same policy. As it turns out, this kind of thing happens a lot, and it is not always clear whether the new document is a new executive action. If you decide, for example, that the total number of executive actions over some arbitrary time period is a good measure of how productive presidents have been, counting both memos on transgender military service members gives President Trump twice the credit for the same policy. This, too, has to be dealt with if we are to get an accurate picture of presidents' strategies.

3.3 Tracking Executive Action

To track executive action by U.S. presidents, I produced a dataset of both presidential documents and other related, less formal actions.[7] The list covers five presidents and their eight presidential terms, or from January 1989 to January 2021. In total, the list contains 1646 actions. Describing the nuts and bolts of creating a list like this is necessary, though it can be tedious. It shows, most importantly, that presidents are innovators who improvise executive action as they go along. Creating the list had two parts—first, collecting presidential directives, which are the documents with the president's signature; and second, collecting informal directives, which are those without it. I tried to collect as close to the universe of each category from good sources, then prune out the things that do not count.

Presidential directives from the George H. W. Bush through the Donald Trump presidencies were obtained from two sources. The primary source is the *Compilation of Presidential Documents* (CPD), which has been published online by the Government Publishing Office (GPO) since 1993. Prior to 1993 I used plain text versions of the *Weekly Compilation of Presidential Documents* (WCPD) maintained by HathiTrust. The WCPD antedates the online publication of the CPD. They are indexed differently but are otherwise similar. Each entry can be treated as a potential executive action. In total, the WCPD and CPD contain more than 35,000 entries during this period. They include appointee nominations, speeches, press releases, conversations with reporters, legislative commentary, reorganization plans, and more.

Why this source? An alternative, the *Federal Register*, is underinclusive. It excludes many presidential directives that presidents, for whatever reason, decided not to publish. Categorically speaking, they are only required to publish two kinds of directives in the FR: executive orders and proclamations (P.L. 74-220, Section 5[a]). Phillip J. Cooper found cases in which presidents did not publish certain directives for strategic reasons (Cooper 2002). In a survey experiment, Thomas Gray and I found evidence that respondents seemed to disapprove of the term "executive order" relative to "memorandum" (Lowande and Gray 2017). It is also possible certain presidents opt to publish more than others for nonstrategic reasons. To remove the possibility the final list would be influenced by these idiosyncrasies, I began with the more inclusive list. I then found all identifiable directives, specifically executive orders, letters, presidential memoranda, proclamations, determinations, military orders, directives, and those labeled as "other." In total, these were 7,030 entries.

The second source for directives is declassified lists of national security–related orders, sought out for the same reason I avoid the FR. While I expect

the vast majority of these are not initially unpublished for nonpolitical reasons (e.g., operational security), occasionally presidents may classify actions
because of the potential reaction of some audience—be it Congress, the public, or some interest group. These are cataloged by the Federation of American Scientists (FAS). Some of these orders are also published in the WCPD
or CPD simultaneously, but most are not. In total, these national security–
related directives add another 301 entries.

The next step, of course, is to prune the things that do not qualify as executive action. As it turns out, this means most entries. This fact should be the
first thing you think of the next time some news outlet produces a figure pur-
porting to show how productive the current president has been. If you simply
downloaded a list and made pictures with it, the vast majority of presidential
directives would be administrative junk.

To apply my definition, I and a team of research assistants went through
a standard search procedure. I first defined a set of policy areas—forty-five
in total—that would be the starting point for the universe of relevant executive actions during this period.[8] This set was adapted from the set of policy questions Vote Smart asks congressional candidates each election cycle.
Vote Smart refers to this as their "political courage test," because it requires
politicians to take a position on pressing policy issues. The questions reflect,
in the words of Vote Smart, "the top concerns of the American people [. . .]
likely to come up in the next legislative session."[9] These topics are listed in
the appendix of this book, but they are fairly exhaustive—so exhaustive, in
fact, that there are some areas where one could hardly expect presidents to
act at all. There is a point to this. Describing where executive action is *not*
occurring can be illuminating. Two topics not included (because they are
apparently not "top concerns of the American people") are actions related
to government transparency and ethics. Presidents routinely write rules for
disclosures of financial entanglements by White House aides. Otherwise, almost every policy area is covered—from housing, education, and welfare to
affirmative action, direct military action, diplomacy with China, gun control, and abortion.

Those defined, we went topic by topic, searching for relevant directives.
To assist in this enterprise, I came up with a set of key words for each topic
and used them to sort documents by their likelihood of relevance. I matched
these to the full text of each document. These dictionaries and match fre-
quencies are also listed in the appendix. At least one coder then read and labeled directives that were relevant to the policy topic. There were a total of
five unique raters, with the typical rater hand coding around twenty policy
areas. Most of these were straightforward and can be collected quickly. For
example, all adjustments to national historic sites and monuments occur via

proclamation, and there are several policy topics in which very few presidential directives ever occur, such as taxation. Some topics are more difficult, and to gauge these, intercoder reliability statistics were obtained for those areas coded by multiple raters. Difficult topics with low ratings were typically broad (e.g., homeland security and defense). To eliminate any remaining false positives and ensure the topics had been applied correctly, I reviewed the entire list of directives and repaired any errors. Orders that did not meet the definition were removed, and one that had been included or excluded inconsistently across administrations were made consistent. In the end, this procedure found 1,460 executive actions, 1,371 from the GPO and another 89 from the FAS.[10]

Next, I searched for executive actions without the president's signature. But without the president's signature, how can we say that the president was responsible? It is important to remember that even with the president's signature, we cannot always attribute an order to the president. President Trump punched out the tweets on transgender military service members himself, but presidents these days do not write their own orders. Thanks to the work of Andrew Rudalevige (2021), we know that often no one in the White House writes them, either. Many executive orders emerge out of the bureaucracy the order purports to control. Presidents sign them, but they may not understand them—or, more important, they may not reflect the president's preferences. All a signature guarantees is that the president consented.

For nondirective orders, we do not even have that. Plenty of policymaking in the vast federal bureaucracy occurs with no White House involvement. To understand whether these policies can be reasonably attributed to the president, I rely on the judgment of legal scholars. The primary source for identifying these executive actions is articles written by lawyers. What are these scholars using to make this determination? Sometimes it is that the White House took credit for the action in some way. There was a press conference by a cabinet secretary, or a later speech in which the president explicitly promotes what "his administration" is doing. Sometimes the attribution is more of a leap. There was no ribbon cutting, but the author might conclude that a sudden shift in the regulation from an agency was the result of the president's priorities. This has a "you know it when you see it" quality that is unsatisfying. But the antidote is sunlight, and I have made the dataset freely available. Anyone can eliminate a case they deem not to have been presidentially driven.

These nondirective actions were taken from two sources, though the second ended up being much more informative. The first is the *Congressional Quarterly Almanac*, which summarizes action in Congress on key issues. These articles occasionally reference executive actions relevant to congressional debates over bills. I used synonyms for "presidential action" to find relevant entries for each policy area. This resulted in thirty-eight matches, of which only four were relevant and did not already appear in the set of directives.

The more significant source was law reviews. Legal scholars write about executive action, often using policy history as a way to make their arguments. It is a collection of judgments by administrative law scholars about which executive actions are important enough to write about. I used *LexisNexis Uni*, where I batch-downloaded and then reviewed four hundred articles. To be included, the article had to mention a president in the time period I am interested in, along with some synonym of "executive action," and to have been published between January 1, 1989, and June 1, 2021. The first few hundred (sorted by key-word relevance) were looked at because by the 400th article, there had not been a new, relevant executive action to include for over 50 articles. I found 182 nondirective executive actions this way. This is how I arrived at the final list of 1,646.

3.4 Presidential Unilateralism in Recent Politics

To anyone who pays attention to American politics these days, it may seem as though presidents act alone all the time, and there is no issue that escapes their influence. Figure 3.1 shows why. It is a map of executive action showing where presidents tend to be most active and where they are most silent. Over the complete time series, there is essentially nothing presidents have not tried to touch. Even taxation, generally thought to be the sole purview of Congress, has seen regulatory moves initiated by the president's appointees. Of course, it would be straightforward enough to find some arbitrary number of policy areas unaddressed by presidential action. But as more were added, they would have to be increasingly obscure. Setting aside the question of whether these actions did anything of consequence, the main fact is that presidents have tried to do something almost everywhere.

Nonetheless, presidents' attention is skewed. They are most active, numerically speaking, in defense, trade, and the environment, and homeland security. The numbers are even more skewed than this figure indicates, because in terms of raw frequency, these four account for about 43 percent of the total. Presidents are least active in so-called pocketbook issues like taxes and the minimum wage. The map also seems to show clear partisan differences. The issues at the top unite presidents in action, but as you move further down, there are clear partisan priorities. Democratic presidents cover more domestic social issues. For instance, gun-control initiatives appear among Democratic presidents. If we exclude President Trump, this pattern is much more pronounced. Until President Trump, executive action on immigration

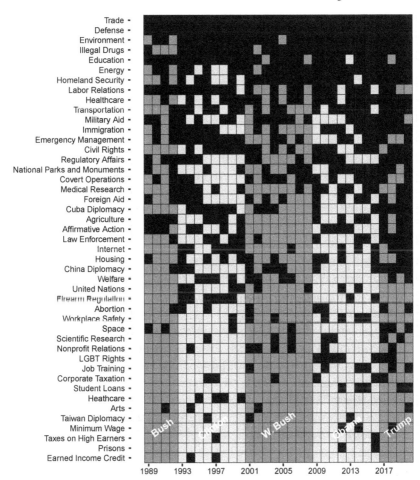

FIGURE 3.1 Executive action is everywhere

Darkened tiles indicate the president took at least one action in that policy area, in that year. Actions taken in the last twenty days of an administration are recoded to the previous year. Topics are not mutually exclusive, so directives may appear twice for the purposes of the figure.

was mostly a Democratic phenomenon. There are also clear sea changes as new policy areas become impacted by executive action. Homeland security and clandestine operations are most impacted by sweeping executive actions after September 11, 2001. LGBTQ rights become a subject of executive intervention only after the Obama administration.

With a general sense of *what* executive action has addressed, we can turn to *how* it tends to happen. There are many tools that help presidents take executive action, so saying something about each is unavoidable. Again, if this kind of detail is not important to you, you can skip to the next paragraph break (on page 70). It is helpful to group actions into two classes: directive and nondirective. The key distinction is whether there is a public document signed by the president. This is a subtle but important point. When I make distinctions between types of executive action, I am always referring to the highest-level document for this particular action. Executive orders, proclamations, and any other directive with the president's signature will usually have a docket of other documents, authored at some lower administrative rung. These provide the official legalese and operating procedures for implementation. For the nondirective class of executive actions, these are all there is.

Within each class, directive and nondirective, there are yet more instruments with variable features to distinguish them. There are at least two dozen types of directives (Relyea 2008), not all of which are represented in these data, for reasons I discuss in the next section. The most common directive types—executive orders and proclamations—have been published, signed, and numbered since the 1930s. The completeness makes them a convenient data source, which is partly why they are the sole focus of most research on executive action. They tend to be the most wide-ranging and significant. We should be careful about these central tendencies, though, because they also contain unimportant tedium. There are executive orders that close government offices on Christmas Eve, and the most common use of a proclamation is to do something like declare it "Wright Brothers Day." This distinguishes the two. Executive orders are directed at administrators, whereas proclamations do exactly what their name implies: proclaim something to be so. This distinction ends up being unimportant, since absent the implicit instructions that come with these declarations, presidential proclamations would not be worth the paper they are printed on.

Next, there are numerous types of national security–related directives. There are national security directives, presidential review directives, national security presidential memoranda, homeland security presidential directives, and national security presidential directives. If the time series went back farther, there would be more names with a similar flavor. But their obvious, defining feature is their subject. They describe procedures for detaining suspected terrorists, describe the steps in normalizing relations with Cuba, and outline U.S. policy on the Arctic. Many are still classified. In some cases we know their title but not their content. In others we do not even know that— just that there is a gap between, for example, National Security Directive no. 10 and National Security Directive no. 12, which is filled with something too sensitive to release to the public.

Beyond these other signed orders, there are many types of unnumbered directives: memoranda, letters, determinations, orders, findings, notices, and permits. Though nothing precludes any of them from having major impacts on policy, they tend to be shorter and narrower. One permit, for example, is the one signed by President Trump to authorize the Keystone XL pipeline. This accomplished something quite specific, but it was politically contested and received media coverage.

The other class, nondirective actions, is even more varied and difficult to define. There are directives that look much like executive orders or presidential memoranda but are signed by other officials, not the president. For example, in 2001 the Centers for Medicare and Medicaid Services launched an initiative that encouraged states to apply for waivers from the provisions of the Medicaid Act and the State Children's Health Insurance Program. Its effect was to incentivize states to add strings to these entitlement programs and effectively reduce their cost to taxpayers. But it was planned and carried out entirely within the agency and its parent department, without an explicit presidential directive. Nonetheless, it was widely attributed to the Bush administration and its politically appointed officials.

In some cases, presidents took explicit credit for regulatory actions like new proposed rules or even had a hand in killing proposed rules. President George W. Bush, for example, proposed rules governing everything from new power-plant construction to endangered species, which were attributed by legal scholars and the press to the White House. More recently, there are less legally consequential but still important "guidance" documents issued by cabinet departments. President Obama's Department of Education issued guidance on transgender bathroom use in public schools.

Then, there are what could be called "enforcement" actions, which I define as some concerted attempt to change the way the government carried out some policy already the books. People often overlook the fact that much of the time, to have a meaningful impact on public policy, presidents need not write anything new. Many existing policies are more like gas pedals, with presidents acting more or less lead-footed. What falls under this category is quite diverse. During this time period, presidents occasionally ignore the throttle entirely. Presidents tell their attorneys general to refrain from litigating, or even to switch sides, in a lawsuit involving the government. President George H. W. Bush, for example, refused to have his department of justice defend a statute that required the Federal Communications Commission to consider racial and ethnic diversity when it granted broadcasting licenses (*Metro Broadcasting v. FCC*, 497 U.S. 547). Similarly, presidents sometimes exempt states from the requirements of federal law. At other times presidents emphasize existing policies by directing more resources toward them or incentivizing subordinates to make extra effort. This is often the case in immigration. DACA and DAPA, of course, are hugely consequential executive actions; but at their core, they are billed as nothing more than simple changes to the way the government enforces existing law. On the other end of the spectrum, encouraging immigration raids on employers in the United States is also a change in enforcement.

Finally, the dataset includes military actions and international agreements. These are generally excluded from studies of unilateral action, but in my view such an exclusion is difficult to justify. After all, these actions and agreements are the most dramatic and violent examples of "orders to administrators that change some existing policy." How can we talk about presidential unilateralism without discussing the bombing campaigns, assassinations, and troop deployments abroad? Likewise, presidents' unilateral decisions about international agreements also bind the government to act in ways that satisfy my definition.

Including these nondirective actions has drawbacks. I freely admit that some of these categories are difficult to define, and it is hard to be certain the dataset includes all actions when there is no neatly organized series to reference. But this difficulty is no justification for giving up. It just means that whenever these data are used, they must be used carefully. When findings change with the particular data points included, I will say so. But ultimately, simply reading them makes the value of including them clear. They satisfy the definition, so they cannot be ignored.

How often has each of these various types of executive actions been used over time? Figure 3.2 plots this usage. I collapsed some categories of the many kinds of actions I just described solely for the purpose of data visualization. National security directives are aggregated and also grouped with military actions. Findings, determinations, permits, and notices are all labeled "determinations," since each involves presidents deciding that some circumstance exists. Reprogramming or withholding funds is labeled a "budgetary action." Enforcement actions include agency guidance documents, other internal memoranda, and pardons. Executive orders, proclamations, and presidential memoranda are stand-alone, unaggregated categories.

As figure 3.2 demonstrates, executive action is constant yet diverse over this period in U.S. history. The figure reveals clear differences in the prevalence of type of action by party and administration. President George W. Bush issued many more national security directives than his Democratic counterparts or Trump. The second Bush administration was clearly driven to this by September 11, 2001, and the subsequent war on terrorism. The Obama and Clinton administrations, on the other hand, appear more active on enforcement and regulation.

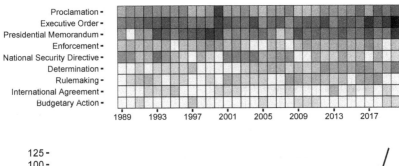

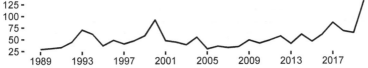

FIGURE 3.2 Executive action is diverse but not consistently going up
Darker tiles indicate that the president took more actions of that type in that year. Actions taken in the last twenty days of an administration are recoded to show them occurring in the previous year.

This may reflect a fundamental difference between conservative and liberal policymaking. Moving something in a liberal direction usually requires more government activity, whereas simple neglect can sometimes be a conservative win. These partisan differences may have less to do with preferences than with managerial style and personnel. Within political parties, there is a nontrivial overlap in the people who make these decisions. Presidents' personal management style may show up in the data. Whatever the reason, this is a reminder that picking any one type could mislead, especially if there are partisan differences in the way executive actions are carried out.

The data also demonstrate what I wrote earlier: there is no raw increase in the frequency of executive action. But there are some local trends. Most notably, the last year in the data appears to be a banner year for executive action, for obvious reasons. It coincides with the SARS-CoV-2 pandemic and presidential election year. The dataset contains dozens of emergency orders meant to respond to the crisis. More generally, if you removed President Trump from the data, the Democratic presidents would appear more active than the Bush administrations.

Each of these patterns invites descriptive speculation that approaches causal inference, which I try to avoid. The main facts are just a basis for a more careful look at the argument I make. Executive action is a diverse, prominent feature of politics in the United States. It is has touched nearly every part of the federal government's policymaking, and even to some extent at the state and local levels. It demands we ask the kinds of questions with which I began this book—about when it occurs and why, and when it will be impactful or symbolic.

3.5 Adapting for Audiences

To understand presidents' underlying motivations, we can start by looking at how executive actions are written. Collecting these data was hard because executive action is so varied, and it is varied because presidents have a lot of say over how it occurs. That also gives them an opportunity to adapt it to suit their needs. This goes back farther than you might think.

By January 1862 Abraham Lincoln was well into the arc of the American Civil War that prompted him to remark: "If there is a place worse than Hell, I am in it."[11] In the opening battles of the war, Union armies were routed and nearly disintegrated after attacks on entrenched Confederates. For the next five months there was little good news. During that period of reorganization, drilling, supply, and logistics—all funded at great expense by Congress— numerically superior Union armies sat idle. Criticism of the president mounted, even in Republican-controlled newspapers. The secretary of war informed the president the Army would soon bankrupt the government. Something had to be done.

What President Lincoln did was sign the President's General War Order No. 1 on January 27, 1862. He made the handwritten order available for publication in newspapers without consulting his cabinet. It ordered all Union forces on land and sea to move against the Confederacy on George Washington's birthday. The order did little to move the Army. But the public reaction was different. In a stroke of luck for Lincoln, the order came shortly before Union victories at Fort Donelson and Roanoke. The *Cincinnati Gazette* called it "the stroke that cut the cords which kept our great armies tied up in a state of inactivity" (Burlingame 2008).

Where did this particular stroke come from, and what is a "President's General War Order"? Lincoln invented it. His was the first general war order, not because the United States had never been at war, but because no president had needed to browbeat his generals in public. To that point, the president tried prodding them in private meetings and correspondence, to no effect. So he resorted to the war order, which was most important for what it said about *the president's position* on the need for offensive operations. There would be more of these, each not an operational document but a public declaration of what the president wanted—just in case newspaper editors got the impression it was he who was responsible for the behavior of some subordinate. These were symbolically important actions.

Lincoln adapted a tool to meet his needs as president: he invented a new kind of directive, which would go out of existence at the end of the war. Though his circumstances were exceptional, his innovation is not. Every president does this, especially when it comes to executive action. Relative to other kinds of political actions, it is diverse and changing because presidents invent new means to accomplish it. There is very little to prevent them from doing so. There is nothing in the Constitution and little in the U.S. Code about the type, format, and procedure of presidential directives. Viewing the documents today, especially those published in the *Federal Register*, you might think otherwise. Their rigid, formal, and legalistic appearance gives them authority. But this masks the degree to which presidents make this up as they go along.

Another example is the transition of presidential "letters" to presidential "memoranda." Until 1960 presidents called these documents "letters" to particular administrators. Then they issued both letters and memoranda, and by 1995 only memoranda. What is the substantive difference between these documents? None. They differ only in name (Lowande 2014). This example, of course, is more mundane than the invention of Lincoln's war order. The point is, there was nothing constraining presidents from renaming or inventing a new kind of directive.

These seemingly innocuous decisions can be very instructive about whom the president intends to reach. Nothing stops a president from beginning their executive orders with a sonnet in iambic pentameter or rap lyrics. These would reach different audiences. Either would be preposterous, but the point about audiences is not. If presidents have the kind of discretion I have alleged and are aware of the symbolic aspects of executive action, then we should see evidence of it. We should see it reflected in the format and language of the executive action. If executive action has a messaging component that informs presidents' incentives, there should be systematic evidence of these messages.

What part of these documents could contain such messages? The preamble, which immediately proceeds the actual orders to administrators. Though the preamble also cites the authority under which the president acts, this portion of the document often contains flowery and descriptive justifications for the action itself. For example, consider the presidential memorandum President Clinton issued on August 16, 1993. It contains over five hundred words of preamble, featuring sentences such as:

> A major problem facing the Nation today is the ease with which criminals, the mentally deranged, and even children can acquire firearms. The gruesome consequences of this ready availability of guns is found in the senseless

violence occurring throughout the country with numbing regularity. [. . .] Today there are in excess of 287,000 Federal firearms licensees, and a great number of these persons probably should not be licensed.

These statements have no legal effect. Rather, they are messages about the president's position and arguments justifying his decision. So extensive are these in this particular order that they account for almost half the words in the directive. The length of this section alone is a useful marker of how presidents adapt executive action to their audience—in this case, elite observers the president would like to convince that he is addressing gun violence.

There are two kinds of documents, executive orders and presidential memoranda, known to be roughly equivalent. Yet, executive orders are indexed, and governed by some of the only formal rules imposed on executive action, while presidential memoranda are not. In other words, presidents have more leeway to decide what a memo is, what it does, and who its audience is relative to an executive order. This makes them a useful pairing.

Thus, if messaging concerns are informing the issuance of executive action, it ought to be more prominent in presidential memoranda, which are more ripe for innovation. We can gather other expectations, too, from the theory in the last chapter. In general, presidents should be more symbolic as elections approach, and when their discretion is limited. These rhetorical flourishes are just that—attempts by presidents to frame their action as a response to some problem, as credit-claiming.

Figure 3.3 describes how presidents' leeway has impacted the executive action over this period. The white line plots the average character length of preambles in presidential memoranda, identified by the many ways in which presidents mark the break between preamble and actual orders.[12] A number of instructive patterns show up. First, over this period, presidential memoranda contain significantly more language that can contain the kind of messaging present in Clinton's gun-control memo. Both directives, on average, contain more symbolic language over time. Another important fact is that memoranda tend to be more variable in the amount of symbolic language across order. This is, again, consistent with the idea that presidents have more leeway in how to use this document.

Finally, within these orders, presidents tend to use more symbolic language when they have less legal discretion. They also tend to use more symbolic language during presidential election years. In the next chapter I will describe how we know this in more detail, but for now it is a first indication that my argument helps explain how presidents tend act unilaterally.

This comparison of preambles across action type is instructive, but so is a broader historical one. It would be a waste of ink to plot the mean preamble

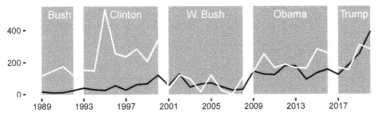

FIGURE 3.3 Less formal presidential directives have more symbolic language
This plots the average character length of preambles by year for executive orders (black) and presidential memoranda (white). Actions taken in the last twenty days of an administration are recoded to show them occurring in the previous year.

length of Theodore Roosevelt's executive orders, because they do not contain any. They begin and end with orders to administrators. On November 15, 1901, Roosevelt wrote in one such order: "It is hereby ordered that San Nicolas Island, California, be and it is hereby reserved for lighthouse purposes."[13] This is not an excerpt—it is the entire order. This tendency extends to more substantive orders, such as those that set aside public lands for conservation purposes. They contain no long justifications extolling the virtues of the preservation of natural resources, no John Muir poetry. Their target audience has no need for any of those things.

When given leeway, presidents adapt official documents to clarify their position on the issue at hand. They are aware of such documents' symbolic importance and act accordingly. The audience for executive action has changed, and presidents have adapted. Today, the executive actions that bear their signature have a lot more in common with the press releases members of Congress issue for constituents than they do with the orders of Theodore Roosevelt or any president of a similar or earlier era.

These are just words. But the basic patterns are circumstantial evidence of a much more important story about how the office of the presidency has been warped by the demands for action. Action itself has political value, and presidents adapt and even invent these tools at will to take advantage of it.

4: HOW PRESIDENTS ACT

Gregory Korte noticed differences from the start. Years into covering the White House, he had been to many signing ceremonies, even for executive orders. This new administration seemed to have them for *every* order. The president would sign with many pens, to be given out as mementos—a practice typically reserved for major new legislation. But officials now did not give reporters copies of what the president was actually signing. After a few rounds of this, Korte asked photographers to get close-ups of the documents when the president held it up to show his signature. Korte compared the images to directives submitted to the *Federal Register*, the place where they go to become law. The originals had typos. Some cited the wrong statutes.[1]

The directives themselves, with a few big exceptions, were vague. Below the long rhetorical windup, there were short, ambiguous requests that administrators make a plan and get back to him. Most orders were directed at appointees who would not be confirmed for months.[2] At the hundred-day mark, the press office boasted about the number of executive actions the president had taken.

Most people are comfortable with the idea that the Trump administration had a flair for the theatrical. It would not surprise them to learn President Trump and his staff cut a few corners to get an executive action out the door and into the press. For some, this just highlights plain incompetence and shows that the Trump White House was filled with political hacks from the campaign who could not help but write their executive orders in crayon. The mistakes would have not happened if there were adults in the room who knew the right way to do things.

I do not see it this way. I think the Trump administration was uniquely *successful* in the way it deployed executive action in service of politics. It is a mistake to assume that when a president disregards procedure and effectiveness, that can only be an error. Presidents can choose to be ineffective policymakers when the situation calls for it.

The Trump administration decided to hold ceremonies and sign directives before they were finished—before they were proofed, and before the people who would carry them out were ready to go. A few times the president even left the ceremony without signing the actual document. His staff decided to move forward on orders that made no immediate changes to existing policy and at best only started a longer process that might. These were conscious choices, revealed by behavior we can see. Moreover, these behaviors are not peculiar to Trump. Every presidential administration treated in this book drafts vague orders of the kind President Trump signed. Every recent administration held signing ceremonies. All presidents display the kinds of behaviors that suggest they care about things beyond just changing policy.

This chapter digs deeper into what presidents actually do. My theory of presidential power should help explain patterns in executive action over the last several presidencies. The implications of my argument, in brief, are that presidents' actions are less substantive in the lead-up to elections and when they have less legal authority. Their actions are more substantive once presidents become lame ducks, and also when they have more support in Congress. Put differently, symbolic orders without substantive backing should be concentrated during election season and when the president lacks the discretion to act.

These are hypotheses about general relationships. They are mostly supported by the data. The reason to actually go through the data, measures, and tests is to learn about the *extent* to which they are supported. Some patterns are stronger than others, and some exceptions are more informative than others. Moreover, as discussed in chapter 8, if you want to decide for yourself whether this turn in the presidency is good or bad, it helps to have a sense of degree. How much has symbolic politics warped the way presidents govern?

4.1 Measuring Minimal Direct Effects

Right away we have a problem. This book is littered with stories about executive actions that fell short of their own ambitions. But, in each case this ineffectiveness was not obvious from the get-go. That is part of the point. If the implications and substantive impacts of executive action were easy to see, then their symbolic component would not be valuable. But how, then, are we supposed to say anything about patterns in the effects of hundreds (or thousands) of executive actions without years of tedious work? Most presidential directives need their own study. Some even need their own book.

In general, scholars do remarkably little of this.[3] While good-government types everywhere implore bureaucratic agencies to be self-critical, to look back at regulations and evaluate their performance, few demand the same discipline of presidents, who muck around in government all the time. Very little, in general, is known about the effects of *presidential* interventions on governance. So little that it is worth returning to at the end of this book as a guide for future research.

But that is no help now. There are sixteen hundred executive actions from 1989 to 2021. We have to have some way of indicating their substantive effect. Fortunately, there are systematic ways of doing this without digging deeply into what happened years after the order. You just need to read them.

Start with a few simple and extreme cases. There are very substantive and symbolic actions. Take, for instance, restrictions on funding abortion as part of a given foreign-aid package. Shortly after the Supreme Court's decision in *Roe v. Wade* (1973), Congress forbade direct funding of abortion in family-planning programs the United States funds abroad. But since 1984, every partisan change in the control of the presidency has led to a change in whether foreign-aid dollars can go to organizations that provide abortion. Come January 20, the acting administrator of the Agency for International Development (AID) receives a phone call saying the president has signed a memorandum adding or subtracting language from AID contracts about abortion prohibitions.

The memorandums leave little to the imagination. President Clinton's, for example, says these "excessively broad anti-abortion conditions are unwarranted. [. . .] I hereby direct that AID remove the conditions [. . .] from all current AID grants to NGO's and exclude them from future grants."[4] This is clear, direct, and peremptory. It is still just a direction, whose details must be worked out by bureaucrats, and whose effects are debatable. But as far as presidential orders go, these have the best shot at change. They tend to be the most substantive.

These orders are also very common, even if almost none are about such highly charged issues as abortion. The president has some clear authority and makes a determination, and that's that. This is most common in trade and national defense. Do some of these lack substance or have symbolic content? Certainly. Some end up being sanctions against persons or foreign entities the United States has little capacity to enforce. Some are exemptions from tariffs that impact a sliver of some relevant industry. But introducing additional judgments like that quickly devolves into the kind of case-by-case investigation that needs to be avoided, at least for now.

Then there are orders that leave the substantive impact—to be on the generous side—up for debate. There was the 1776 Commission, announced by President Trump the month before the 2020 presidential election.[5] Section 1 of the executive order reads, "The American founding [fathers] envisioned a political order in harmony with the design of 'the Laws of Nature and of

Nature's God,' seeing the rights to life, liberty, and the pursuit of happiness as embodied in and sanctioned by natural law." It blathers on for another 650 words.[6] The order creates a body endowed with no power other than to meet and talk. It would put out a forty-one-page unsigned report two days before President Trump vacated the White House, a month after the president appointed the commission's membership.[7] This is a long way from tariff modifications and abortion restrictions in foreign aid. In terms of altering the doings of government, it did nothing. This is the kind of action I referred to in chapter 2 as a "think piece."

The 1776 Commission highlights features of orders that are themselves giveaways for this kind of impotence. It contained a long rhetorical preamble. It specified an exceedingly vague policy: the promotion of a particular kind of civic education. It contained almost no detail about how that goal was to be achieved. It created an advisory body with no authority. It asked that body to produce a report and recommendations.

And then there is what it did not do. It did not cite any statutory authority the president could deploy in pursuit of his goals. It did not order any administrator to promulgate regulations. It did not specify what would and would not count as the kind of civic education the order sought to promote. Any of those things might have brought the instructions closer to the order's announced purpose.

Those details do not demonstrate the impact of the policy—at least, not on their own. They reveal the gap between the apparent policy objective of the order and what the order actually does. Presidents are not allowed to lack ambition. They want to cure cancer, end gun violence, defeat antibiotic-resistant bacteria, raise wages, and increase exports. But they have plenty of latitude in how to order administrators around on the way to those goals. Sometimes they make big changes. DACA was a big change. It was peremptory. It was abundantly clear what the president was doing. There was no daylight between what Obama asked for and the goal of shielding a select group of undocumented residents from deportation.

Imagine that there had been. John Lennon and Yoko Ono broke up, and Lennon went back to the United Kingdom and recorded another Beatles album. So there was now no existing designation called "deferred action" that could be conferred upon dreamers. What could Obama do? Form a working group or commission, or create an office. Call it the President's Task Force on Dreamers. Direct them to come up with a plan, to piece together ways to limit the impact of deportations on that population. The task force could lobby for legislative changes and disseminate information. It could issue guidance to immigration agents and to states and localities. It could start a conversation.

Perhaps one day this would lead to substantive changes, perhaps not. The point is, the substantive effects would be up in the air. All the president did was create a task force and set them on the trail. It would be a think piece.

This is how the actions themselves hint at their effects. Some are clear and peremptory, while others are contingent. It is all a matter of degree, something you can take stock of by reading and making a series of judgments—some more subjective than others. Relying on quick judgments based on the orders themselves is, of course, more indirect than delving deeply into each case. When I later show differences in the proportion of executive actions counted as "nonsubstantive" by this method, I am really describing differences in the *expected* or *immediate* implications of presidential actions, based on factors apparent from the way they are written.

These considerations lay the groundwork for measuring what I refer to as "minimal direct effects," which is what is needed to test the hypotheses from chapter 2. This section details those steps and describes the measure. If you are short on time or uninterested, you can safely skip to page 83.

The clearest, most *objective* factors that indicate that an action is a think piece come from asking the following questions:

1. Did the order create a new body or organization?
2. Did its preamble cite a specific statute or law?
3. Were its orders directed exclusively at persons within the White House or Executive Office of the President?
4. Did it contain a rhetorical preamble?

Then, there are more *subjective* questions, such as:

5. If the order created a new organization, is that organization's role primarily informational or advisory?
6. Were its instructions or goals vague and general?
7. Was it primarily a request for information or advice?

These factors lead to the most subjective determination, which is:

8. Did the order have minimal direct effects on policy?

Was it, in other words, more like a 1776 Commission or an abortion ban? Answering these questions for each executive action should, in the aggregate, reveal predicted patterns in symbolic action. They should show us when the president consciously chooses to take some action, with little immediate effects on what the government does.

This indirect measurement strategy will undercount symbolic actions. Plenty of actions *do* make immediate changes, but those changes end up having little substantive effect, for various reasons. There are at least two other kinds of symbolic, nonsubstantive actions, which I cannot measure easily and which will depress the total number of nonsubstantive actions identified. For example, President Clinton issued a memorandum directing the Environmental Protection Agency (EPA) to receive and act upon complaints under Title VI of the Civil Rights Act of 1964.[8] He called this the legal basis for addressing inequities in the distribution of toxic waste and pollution, or what activists call "environmental justice." But in the years that followed, the EPA was able to act on almost none of the complaints it received (Foreman 2011, 56–59). This was what I called a "basket bet" in chapter 2.

Another example, Executive Order 13043, titled "Increasing Seat Belt Use in the United States," ordered federal employees to wear seat belts on the job.[9] How many were covered by this order? How many of those were not already wearing seatbelts? How many changed their habits as a result? No one knows. But at the time, President Clinton was pushing for a nationwide seat-belt law, so this certainly looks like another case of using federal employees as props in service of the president's political goals. This was what I called a "non sequitur" in chapter 2. In both of these cases, the orders were direct and peremptory, so they will not be coded as having minimal direct effects.

Before describing how I read and coded, it is important to head off other sources of confusion. Minimal direct effects is not the same as *ceremonial*. When President George W. Bush created an award for service in the "war on terror," he was acting ceremonially.[10] He acted the way kings and queens do when they bestow honorifics on people. The order's impact on military morale, let alone anything related to the war on terror, is unknowable. But this analysis does not even speculate. There is no distance between the directive and the outcome. The president created the medals. There they are, so it has something other than minimal direct effects.

There is another problem to confront, common to anyone who implements a measurement strategy with a theory in mind and best summarized by the physicist Richard Feynman: "You must not fool yourself and you are the easiest person to fool."[11] Authors write books that advance arguments. While well qualified, they are also the least impartial coder. How do you reduce the potential impact of that bias on the data?

In this analysis, there are a few guardrails. First, the coding rules build in diagnostics. The last judgment—question 8—is the clearest and will be used for most of the results reported in this chapter. But it is also the most subjective. I also label more cut-and-dried characteristics of orders. If I am correct, they should be related to the last question. Creating an advisory body, producing a vague order, and including a rhetorical preamble while citing no underlying statute all should be positive indicators of an order with minimal direct effects. It should be reassuring that my subjective judgment correlates with the objective features of orders.

Another key check is that some orders can be coded immediately based on their title. Trade-related determinations are like this. The president says the goods of a foreign country get preferential treatment, and that's that. Likewise, there are releases (or drawdowns) of military aid, renewals of states of emergency, or declarations of disasters. These kinds of orders are simple and formulaic. None of them qualify as orders with "minimal direct effects." Therefore, they can be autocoded. About 45 percent of orders were coded this way.[12]

The most important check on potential bias is that the vast majority of actions were date-blinded. They were coded without my knowing *when* they took place. Most of the implications of my theory of the presidency have to do with the timing of executive action. I teach politics. Unfortunately, I cannot un-know election years or partisan control of Congress over the last few decades. The best opportunity for me to fool myself is to read an action, see it took place near an election, and then unconsciously make judgments based on that. Here is the tautologist.

Unfortunately, that is not always possible. Why? Some orders reveal their timing. Orders in response to the SARS-CoV-2 pandemic, for example, were all obviously produced after March of 2020. Some orders include an effective date at the end. Some orders have duplicate titles, and thus can be differentiated only by their date of issue. Because of these exceptions, 87.1 percent of actions were date-blinded.[13]

The last line of defense is that I have not hidden my work. Again, freely given with this book are the rules I followed, the data, and the code reproducing every figure. The skeptical and curious can decide for themselves, and those better equipped to assess my assessments can do so. If others find another method, they can compare my judgments against their innovation. Have at it. My word on these patterns and data should not be the last.

As it turns out, orders with minimal direct effects are a nontrivial proportion of all action, and especially of those dealing with domestic policy. About 12.5 percent of all actions were coded as having minimal direct effects. For domestic policy, that figure is 19.7 percent—or about one in five.

Now, it is reasonable to wonder: Is it even worth explaining a political phenomenon that seems to occur so infrequently? Yes, and not just because infrequent political phenomena are still worth studying. Presidential vetoes occur rarely (on around 2 percent of all bills) and are even more rare in the modern era, but as Charles Cameron (2000) shows, they resonate throughout the legislative process. In this case, a huge number of actions—almost half—are mere determinations, with immediate effects. As it turns out, these are almost always so administratively mundane they are completely ignored by the press, the public, and—quite frankly—the White House. That means that while one in five has minimal direct effects, only one in three of the remainder falls into that other category of orders that are both substantively impactful and unique enough that they had to be read to be coded.

In other words, actions with minimal direct effects are a large proportion of the actions presidents take with some willful, strategic reason in mind. Recall, also, that this is probably an undercount of actions that turn out to be nonsubstantive. I decided on an indirect measure to remove as many subjective judgments from the coding process as possible. The price was a conservative benchmark on what could be called mostly symbolic.

The next question should be: Does this benchmark look as though it is capturing what I say it is? In other words, is it a valid measure of the concept I have described? To investigate this, I first examined whether the objective and subjective features of orders (questions 1–7) were correlated with my dichotomous measure (question 8) in ways that make sense. They are. The first characteristic is whether the order created a new organization or body. About one in six executive actions creates at least one—a task force, an initiative, an advisory council, a presidential board, a commission, or a working group. There is a moderate correlation ($r = 0.27$) between the creation of a new organization like this and being coded as having minimal direct effects, but that correlation goes up for orders that create informational or advisory groups ($r = 0.48$). In fact, if you remove these informational bodies, there is no correlation between an order being coded as nonsubstantive and the creation of these kinds of groups. This is reassuring. If the president creates a new unit with decision-making authority, it indicates their order *does* have direct effects on policy.

There are other intuitive patterns. Citations to the U.S. Constitution and congressional statutes are *negatively correlated* with indirect orders ($r = -0.30$). When presidents are relying on some underlying authority to act, the orders that follow are likely to tell bureaucrats to do something specific. About 1 in 4 orders had a rhetorical preamble—the kind I measured more precisely for executive orders and memoranda in chapter 3. These preambles are positively correlated with nonsubstantive actions ($r = 0.37$). In other words, when presidents present long, flowery justifications for their orders, the orders are less likely to contain explicit directives.[14]

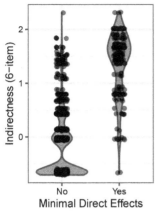 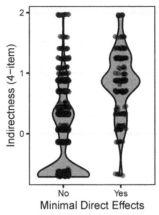

FIGURE 4.1 Measuring minimal direct effects
Points are individual executive actions, plotted by their question 8 coding (i.e., "Did this order have minimal direct effects?") and one of two latent measures estimated with 2-parameter item response theory models. The left panel uses 6 questions, whereas the right uses only the "objective" indicators from questions 1–4.

These are only descriptive patterns. Some characteristics are more prevalent than others, and some may be better than others at distinguishing between substantive and nonsubstantive orders. We need a statistical model flexible enough to account for these possibilities, which would produce a composite measure to compare to my main measure.

Therefore, I used these indicators to estimate two other, latent measures of policy substance. The first uses all dichotomous indicators (questions 1–4 and 6–7). The second uses only the objective ones (questions 1–4). Specifically, I estimated (two-parameter) item response theory models, in which each "item" was a feature of the order and each "subject" was an executive action.[15] I plot all three measures in figure 4.1. As anticipated, these features of executive action are strongly related to the dichotomous measure. The relationship is stronger for the six-item measure (left panel), which contains more information. The findings in the following sections are usually not sensitive to the measure used. When they are, I will tell you.

A first look at the substance of the policy allows us to assess a challenge to my theory. Maybe the media see through the lack of immediate effects and tend to avoid reporting them. If that were the case, then the supposed benefits of symbolic actions would be dubious. They would be limited to some specialized audience that does not get its news from news sources. We can examine this by using data on executive-action news articles. I describe and use these data in chapter 6. But for now, it is worth noting that newspapers do not ignore indirect orders.

First, actions with minimal direct effects received, on average, fewer news articles—9.6 articles, relative to 13.2 (though the difference is not statistically significant by convention; p = 0.22). If you look at total coverage, there are more articles that mention what I have labeled substantive executive actions. But, this is driven by a few extreme cases such as DACA and the Trump executive order on sanctuary cities. Substantive actions are not more likely to be covered, period. If anything, it is the opposite. Actions with minimal direct effects have a mean coverage rate of 62.4 percent, while substantive ones have a coverage rate of 54.2 percent (p = 0.07). This does not mean the media do not know the difference. But it is important to know that when presidents produced orders that lacked substance during this period, the media did not ignore or even underreport them.

4.2 Going Symbolic in a Power Vacuum

Presidents go symbolic when they have few other options. There is some problem they would like to do something about, but they lack the means to have direct, substantive impacts. They do not have the legal authority, personnel, or available funds—or some combination of all three. That makes investment in high-quality, substantive policy also more costly in terms of effort. This is the most obvious implication of my argument.

But even though it is consistent with common sense, it is orthogonal to existing theories of presidential power. In arguments past, it was maintained that if the president has little (or no) discretion, the president does not act, because the focus of these theories is explaining actions that have substantive effects. Actions with minimal direct effects, these arguments would say, are not unilateral action at all. They are outside the theory. But they cannot be set aside. They cost the president's most valuable asset—time—and soak up significant resources in the White House and elsewhere. Moreover, this drives innovation. Presidents may take risky action they expect will fail. Some of these will succeed against all the odds and set a precedent for future presidents.

This means it is important to evaluate the implication that presidents should perform when they lack the forceful discretion to act—which is overwhelmingly the case. I have already hinted that there are far fewer substantive actions in domestic, as opposed to foreign, policy. In terms of probability, foreign-affairs actions are 13.9 percentage points less likely to have minimal direct effects.[16] That itself indicates that presidents are more substantive in affairs over which they tend to have more direct control. But this simple distinction obscures a lot of variation within those categories. Presidents have quite a lot of direct authority over the management of public lands, and far less over taxes, gun control, and abortion—though all are domestic-policy issues.

If the theory is useful, it should organize a simple pattern. The more discretion there is, the more substantive the president's actions should be. This seems simple enough. To test this expectation, I rely on a measure Charles Shipan and I developed that examines how much leeway presidents have in various areas of public policy (Lowande and Shipan, 2022). I discuss this measure more in chapter 5.

There is, however, one complication, which is that the fifty-two policy areas that Shipan and I examined in this study are often too general to describe specific executive actions. Take, for example, the so-called Mexico City Policy, the one that prevents family-planning funds in foreign aid from going to organizations that provide abortion services. This could be classified as either foreign aid or abortion; the two are not mutually exclusive. Some actions cross-cut topics where the president's discretion over policy is quite different. President Obama signed a directive requiring national security decisions to incorporate climate change.[17] Presidents in general have far more authority over national security than they do over things that impact climate change, which means assigning one topic would introduce more error. So I allowed actions to fall into up to two categories, then took the average of the two.[18]

Discretion, measured this way, is negatively associated with symbolic, nonsubstantive acts. More specifically, for a typical (i.e., standard-deviation) increase in discretion, there is a 6.9 percentage point reduction in the likelihood of the action having minimal direct effects.[19] In terms of the topics themselves, a "typical" increase in discretion means something like moving from the area of air pollution to responses to terrorism, or from abortion to civil service issues. The baseline probability an action has minimal direct effects is 12.5 percent, so a 6.9 percentage point difference is huge.

It is also reassuring this pattern is consistent across the other measures of nonsubstantive, symbolic action. First, the association is robust to the latent measures of indirectness in figure 4.1. Both have strong negative associations with discretion. If you look only at executive orders and presidential memoranda, you will find that those with longer rhetorical preambles tend to rely on less legal authority. A standard-deviation increase in discretion is associated with a 6.4-percentage-point decrease in the proportion of an order that is rhetorical.

This only tells us about nonsubstantive actions from topic to topic, because the discretion measures are based on general judgments about presidential discretion during this period. But in these same periods, presidents could have—and did—receive or lose legal discretion. The substance of executive action should respond to these changes in authority. Likewise, if there are no changes in discretion, the substance of executive action should remain stable.

There are many policy areas that tell that basic story, but education policy is particularly illustrative. Beginning in 2001 with the No Child Left Behind (NCLB) Act, then continuing with a little-known part of the Affordable Care Act that made the federal government the main holder of student loans, the president acquired significantly more authority and resources to influence education policy.[20] Specifically, the NCLB Act funded and imposed regulatory requirements on state-level education programs but left both to the secretary of education.[21] The reconciliation bill that contained the ACA changed the federal government's role in student loans from guarantor to direct funder. Since the secretary is a political appointee, this federal intervention dramatically expanded the power of the president. Before the act, about two of every three education-related executive actions were indirect. Afterward, this figure was one in three.

That increase in policy substance was driven by a slew of important actions during the Obama and Trump administrations—most notably, waivers from the NCLB Act, "Race to the Top," and actions on student loans. Executive actions taken during the administrations of George H. W. Bush and Clinton look meek by comparison. They are mostly commissions and working groups on improving the educational outcomes of particular racial and ethnic groups. One of Clinton's nominees to these groups grew so dissatisfied with its lack of policy depth that he resigned. In another case, Clinton issued a memorandum designed to help "schools end social promotions."[22] After its extensive rhetorical windup, the president ordered the secretary of education to produce what would eventually be an eighty-five-page document that included such banal advice as "set high standards" and "concentrate on providing high quality curriculum and instruction."[23] There are, by contrast, some policy areas that saw no serious changes in presidential discretion. And as expected, the substance of this mix of orders is essentially flat. Over this period there were no significant changes to the president's authority over trade and national defense, and in both cases there are almost no actions with minimal direct effects over the complete time series.

Overall, the evidence supports the basic intuition. Presidents tend to go symbolic when they do not have the capacity to make serious changes. In the absence of the tools necessary to make a difference, they are incentivized to produce the *appearance* of governing.

4.3 Policy Substance and Congressional Opposition

When presidents take executive actions with little substance, it is not just second-best or because of the limits of their office. For presidents, symbolic orders require less costly effort than clear, substantive orders. The political risks of substantive orders almost never have anything to do with the order being overturned outright, because that rarely happens. Most substantive and impactful orders involve a longer policy process that is vulnerable to sabotage and requires a lot of time and resources on the part of the White House.

Congress poses the acute threat. They gum up the policy process, either formally or informally. They can reduce the capacity of the organization tasked with implementing the order. They might support lawsuits, conduct oversight, or otherwise demonstrate their disapproval to the administrators carrying out it out. When successful, these tools sink the resources the president deployed. Even if unsuccessful they can become a tax on the White House's time. All that, however, assumes that the order is substantive. If an order lacks substance, that fact may blunt Congress's efforts or desire to undo it. For these reasons, Congress is a natural place to look to evaluate the idea that presidents go symbolic in response to stronger political opposition.

There is an immediate challenge to gauging that effect. In general, it varies every two years, which is another way of saying it does not vary much. Each election cycle brings a new Congress, and though there are resignations, deaths, and party switches, these changes do not usually shift the balance of power in ways that would cause the White House to take note. Without many election cycles (which we do not have), and significant variation in those cycles (which is not present), it is difficult to reliably estimate the effect of congressional opposition on the kind of unilateral action the president undertakes. This is the same generic statistical problem I discussed in chapter 1, the one pointed out thirty years ago by Gary King, which makes studying the presidency difficult.

However, this does not mean that the data can say nothing. It only means that the findings in this section should be treated with more scrutiny. Whatever patterns there are, or whatever ones are absent, it could simply be that a longer period of history would be needed to find the true relationship. But I am skeptical about looking backward, partly because of evidence from other chapters. The data in this book come from George H. W. Bush to Donald Trump. That is partly because the argument in this book is about what the presidency has become over that period of politics. Some of the political conditions I described in chapter 2 predate the first Bush presidency. But it is more difficult to imagine executive action, as a political strategy, being deployed by past presidents in the same way that Biden, Trump, or Obama did. Presidents take cues from their predecessors, so it is more reasonable to think that reanalyzing these data after another few decades would be more informative.

With those caveats in mind, I first examine systematic patterns in executive action using industry-standard statistical summaries. These confirm the uncertainty inherent in examining this question with these data. Under unified government, defined as both chambers run by majorities of the president's party, the proportion of orders with minimal direct effects is 11 percent; under a divided government, it is 13.2 percent.[24] Another way to look at this is monthly, simply counting the number of minimal-direct-effect orders issued under one administration compared with other. There are 0.55 minimal-direct-effect orders per month under divided government, compared with 0.48 under unified. In contrast, for substantive orders, there are 3.89 under a unified government, but 3.61 under a divided one.

The strongest evidence in favor of my hypothesis comes from the rhetorical preambles. Executive orders and presidential memoranda signed under a divided government tend to have 4 percent more of the text of their order taken up by rhetorical language. This hints at the idea I raised in chapter 2 that the performance of executive action was one explanation for why so many have found different patterns for the *frequency* of actions under a divided versus a unified government.

These associations are all in the expected direction, but I would not take them to the bank. With the exception of some specifications of the rhetorical-language relationship, none are statistically significant by conventional standards. Likewise, the fallback measures I have mentioned—both the latent-trait measures from figure 4.1—show no consistent patterns within this time period. In an analysis at the directive level, the 95 percent confidence interval for the effect of divided government is wide: between -2.2 percent and +6.7 percent.[25] That interval tells us that the data *are* consistent with the idea that the effect of changes in party support, generally, is small or moderate. Put differently, if congressional opposition does influence the president's strategic calculus, it probably is not as significant as, say, the effect of the president's legal discretion or the effects of election cycles. For those other factors, there *is* enough variation to benchmark the size of the effects, and both appear large and important. The effect of congressional opposition might simply be smaller.[26]

But this treats congressional opposition generically, which is a blunt fit for many executive actions. Suppose the president is deciding whether or not to declare something a national monument in rural California. The delegate representing the fine people of eastern Rhode Island may have no opinion on the matter at all. The previous analysis counted them and the delegate representing the land area to be declared a national monument as equal. Executive action has regional significance, itself evident in patterns of media coverage, which I discuss in chapter 6.

All this calls for a different approach. Since there so few cases, it may be more informative to identify critical moments and describe them in detail.

That means political scenarios from 1989–2021 in which presidents were suddenly faced with a change in party support in Congress. There was President Clinton and the 1994 "Gingrich revolution," the second President Bush and the "Jeffords switch," the second President Bush and the 2006 Democratic referendum, President Obama and the 2010 "red wave," and finally, President Trump and the 2018 midterms. In each of these situations, the key question is whether the president's executive actions became less substantive after the loss of partisan support.

The best case for this hypothesis comes from the Clinton administration. Many scholars think the 1994 congressional midterm elections were a turning point in American politics. Despite the fact that Republicans had lost the presidency two years before, they took control of the House and Senate for the first time since before Alaska and Hawaii were states. The Republican caucus changed its style, or rather, as the political scientist Barbara Sinclair describes in her book *Party Wars* (2006), they had their style changed by decades as a minority party. Newt Gingrich, at the time Speaker of the House, believed the most effective strategy was to "'use the chamber as a political forum to express opposition and build electoral support'" (113). Congress saw direct confrontation with the Democratic president as a winning strategy, and their takeover surprised most pundits.[27] Did President Clinton's executive action become less substantive after the change?

In general, the answer is probably "yes"—but it did not happen immediately. There are actions with minimal direct effects in the second half of his first term, and they account for a larger share of all his executive actions. The big increase takes place in 1996 and coincides with his reelection campaign. The high proportion of minimal-direct-effect actions sticks for the second term. That is reassuring, because it remains outside of election cycles, and as Republicans stay numerically strong in Congress. In one illustrative case, shortly after the Republican congressional takeover, the president issued a memorandum requesting a "study" of affirmative action programs. The new majority intended to do away with race and gender preferences in federal contracts. Instead of issuing an order that directly reformed, replaced, or expanded these orders, he ordered the report. Once it was delivered, President Clinton gave a speech in favor of affirmative action at the National Archives that drew praise from his diverse political coalition ("Affirmative Action" 1995).

The midterm defeats endured by President George W. Bush in 2006 and President Obama in 2010, however, are far less convincing cases. For Bush, only eight actions in his entire second term are coded as having minimal direct effects, and they are not concentrated after the midterm loss. For Obama, there are more, many them included as part of the "We Can't Wait" campaign. But these coincided with the 2012 election, so it is difficult to say which factor was determinative.

The other important cases of changes in congressional opposition strength are not as useful as they initially seem. On May 24, 2001, Jim Jeffords, a Republican senator from Vermont, announced that he intended to caucus with Democrats. This created a new fifty-one-seat Democratic majority, mid-Congress, which was so unusual there is now an entire book on it (Hartog and Monroe 2019). This meant a meaningful increase in the strength of Democrats. It seems like a clear-cut case of "as-if random" variation. But later that same year, terrorists flew planes into the World Trade Center and the Pentagon. The focus of the Bush administration immediately changed, and Congress subsequently granted the president vast new powers in the primary policy area of concern. A similar situation obtains for the Trump administration. Even if we depart from the measurement rules I discussed earlier in this chapter, the last year of his term is filled with substantive actions responding to the COVID-19 pandemic. This, of course, highlights the degree to which the factors mix and cut against one another in the real world.

Thus, there is suggestive but weak evidence that opposition strength has impacted the substance of executive action. There are expected but usually small and imprecise differences across divided and unified governments. The strongest case-based evidence comes from the Clinton presidency.

4.4 Timing Is Everything

George Bush is 16 feet wide and over 245 feet tall. Standing below the giant sequoia in 1992, the president signed a proclamation meant to protect these trees, with the largest one taking his name. The Democratic primary had concluded the month before. Political advisors believed the young challenger could be bested by highlighting the president's environmental record. As governor of Arkansas, Bill Clinton had taken heat over his typical policy approach—which included study committees and voluntary guidelines, thought to be too soft on the state's most significant polluters.[28] Later in the campaign, the *Los Angeles Times* wrote that "no two presidential candidates ever have devoted more attention to the issue of environmental protection than George Bush and Bill Clinton."[29]

The president's nineteen-hour trip to California was part of the reason. Press invites went out shortly after Clinton made "Albert Gore, 'the Environmental Senator,'" his running mate.[30] Newspapers ran the story of the president's trip—one about his effort to protect the grove of trees he called "a great cathedral" and the defense of his defense of the environment.[31]

Whether the order protected that cathedral was another question. The proclamation did not specify which groves would be protected, or when.[32] The areas eventually protected would have been subject to logging, had a Forest Service plan early in the presidential term gone into effect. It did not, because of successful lawsuits brought by environmental groups.[33] At first invited to the ceremony by the White House, the Sierra Club now picketed, describing the event as an "election gimmick."[34] The president, they said, was rebranding a loss in court as an accomplishment. Freeman Creek Grove, where George Bush (the tree) lives, is the easternmost grove of sequoias, and the trees in it are much younger than the famous Mariposa Grove old-growth trees to the northwest. It had never been logged because of the trees' size and location.[35] Beyond the grove, however, the logging of giant sequoias continued after 1992 because of contracts grandfathered into the new protection regime. Conservationists asked for more and got it only eight years later, when President Clinton signed a proclamation creating Giant Sequoia National Monument. There is no Bill Clinton sequoia.

George Bush and the 1992 campaign were no mere coincidence. George Bush and President Bush created a few days of positive press on the campaign trail, trying to pitch the president as a promise keeper, a candidate who had run as a conservationist in 1988 and followed through. The summer of 1992 was the time to do it.

If presidents use executive action to secure the political benefits of symbolic policymaking and those benefits are indeed short-lived, then this should influence when they decide to act. Executive action should reflect the political calendar. The key dates for the president are the first Tuesday after the first Monday in November and January 20, every four years. Nonsubstantive actions carry less administrative headache, and their symbolic benefits are short-lived. More substantive actions on the other hand, are high risk and high reward—only their substantive rewards take years to manifest. As the election approaches, presidents' actions should be symbolic and nonsubstantive. Then, once they are in the lame-duck period (or approaching a second term), their actions should become more substantive. They pursue short-term political benefits, convenient headlines, and the appearance of solving problems as election day approaches.

Executive-action theories are usually about the separation of powers and say almost nothing about when executive action occurs within a president's term. Elections happen, the offices—the president and Congress—are filled, and the rest is the game playing out.

Of course, that way of thinking sets aside important facts about how any given White House operates. Peruse the memos written by domestic-policy aides of presidents past and you will find an obsessive focus on time. When will they roll out this new program? When can the president sign this document? How will this or that action fit into the themes of the administration? When is the best time to go forward? There is, by contrast, much less discussion of the opposition in Congress. This does not mean Congress is absent from their thoughts. It certainly is not. But the difference in emphasis suggests that something important to practitioners has gone unexplained by scholars. This is one value added of the way of looking at the presidency I propose. It recognizes something that seems to be important to people who work in politics.

Examining the patterns of timing is relatively straightforward. Actions are issued on a date. But there are some minor complications. First, a half dozen actions have an ambiguous date. In all but one case, the date of the action could be narrowed down to a particular month.[36] Second, some actions, though signed on a particular day, might be leaked or announced months earlier. I discuss this more in chapter 6 on media coverage. Most important, though, some policymaking might be designed to generate headlines at a later date. President George W. Bush issued Executive Order 13443, which purported to expand hunting on federal lands.[37] Contrary to the headlines it garnered, it ordered the secretary of the interior to produce a set of proposals for expanding hunting on federal lands. Those proposals were due one year from the date of signage, during the 2008 presidential election season. Development of the action plan took place through a White House conference organized in October of 2008.[38] Most of the final proposals required legislation. The action date may be one of several dates presidents expect to accrue political benefits. This is a source of error to keep in mind.

Nonetheless, executive actions are seasonal in a way that is consistent with my argument, with one unexpected pattern. The most informative way to summarize these patterns is to look at executive action over the life cycle of a presidential term—that is, beginning with month 1 (January 20–31) in the first year and ending with month 48 (December of year 4) and month 49 (January 1–20, just before inauguration). Figure 4.2 plots the proportion of orders coded as minimal direct effect by these sequential months, averaged across eight presidential terms in the dataset. As expected, actions with minimal direct effects rise and peak before a presidential election, then almost bottom out during the lame-duck months. The actual peak occurs in the forty-third month, which is July of the presidential election year and well into the campaign. In that month, actions likely to be less substantive make up 27.5 percent of the total, which is more than double the baseline figure.

But surprisingly, the trough of indirect actions occurs not at the start, but in the middle of the term, shortly after the midterm elections. During this

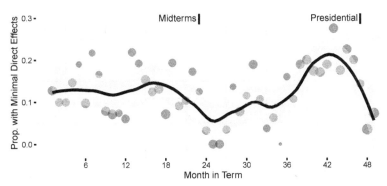

FIGURE 4.2 Less effectual orders peak near the presidential election
Points are the proportion of executive actions in that month coded as minimal-direct-effect orders. Larger points indicate more orders were issued in that month. LOESS line with $\alpha = 0.4$. Month 1 is January 20–31, and month 49 is January 1–19.

period there are several months in which all actions issued in any presidential term have some immediate, direct effect. There are also plenty of orders with minimal direct effects early in the term, especially in the first year and the year of the midterm cycle. There are many possible explanations. During the midterms, presidents might care about the fate of their co-partisans and try to aid their reelection. Early in the term presidents might be using nonsubstantive actions as a tool to push their legislative agenda, as I hypothesized in chapter 2. I remain agnostic about interpreting the evidence this way because I have not measured the president's legislative agenda or connected these orders to it with anything but anecdotes.[39]

In general, these patterns hold up to different summaries, which are more precise in describing the change in the odds of an indirect order based on timing. I estimated the likelihood that an order has minimal direct effects as a function of the key factors highlighted by my argument. In this case, that means the discretion the president has in that particular policy area, whether it was issued in a lame-duck period and whether it was issued near a presidential election.[40] Estimated in this way, orders issued within a presidential election year (but prior to the election) are 7 percentage points more likely to have minimal impact.[41] Those issued during a lame-duck period are 6.1 percentage points less likely to have minimal direct effects. Estimating the effect of lame-duck periods is less precise because there are just fewer orders. Finally, these patterns are mostly robust to different measures of policy directness. The six-item latent measure from figure 4.1 shows similar patterns: it is negatively associated with lame-duck periods and positively associated with proximity to the presidential election. The exception is the four-item measure based only on "objective" features of executive action. Both relationships are in the expected direction, but they are less precisely estimated.

These patterns cut against a potential criticism of the way I have measured minimal direct effects. A lot of these create groups that produce policy recommendations. Let's be generous. Suppose these organizations do a lot of good. Maybe they get the ball rolling. They start conversations or set the agenda. They are the preliminary steps toward something bigger. This is what many who worked in the White House say, and there are examples consistent with that story. President Obama, for example, signed a memorandum that asked administrators to develop a plan to promote "job-driven" training.[42] The plan came three months later and was followed up by bipartisan legislation that incorporated many of its recommendations.[43]

But even if these orders always had a happy ending, the optimal time to take this kind of preparatory action would not be as the president approached the end of his term. The right time would be at the start. The actions would be concentrated at the beginning of the term, each a first step toward changes the president knows will take years. That is not in the data. Presidents seem preoccupied with using their power to assemble others as a way of bolstering their brand in the months prior the election.

What do these patterns mean in terms of typical executive actions? Presidents rarely, if ever, sign orders that are not immediately substantive in the period between election day and inauguration. Domestically, they establish new national monuments, sign permits, grant pardons, release fuel stockpiles, and finalize regulations. In foreign affairs, they release military aid, levy sanctions, and extend duty-free treatment of imports.

There are exceptions. President Trump signed a memorandum billed as prohibiting immigrants with affiliations to antifa, a loosely organized leftist movement in the United States.[44] The order had no impact on immigration laws or enforcement. It asked the secretary of state to consider adding antifa to a list of terrorist organizations. Trump administration officials had previously testified in Congress that antifa was not itself an organization.[45] Whether any designation could occur in the remaining fifteen days of the term was beside the point, because the law already permitted denial of entry for any persons suspected of organized criminal activity. It will be years before records are released that might piece together why such an order was signed at all. As far as outliers go, this one occurred during a transition period that was, itself, an outlier in American history—owing mostly to President Trump's refusal to concede he lost the election, the attempted coup, and the violent attack on the Capitol.

In general, however, the orders that are given between election and inauguration tend to be more substantive, especially when considered alongside ones given before the presidential election. President Clinton asked his appointees to get back to him with recommendations for reducing teen drinking and driving and promoting the use of uniforms in schools.[46] President Bush asked agencies to put on a conference to promote "cooperative conservation,"[47] and for the secretary of the interior to give him recommendations about whether to declare Pearl Harbor a national monument.[48] President Obama asked the defense department to release generic tabulations of persons killed by U.S. drones abroad.[49] President Trump asked appointees to report back to him about federal funds spent in cities he deemed to be permitting "violence" and "anarchy."[50]

Depending upon your own political preferences, these may seem like laudable goals. Again, it is not my argument that such orders will never lead to policy change or anything of substance. Some can and have. The pattern, though, is that orders with the combination of high-minded goals and vague directions are concentrated just as the retention of political office—by both the president and their party—is top of mind. Even if we give them the benefit of the doubt, this is not an opportune time for such actions. The end of a presidential term is no time for listening sessions, policy development, and nonbinding reports. The best explanation is not that presidents and their staffs are making systematic mistakes. The best explanation is that they believe executive action itself has symbolic value beyond what it does to change policy. Presidents use the machinery of government bolster their political brand when the time is right.

A nontrivial portion of the directives presidents sign has little immediate connection with changing the status quo. But many of them manifest a sincere desire and a policy position. They say that the president is a conservative or a liberal who is going to fix some problem. Even when the scope of the president's authority is limited, he can earn a symbolic win by acting. When the electoral fate of his presidency is on the line, he has stronger incentives to push out actions that will only indirectly change what the government does, if they ever do. Presidents adapt the things most immediately within their control to political circumstances. They are strategically ineffective.

But the evidence in this chapter can only take us so far. I relied on an indirect measurement strategy to test the theory. But my argument also makes claims about the way people view executive action, and the way the press covers it. These are what I turn to in chapters 5 and 6. If they are confirmed, we can be more confident in the argument.

This chapter also has said nothing about where these actions come from. Presidents' resources and capacity have always been in the background. The same incentives that drive presidents to change the way they act unilaterally also inform the way they organize their presidencies. Ultimately, nothing gets the president's sign-off without working its way through the White House. So the White House is the place to look for evidence of their underlying motivations. As I show in chapter 7, presidents build their own capacity not only to govern effectively and control the bureaucracy, but also to enhance the symbolic component of the policies they pursue.

5: THE PUBLIC DEMANDS

Congressman Paul Broun addressed a group of women in Columbus, Georgia, who he hoped would become his constituents. Then vying for a Senate seat, he waved a pocket Constitution while listing all the ways the Obama administration had "left the bounds" of that document and was now "totally out of control" (Parker 2014). It was a theme for Republican candidates that election cycle. One candidate wrote the president "declared war" on Congress by implementing his plans with nothing but the consent of bureaucrats (Neugebauer 2014). Another, who would best Broun in the 2014 Senate contest, later declared that Obama had "disrupted the Constitutional balance of powers" (Perdue 2015).

It is easy to imagine that charges like those could reflect something deeper in the American electorate—that alongside the demands for action from activists like Hong, there are accusations of presidential imperialism from people like Broun, which also resonate with some segment of the public. Modern presidents might be caught in a trap, with public expectations and public skepticism jointly immobilizing the president.

This is less than half right. The public does expect action from the president, and when the president acts, criticism tends to include high-minded references to the Constitution, the separation of powers, and the rule of law. But the way both of those facts impact how presidents behave is not as obvious as the case of President Obama and Congressman Broun implies, for two reasons that form the argument of this chapter.

First, while the public demands action, it does not hold presidents accountable for results. Their demands are not like orders that, if ignored or botched, pose consequences at the ballot box or in the history books. They are, instead, vague expectations that the president has the ability to make a difference. Public demands are closer to *desires* in the market, the way we talk about consumer demand for toilet paper and athleisure wear. They can burden and strain the people in the White House. But make no mistake: they are also an opportunity. This opportunity has not always been there, because public demand is a recent phenomenon relative to the complete history of the office. There are many good books on the historical development of these expectations.[1] The history is instructive because the recency implies something most would find hard to believe: that those expectations could change. I pick this thread up again in the final chapter.

Most would probably agree that public demands present a political opportunity. But the second point—that the public does not hold the president accountable for the results—might strike some as bizarre. Any book on the modern presidency includes a few lines like this: "When bad (or good) things happen in America and elsewhere, presidents are punished (or rewarded), regardless of whether they had anything to do with those bad (or good) things." Let's say this is true.[2] This sounds a lot like being held accountable for results, but it is not. The public is blaming presidents for circumstances, not reacting to individual actions the president has taken. This is an important distinction. When I argue that the public does not hold the president accountable for "results," I mean the results of the actions they take. I mean that presidents are mostly free from criticism for the direct consequences of their executive actions. The main reason is that for most executive actions, practically no one knows what those results are. Experts, who do sometimes know, do not matter.

There is a second reason these demands do not cripple the president. Critics of executive action may raise procedural issues—it circumvents Congress, it is not constitutional, we live in a democracy—but the consequences of those criticisms are not as dire as they sound. There was a time when they were, and it is instructive. For much of American history, executive initiatives like the ones launched by presidents today would be considered radically inappropriate, even impeachable, by a consensus in Congress and among people who could vote. Even in 1952, when President Truman famously seized the steel mills, the criticism was overwhelming and bipartisan (Reeves and Rogowski 2021, 174–75). These sentiments still exist, as Andrew Reeves and Jon Rogowski's account clearly demonstrates.

What has changed is these sentiments' relative weight. It is easy to imagine President Trump, Biden, or Obama doing the same thing, and the partisan Venn diagram of their critics having little or no overlap. The electoral fortunes of same-party members of Congress are now so closely tied to the president that they cannot afford to cross the aisle over procedural traditions. When members of Congress deploy America's civic religion and cry blasphemy, you can usually predict their party, even if you do not recognize their name.

Let's check in with Congressman Broun after he and President Obama left office. In 2019 President Trump reprogrammed $8 billion in military construction funds to build a border wall, which he had promised during the campaign. It was an executive action on immigration, taken after Congress did not agree to the measure—just like DACA. But it will surprise no one that Broun did not raise constitutional objections to this particular use of executive power. In fact, he cheered it on—both because he agreed with the policy, and because he and President Trump are both Republicans (Barr 2019). Democrats do this too. They cheered DACA and called the border wall a violation of the legacy bequeathed by the founding fathers. When Presidents Trump and Obama undertook their initiatives, they said it was Congress who had invited the moves by being slow and ignoring the will of the people.

This inconsistency does not make modern politics look good. But politicians today are not uniquely scurrilous. Appeals to the Constitution and the supremacy of the legislature were bipartisan when the parties could expect Congress to do something about major policy issues. Today, the best opportunities for quick-kill, public-facing policy wins are presidential. The executive branch is the center of governance in the United States, and Congress is in no hurry to change that. So civic tradition now cuts against other desires. If you would like almost a million resident aliens who go to school, do not commit crimes, and like America to be able to stay here, your choice in 2012 was DACA or nothing. Likewise, if you would like more physical barriers between the United States and Mexico to answer flagrant disregard for the border, your choice was a national-emergency decree or nothing. Nonetheless, the tradition is there, and it is persuasive enough that politicians deploy it as a rhetorical device. The point is, it is just that: rhetorical. The rhetoric has no legal or policy consequences, and it is telling that most often, when members of Congress raise these points, they are deemed wrong in court. The Supreme Court of the United States determined that both DACA and the border wall were constitutional. The criticisms remain to dress the windows of the Capitol.

In this way, the public helps *enable* executive action more than it curbs it. Its desires and limitations help make symbolic executive action both viable and strategically advantageous. The results of executive action are often imperceptible, even to careful observers and experts. I teach government, and therefore I think politicians who force students to take classes on government are doing God's work. But there is not some great deficiency in civic education to be rectified. Nor are the smartphone-scrolling generations of today somehow uniquely inattentive and shortsighted. It is not even a problem unique to democracy, as research on performative governance in China by Ding (2022) teaches us. The information gap between the public and executives is fundamental to almost every problem of how people organize and govern themselves.

Another thing that makes presidential orders in the United States different is that in this case, even the opposition party does not have an incentive to bridge that gap. If Republicans had argued that President Obama's memorandum on gun-violence research was ineffective, they would have undercut their assertions that it was part of an unconstitutional power grab. If Democrats had pointed out that barely eighty of the hundreds of miles of wall built during the Trump administration were, in fact, new barriers not replacing old ones, they would be playing down its importance to their own supporters—deflating the same constituents they need to mobilize.

This means the public has no choice but to make the best assessment based on *expectations* about results. They have outsized expectations about the scope of presidents' authority. They treat new information about executive action as a signal about the president's position. By default, they treat that new action as if it had already been carried out.

What does this all mean for a sitting president? The symbolic and substantive dimensions of their actions are separable. When presidents announce a policy, this public audience responds based on its symbolic content. The fact that the president acted alone is not itself negative. At the end of those first days, executive action is the political equivalent of a very loud press release. This is critical for presidents' incentives. Because presidents do regularly make substantive policy changes, the public tends to treat *all* such actions as substantive, which opens up the opportunity to get away with being mostly symbolic. This is what makes the strategies uncovered in the last chapter appealing.

These are all assertions about how the public views and reacts to executive action. Evaluating those assertions means first looking at public opinion. We have to know how the public views the president's job and how they respond to what the president does. In a nutshell, this means demonstrating that executive actions are powerful credit-claiming opportunities for presidents, and that the public downsides—such as punishments for failure or constitutional critiques—are not really relevant for presidents' decision-making.

5.1 The Pageant

John H. Hartig watched as several thousand kids converged on the lagoon. Bused there by Nickelodeon, they were then given trowels, shovels, nesting boxes, garbage bags, and potted greenery—tools needed this summer morning to carry out an executive order signed by the president of the United States. The kids did not know that, of course. They just knew there would be orange semitrailers, a mobile stage, games, blaring music, hot dogs, and green slime. With his own daughters among them, Hartig told a reporter,

"This is the first of many big steps to come on Belle Isle." It was August 6, 2000, on the island park in Detroit, Michigan, which sits a third of a mile into the river near the upper mouth that opens into Lake St. Clair.

In the century since it became a public park, a lot changed. Detroit mass-produced weapons, vehicles, and equipment for World War II. After these products were shipped downriver, the dregs of the assembly lines remained for decades. In the three-year period after the war, the government guessed that eighteen million gallons of oil were dumped into the Rouge and Detroit Rivers. This is enough to contaminate about a million times as much water, or every drop of the western basin of Lake Erie. Before the late 1960s waste-water plants discharged hundreds of millions of gallons of raw sewage each year. Even in the early 1980s, a hot summer might bring winds of hydrogen sulfide, which would off-gas as sewage choked oxygen from the river water. By the time of the Belle Isle cleanup in 2000, the most obvious side effects of industrial expansion had been curbed by regulation. But wildlife and wetlands were mostly gone, replaced by concrete breakwater and sheet-steel piling that hid industrial toxins stored in the river sediment.

Hartig, then working at the Coast Guard, knew this history well. Growing up in nearby Allen Park, he was taught not to eat fish caught in the river, and he remembered the day in 1969 the Rouge River caught fire and sent flames almost fifty feet high. For him, these were formative childhood experiences that led to a career in conservation. So when producers from Nickelodeon called wanting Detroit to be the sixth stop on a national tour to promote community service, the neglected shorelines of the Blue Heron Lagoon on Belle Isle came to mind. Hartig gathered donations and volunteers for an event he would later call "typical" for an initiative thought up and executed by the Clinton White House.

President Clinton had announced the program three years earlier, during his 1997 State of the Union address. The American Heritage Rivers Initiative (AHRI) would help communities "revitalize their waterfronts and clean up pollution." He said so at the signing ceremony, overlooking the Potomac, and again the following year at a designation ceremony along the New River in North Carolina. Staff in the Council on Environmental Quality had spent the previous year pitching the program. The recurring opportunities to craft the administration's environmental bona fides were its key upside from the get-go.

Kathleen McGinty, a former legislative aide to Al Gore and then head of the Council, had been asked by advisors to the president to produce "several options for new 'bully pulpit' challenges [. . .] on the environment." To make the pitch for the program, McGinty made a side-by-side comparison of Clinton and the original bully. The initiative could be the president's "signature stewardship creation, much as Teddy Roosevelt created the first wildlife refuge and established the first national forests." The aides liked the sound of that. It made the top tier of a plan—titled "Activist Presidency"—to "give the President three to four substantial message opportunities per week."

The first message was well received. Local and national news outlets ran endorsements from politicians at every level of government. PBS planned a full *NewsHour* piece on the initiative. Communities prepared applications to compete for the official designations, which were to be announced later. The initial buzz was "terrific," McGinty wrote as she appended the good press to a memo. The subsequent milestones promised more. The president would give speeches beside rivers, standing alongside communities around the country. The vice president could be lauded by the current president for "the magnificent record he has established in protecting our environment"—a record McGinty and others hoped would propel Gore into the White House in 2000.

Before any of that, however, there were some important details to attend to. The day the president announced the program with a single sentence in the State of the Union, the executive order he was to sign had not been written. The communities applying did not know what it would mean to be an "American Heritage River." Though scientists such as Hartig carefully defined what qualified as a river, even this basic detail had not been decided (and never would be). So it was anyone's guess which communities would qualify, and whether that designation would mean anything. Would the label mean new federal dollars and environmental protections?

The president and his staff later answered this question with an emphatic "no." There would be an entirely new system of specially designated river communities. But there would be "no federal mandates, no regulations, no restrictions on property holders' rights," Clinton assured ascendant conservatives in Congress. The program would add not a cent of obligation in the budget; what it needed would come from existing programs. It would hire no new employees. It would rebrand what was already on the books.

That did not mean, however, that no one would work on it. In fact, this was the only concrete reward for acquiring the new presidential title. Each river would be given a dedicated employee whose title might lead you to think they spent their days at the helm of a keelboat. This was how Hartig came to be officially known as "John Hartig, River Navigator." Hartig and his peers navigated the bureaucratic morass of federal, state, local, and private entities with jurisdiction over their rivers. The White House would link these waters to resources that already existed but had gone unused simply by providing a dedicated advocate.

Getting even that was not easy. To make it neutral in the eyes of accountants, willing agencies had to house the navigators. No two homes where quite the same, and in some cases the federal government would not even foot the bill. Hartig ended up in a Coast Guard station overlooking the Detroit River. Others were housed in the Geological Survey, the EPA, the Army Corps of Engineers, the Forest Service, and at a mix of local nonprofits. Hiring and keeping them was a challenge. Public employees had to be convinced—as Hartig would later put it—to "give up tenure, effectively," and take a job the White House said would last only five years. Even when they did hire, the insecurity made jumping ship normal. Some hosts cut the position. A few years in, several rivers lost their navigator permanently.

If any of this was clear at the outset, it did not discourage communities around the country from applying. There were over a hundred applicants for ten designations. They were enlivened by the competition. It was not clear how the selection committee—then headed by Dayton Duncan, the documentary filmmaker who produced *Lewis & Clark* with Ken Burns—would choose, or by what reasoning. This fanned creativity. Self-conscious about their status as a postindustrial river, the Detroit organizers gathered stories from thousands of locals and mailed them at the nation's only floating post office, which docks at Belle Isle. The real application went through FedEx. The process turned Clinton into a judge with an audience of hopeful contestants. John Delaney, the Republican mayor of Jacksonville, Florida, and an ardent supporter of the program, called it "a beauty pageant for American rivers."

Others did not see it that way. The president's announcement created confusion that would last for years. Many news reports then and years later said the program included environmental protections. The Heritage Foundation wrote that the program "creates, by executive fiat, the most all encompassing regulatory regime ever to be imposed on private landowners" and that it shook "the balance of power in Washington, D.C." According to critics, President Clinton had "neither the constitutional authority [. . .] nor the intention of asking Congress for such authority." One op-ed called it "a massive power grab by the federal government." A political action committee called "Liberty Matters" circulated claims that "black helicopters" had been sighted near World Heritage sites, that the rivers initiative was a backdoor means to total control by the United Nations. Republican leadership received "tremendous public outrage" in the months following the announcement.

This all resonated with Helen Palmer Chenoweth, a Republican from Idaho who rode the wave of Newt Gingrich's Contract with America into the House in 1995 and who would later be one of the first to support President Clinton's impeachment. She introduced legislation to undo the program, sued the president, and demanded that its principal architect—meaning McGinty—testify before Congress.

On a fall day in Washington, Congresswoman Chenoweth began her questioning by presenting a letter from her state's complete delegation denouncing the program and saying they would not allow their state to participate. "What is your oral response to the delegation letter?" Chenoweth asked. There was a pause before McGinty smiled and said, "Thank you very much." When the laughter stopped, she went on to say, "I think that's just fine. This program isn't for every community, and if the communities of Idaho don't want to be part of it, that's their choice."

By this time, it was clear this basic point would carry the day. The legislation that would have abolished the program died before reaching the floor. Members who wanted to could take their rivers out of the running. The lawsuit would later die too, as the DC Circuit Court reminded Chenoweth that failing to attain a sufficient number of votes in Congress was not grounds for a lawsuit. More important, everything McGinty and the president had said about the program was true. There was nothing for the court to defang. The designations changed nothing as far as the laws and accounts of the United States government were concerned.

This did not mean that the presidential title meant nothing to those who were selected. Hartig and others believed the gesture carried a symbolic weight that opened doors then and into the future: even though the program ended in 2004, with nothing remaining but the name itself, it was a catalyst for tens of millions of dollars in federal grants and the promotion of organizations that would outlast the president. At the same time, however, they would also say that it was their community that had made most of the difference. Other designations had not led to these results, other navigators quit early.

Less visible was the fact that from its earliest beginnings in the White House, aides saw the existing growth of river community organizations as a wellspring of political support to be tapped. "In many places, Regional Watershed Councils are already forming," an associate director under McGinty wrote in 1996. Even more opaque, perhaps, was that thirty years earlier Congress had created a system of "Wild and Scenic Rivers" that did have the regulatory fangs missing from the new designations. The administration chose to create a new system rather than work within the old.

Hartig had no illusions about the impact the designation would have on the Detroit River, any more than he had hopes that his five-year term would be extended once the Bush administration took over the White House. Shortly after the transition, he convened an expert panel asking for the Detroit River to be designated a wildlife refuge—something the president was powerless to effectuate, despite the fact that it had been Teddy Roosevelt who invented the first of these and inspired the creation of the program that paid Hartig's salary. Later that year the Detroit River became the only international wildlife refuge in North America, after a bill introduced by Congressman John Dingell passed by voice vote and was signed by President Bush.

Hartig was hired to run the refuge and did so for the next fourteen years. Today, in its nearly six thousand acres, bald eagles, osprey, and peregrine falcons nest. Having vanished at the low point before the conservation movement, they have returned, along with lake sturgeon, whitefish, mayflies, otter, and beaver—resident legacies of a policy victory that ended, but had not started, with the president's signature.

5.2 Gait Expectations

When President Clinton and his advisors put together the AHRI, they were tapping into expectations that predated their time in office—though not in the way people normally think about those expectations. The conventional wisdom is that it is about success or accomplishments. In a book titled *The Presidential Expectations Gap*, for example, the authors define the gap as a "pattern of declining approval ratings over time" and an "increased dissonance between expectations and reality" (Waterman, Silva, and Jenkins-Smith 2014, 30).

Each new presidency is like a bad marriage, this perspective suggests: it peaks at the opening ceremony. People simply expect presidents to be much more successful than they can be, and over time they become disillusioned by the misalignment of their hopes with realities. There is probably some truth in this, if only because this is a basic feature of human psychology. After all, presidential campaigns are built to raise spirits that are unsustainable. But this idea is not terribly useful if you are a president, beyond fatalistic reassurance that your unpopularity—barring a major terrorist attack or an assassination attempt—is inevitable.

What I have in mind when I refer to public expectations is much more informative for presidents and their advisors. The public has expectations about what the president has say over—about what their domain is and what they can do. Public expectations are not about whether you think the president fixed your car, but whether you think of the president as a mechanic. When the Clinton administration launched the AHRI, the underlying expectation was, "The president does this kind of thing." Presidents anointed rivers, forests, or other natural wonders beautiful and protected them from the incursions of market forces. The public expected the president to have sway. In this case, as McGinty and others made clear, they had that historical reference in mind. Presidents had been protecting lands unilaterally for almost a century, and the first mover, President Theodore Roosevelt, had been lionized for it.

But there was daylight between the Clinton rivers initiative and Teddy Roosevelt, and it makes the AHRI seem almost farcical. There is a gap between what President Clinton could actually accomplish alone and what President Roosevelt had done earlier that century. Some of it was legal. Rivers could only be designated Wild and Scenic Rivers by an act of Congress or the states (P.L. 90-542). The other option—designating portions of the rivers as wildlife refuges—is a bit more complicated. Refuges have been created by the executive branch and by Congress. But the executive-driven refuges got that way because they were on federally owned public land. Decade after decade, as the most agreeable tracts of land were added to this system, there were simply fewer obvious additions. Later, and mostly through innovations by the secretary of the interior, Ken Salazar, the Obama administration added refuges by accepting donations. These "conservation easements" allowed private individuals to retain ownership the land but let it be managed by the government.

Going this route in 1997 would have been complicated and effort-intensive, and may not have worked. This, of course, highlights the fact that the gap also had to do with resources. The final initiative was carried out by the White House and employees on loan from a ragbag of bureaucratic agencies and relied entirely on programs already on the books. Anything more would have required what agencies either did not have or were less than willing to give up. Real, substantive policymaking requires hard work.

The expectations gap, in this case, was not between success and failure—and whether this succeeded or failed was politically irrelevant. On the one hand, the public believes the president has a say over lots of policies and problems. On the other hand is the reality the president is constrained in all facets of governing. These were not always separate, as the journalist John Dickerson (2021) summarizes in *The Hardest Job in the World*. Dickerson illustrates the transition with natural disasters, which presidents used to say almost nothing about. Today presidents have even staged meetings with response teams for show. Do presidents add any value to disaster response when they show up with their shirt sleeves rolled up? Of course not. But these are politicians who have made it to the highest office, and they know people think their presence matters, that addressing the disaster is within their purview.

The gap is often framed as a burden. The fact that George W. Bush took the blame for inadequate response to Hurricane Katrina in 2005 is considered a given by most commentators, Dickerson included. But there are also cases people say boosted the presidents' fortunes, such as President Obama's response to Hurricane Sandy just days before the 2012 presidential election. We can't know whether these claims are true.[3] But people seem to think the expectations gap can generate a political opportunity—one that is not related to presidents' actual accomplishments. This is what executive actions like the rivers initiative take advantage of. They are valuable *because* expectations are high.

These expectations differ from those about success and failure in another important way: they are not uniform. Environmental conservation and disaster relief may have different size gaps because both public expectations and presidential authority vary from issue to issue. Presidents are commonly thought of as more powerful, for instance, in foreign affairs relative to domestic issues, which may or may not parallel public expectations. As it turns out, this can be quantified more systematically. The president's discretion and public expectations should guide us toward areas of policy in which we are more likely to see symbolic actions that do less to change the status quo. In other words, taking stock of the gap can help identify where the president's political opportunities are.

Measuring the expectations gap means understanding both sides of it. It requires knowing something about what the public expects relative to presidents' actual capacity for meeting those expectations. This is not easy. Public expectations about presidents' powers are a topic for public-opinion scholars. The president's discretionary powers are a topic for scholars of institutions or administrative law. In general, the former deploy surveys of the public, the latter examine legal documents. Taken separately, each enterprise might be fine on its own. One could come up with a survey-based ranking of public expectations about where presidential power lies, along with a separate measure of the degree of presidential discretion in various policy areas. But the two ways of doing things are not comparable.

With this challenge in mind, Charles Shipan and I set out to make them comparable—and as a result, identify where the expectation gap is large and where it is small.[4] In the previous chapter I used the data we constructed to measure the leeway presidents have in different policy areas. The following describes how these measures were created. We ran several surveys in which survey takers were presented paired choices at random. This approach is a mainstay of market research. In this case, the choices were not products or services, but areas of policymaking. After reading a prompt defining presidential discretion, they were faced with a simple choice of A or B: "For the following pair [. . .] click on the policy that recent presidents (i.e., Bill Clinton, George W. Bush, Barack Obama, and Donald J. Trump) have had greater discretion to change through executive action." The basic question is, when forced to compare any two, which does the audience think the president has more sway over? These individual decisions can be aggregated to rank-order perceptions about which issues the president has more power to impact.[5]

The key innovation, from our point of view, is who made those individual choices. We fielded the same survey, first with a nationally representative sample of 400 U.S. citizens, then with a group of 128 scholars—mostly political scientists like us, but also lawyers, historians, and economists. The first set provides us with public expectations, the second with something closer to the reality of the president's discretion. It is reasonable to compare them because they were generated with the same procedure. There are many sources of policy discretion for presidents (e.g., available personnel and resources, statutory and constitutional language), so this approach allows experts to condense and weight whatever they believe is relevant. Different survey takers will bring different ideas. All will be somewhat imperfect. But aggregating the judgments of everyone should make for better rankings.

The gaps are significant, and instructive, as figure 5.1 illustrates. The diagonal points are experts' rankings, from most to least presidential direction. Differences between that rank and the rank of the public generate the horizontal lines. These are expectations gaps. They are most significant and noteworthy in domestic-policy issues relative to foreign affairs. Notice that items such as military action, trade, terrorism, exports, arms control, and military aid all have little to no gap, or even a surplus. The public and experts alike tend to understand that the president has a lot of discretion over foreign policy. Beyond this, serious differences in judgment emerge. The American public seems to think the president has a lot of say over big pocketbook issues such as taxation, inflation, monetary policy, welfare, regulating big banks, and direct payments to farmers. There are also deficits in perceptions of the president's control over incendiary issues such as gun control, voting rights, health insurance, foreign aid, and immigration.

The rankings raise a second question: Is it possible for there to be an expectations surplus, rather than a deficit? Could it be that the president actually has *more* control than the public expects him to have? Yes—at least in theory. In this case, our survey cannot tell us one way or another. The public's expectations might be an order of magnitude higher than those of the experts, in which case, all this figure tells us is about the size of the gaps relative to other gaps. It cannot tell us whether the president actually has more or less power than the public thinks. What we can say with confidence, though, is that the gap is likely most sizable in domestic political issues.

The surveys also demonstrate an important point about public expectations: the public is very uncertain about what presidents can and cannot do. Figure 5.1 obscures this, but two properties of the data are illuminating. First, practically speaking, it takes many more members of the public to precisely estimate the rank. That suggests the public does not tap a widely shared understanding of what presidents can do. Second, members of the public were

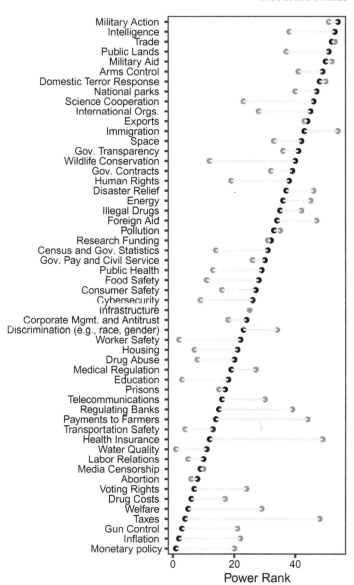

FIGURE 5.1 The expectations gap is larger for domestic affairs
Dark dots indicate expert rankings, while lighter dots indicate the public's ranking of that issue.

likely to violate a basic tenet of rationality: transitivity. If the president has more power over guns than abortion, and more over abortion than space, then the president should have more power over guns than space. On average, the public made six errors like this in a sequence of twenty choices. These seem like obscure statistical properties, but they illustrate how vexing public expectations can be. Even though there are some discernible patterns, their constituents have quite vague ideas about what is within their power. In other words, depending on the circumstances, it is entirely possible that the public is moving the goalpost.

5.3 Just Get It Done

President Clinton and Chair McGinty tried to outflank criticism of the AHRI from the get-go. The whole thing seemed to be crafted to avoid offending conservatives. There were, as both said repeatedly, no mandates, no restrictions on property rights, and no new spending. This was not enough to head off criticisms, which read as though they had been copied from a template. Alongside a program that led to things such as summer cleanup parties for elementary-school kids, there were accusations the president had usurped Congress, that his actions were unconstitutional, and even that he had invited the global domination of the United Nations.[6] That last part is a quirk of this case, but the rest is familiar. No modern president gets out of office without fielding this kind of criticism. The important question is whether that criticism matters for their incentives. Do we have any reason to think they should hesitate in fear of this kind of political attack? The simple answer is "no."

If I asked someone whether they thought the president should be allowed to enact a law by himself, without Congress, what could I expect them to think about before spitting out a response? Probably the sitting president. I have not mentioned his name, but since this is being written in 2024, "the president" means Joe Biden to almost everyone. Next is probably "Congress" and whatever they know about it, which is probably not positive. At present, one in five approve of the job Congress is doing.[7] The third thing is probably the "law" or policy the president wants. It is anyone's guess what specific law or idea they have in mind. It could be the most recent law Congress tried but failed to enact, or whatever single issue matters most to them. We have not gotten to the Constitution and the separation of powers yet, but that is the point. As the adage goes, questions of procedure are questions of policy. In this case, the constitutional questions are inseparable from a particular moment in time: a particular president, the Congress, and the policy.

From a researcher's point of view, this presents two challenges. First, it renders simply asking people how comfortable they are with executive action mostly useless. Their answers are sincere, to be sure, but the relevant question, from the president's point of view, is how they balance these considerations with the rest of the particulars. The president cares about the net effect of these concerns, because the scenario in which all the public has to consider is the sacredness of the Constitution and the separation of powers does not exist. Second, if these concerns are contingent on circumstances, that makes saying anything general about them more difficult.

Benjamin Goehring and I studied this by fielding a panel survey before the 2020 presidential election.[8] We showed members of the public a prompt about the president's position and recorded their opinions. The experiment randomized, among other things, *how* the president acted. It either gave them information about the president's position, said they were lobbying Congress, or showed them signing an executive order. We also varied the president and the policy. The action could have been taken by President Obama or President Trump, and the policy acted on could have been one of fifteen. Like the topics listed in the last section, these ran the gamut from foreign to domestic, and from highly controversial (e.g., abortion and gun control) to relatively bipartisan (e.g., farm payments). The prompt was random, so to determine whether the public had different opinions based on how the president acted, we averaged over these other conditions.

For example, the "President Obama taking executive action on the minimum wage" condition reads, "President Obama supported raising the minimum wage for government contractors. He acted alone by signing an executive order. The order would raise the minimum wage for government contractors," and was accompanied by an image of Obama signing an executive order. If it was the Congress's condition, the survey would include an image of Obama at a table with members of Congress. The Trump conditions would swap Obama for Trump, the minimum wage would be lowered, and the image would show Trump apparently working with Congress or signing an order. By asking many people and varying these particulars, our aim was to get at the impact of executive action on public perceptions in general.

I illustrate those perceptions in figure 5.2. After reading the prompt, respondents recorded their job approval of the president, their approval of the president's handling of that particular topic, whether the president worked with Congress, and whether the president respected the rule of law and the Constitution.[9] The most obvious differences are, in the first place, by president. This survey went out August 2020, so by this time, views on Obama were fairly positive (i.e., north of 60 percent) and views of Trump were generally negative (i.e., south of 45 percent). For any particular president, there isn't much difference between any of the ratings, which are broken down by the type of action viewed by the respondent. Despite the survey takers' being bombarded with short and clear text, along with an associated image, whether the president took executive action did not matter much for opinions.

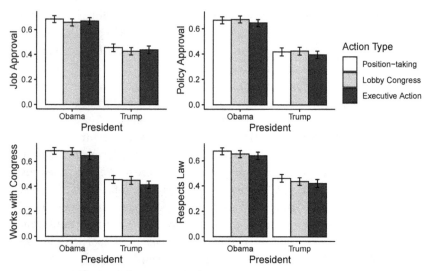

FIGURE 5.2 There is little or no penalty for executive action
Error bars indicate 95 percent confidence intervals.

There were, however, small and statistically distinguishable differences for the questions about working with Congress and respecting the law. These small effects (i.e., about -2.5 percentage points) suggest that the public sees executive action as less cooperative and respectful of civic tradition. The important thing, however, is that these effects are not paralleled when you ask the public about job or policy approval. In other words, for the few who see the actions as inappropriate or uncooperative, that does not seem to relate to their overall assessments of the president's job.

This does not mean the public does not care about the rule of law or the Constitution. What it does is help gauge the relative weight of those considerations next to unavoidable features of politics. In this case, Trump the person swung approval ratings by 20 percentage points. Trump the signer of executive orders made hardly any difference. Trump's personal effect conflates the effects of co-partisanship and approval of the policy direction the president proposed. If there is a general penalty for going outside the civic bounds, it is small, something less than 2 percentage points, or less than 4 percent of the mean approval. The question is whether this is something a president should worry about. Would you?

This is one study, but there are entire books on this subject, which largely support these assertions. In *The Myth of the Imperial Presidency*, for example, the political scientists Dino Christenson and Douglas Kriner report results from surveys about Obama reforming student loans, DACA, and Trump building the border wall (Christenson and Kriner 2020). They used different language that either emphasized the actions were unilateral or did not. These were different surveys, conducted at different times, on different issues. Survey takers still did not respond negatively to executive action itself. Christenson and Kriner conclude that "the dynamics driving public attitudes toward presidential use of unilateral power are remarkably like those driving public opinion on other policy actions" (58).

Another book seems to be much less supportive, at least on its face. In *No Blank Check*, Reeves and Rogowski write that "Americans hold presidents accountable not only for what they accomplish but also for how they wield power" (Reeves and Rogowski 2021, 21). They write compellingly about the civic education and norms of the United States and find, in survey after survey, that the public tends to disapprove of executive action. The main difference is that this disapproval comes out after Reeves and Rogowski carefully excise the political context I have argued is most relevant. They abstract away from the policy, the president, or even the presidential candidate. In most cases they are careful not to cue party, policy, or anything else. This serves their purposes, which is to study these attitudes. The question is whether those attitudes are relevant for an incumbent president (or a presidential candidate).

I think not. The basic reason is that politics is particular, and even in Philadelphia in the summer of 1787, the constitutional delegates probably had in mind a president (e.g., George Washington) and a policy (e.g., tariffs or internal improvements). Another way of putting it is that these types of questions do not reflect how politics plays out outside of surveys. This is an empirical claim, one that cannot be settled until we examine the kind of information available to the public in the wild. This is what I do in chapter 6. But if true, the implication is clear. If the public sets its mind on something, they mostly set aside how it is done, because they just want it done. If you are a president thinking about whether executive action is a good idea, then this is the relevant fact.

5.4 Success Is the Default

Like so many other executive actions, Clinton's AHRI was designed to give the president messaging opportunities at a regular clip. Among the presidential aides McGinty was to supply these opportunities to was Elaine Kamarck, then senior policy advisor to the vice president and manager of the National Performance Review. Kamarck has since written the confidently titled *Why Presidents Fail and How They Can Succeed Again*, which defines failure as some scandal that leads to spectacularly bad press (Kamarck 2016). There was no such scandal for the AHRI, and press about it mostly died after the announcement of the fourteen designated rivers. But the coincidence raises an important point about executive action, success, and failure, which is: why did Clinton's staff think of executive action as a positive messaging opportunity?

The answer has to do with the way the public treats new information about something the president has done. This is clear enough after rereading the survey: "President Obama [. . .] acted alone by signing an executive order. The order would raise the minimum wage for government contractors." The statements are strong and declarative. They do not hedge or embrace contingency. They imply the president has already won. These survey statements are all fictional, but as I show in chapter 6, they are consistent with the way journalists write up the news.

Failure still matters, however, as does the policy itself. There was some proportion of the public that disapproved of the rivers initiative.[10] Despite the work of speechwriters, Clinton was not going to convince them otherwise. This is true in general, as the political scientist George Edwards (2003, 2009) has demonstrated with decades of research. Presidential speeches do little to change public support for policy. Likewise, executive actions are not tools to persuade a skeptical public that a particular action is needed. On the other hand, failure can be a powerful persuader. It might persuade the public that the president is incompetent and not in control.

This seems like a risk of going it alone. Sign an order as president, and you own the results. But a few different issues are wrapped up in this risk. The first is that perhaps presidents own *all* failures of government, regardless of their direct involvement. Many think this is the case. This is what they mean when they write that presidents are held "accountable" for everything that happens in the United States, good or bad. So the question is whether presidents pay an especially high price for policies they have attached their name to by taking executive action. On the other hand, failure may not persuade enough people to inflict a real political cost. After all, views of the president and the policy may be so entrenched that news of failure will not move the public.

This is what the second wave of our 2020 panel survey was designed to sort out. Waiting a few weeks, we recontacted respondents from the first wave, informing them about the outcome of the president's action. We defined failure as the policy the president asked for not happening.[11] In the case of the Obama minimum-wage hike, we informed the respondent that the hike simply did not happen. The same went for Trump, only they had been told the president wanted the wage lowered, but it remained the same. Again, we accompanied this information with images you would likely to see in news stories about failures—the president looking quite vexed, even sad. The idea is to simulate, with as much clarity as feasible, the messages from the kind of press that reports a win or a loss.

We found that the public does indeed punish presidents for failure (fig. 5.3). Specifically, across the board (e.g., among independents, co-partisans, and the opposition), information about failure systematically reduced perceptions of presidents' handling of that policy area by about 6 percentage points. This is fairly large effect, all things considered. In many cases, it will be the difference between majority and minority support on that issue. The penalty is only there for the handling of that issue, not for vote choice or overall job approval. So survey takers were unwilling to change their minds on those more entrenched opinions. Since these were surveys about one small policymaking action, it may be that the accumulation of failures would move the dial on job approval. Subsequent reports of failure can indeed reduce public assessments of the president.

There are questions that have yet to be answered, however, before this effect has any relevance for incumbent presidents looking to act unilaterally. These are topics for chapter 6, but ultimately, my answer is that it does not. The reason is that in the real world, it is very rare for people to get information about the outcomes or results of presidents' decisions. Clear presidential failures are either the stuff of scandals, weakly covered, or otherwise go entirely unnoticed by the public and the media.

Public assessments of success, as it turns out, are much more illuminating. In particular, across all policies and both presidents, responses to success were indistinguishable from responses to the first wave. That first wave was the announcement of a policy, or the kind of flash reporting that occurs

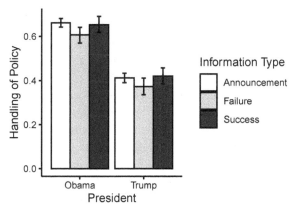

FIGURE 5.3 Public opinion about presidents' handling of the topic at announcement is indistinguishable from success
The figure reports support for presidents' handling of the topic in the first wave (announcement), in the second wave after information about success (success), and information about failure (failure). After accounting for topic, condition, and pretreatment support, the effect of information about failure is about 6 percentage points.

once a president has signed a new order. Respondents treated news that the order had succeeded in its aims the same way they treated announcements of new policy.

This brings us back to the Clinton rivers initiative, and to all considerations of executive action more generally. An upside of action is clear. To be an "activist" president means controlling an important narrative. The president is acting. Their administration is succeeding in its aims. Though orders are pieces of paper until they are implemented, the public still treats signage as an accomplishment in and of itself.

These patterns put the presidency in the same light as Congress and its members. In their book *The Impression of Influence* (2014), Justin Grimmer, Sean Westwood, and Solomon Messing examine congressional behavior through press releases. They show that members often boast about acquiring benefits for their districts, and, more specifically, what matters most is the fact that they boasted, rather than the content of the boast. The amount of money, and whether the money was secured, dispersed, or just proposed, have little impact on perceptions. A similar point can be made about executive action, though on an entirely different scale. If executive action is like a press release, it is one heard around the country. But like those other credit-claiming opportunities, it is treated as a win, regardless of details or the long road that might lie ahead for securing the real win.

For most of the policymaking presidents engage in, the public is not a constraint on executive action. They have outsized expectations of what can be accomplished, combined with the general impression that presidents have the power to act when they do not. Concerns about the way that action is taken are not overriding. Once the action is announced, the public treats the presidential announcement as evidence of a win, so they give the president credit for it. This is what helps to make symbolic policymaking valuable. If there were some deep skepticism of executive action, or if the public saw executive action as cheap talk, presidents would be less apt to go it alone.

All of these are freely contestable points. But if they are true, they present a very different political scenario than the one outlined by others. Alongside the desire to be effective and govern well, there are more immediate and less costly ways to capitalize on the waiting expectations of the public. They may be called undemocratic and unconstitutional, but this will matter little; and by taking executive action, the president may be giving the public exactly what it wants.

6: MOST PRESS IS GOOD PRESS

Presidents hate the press. Or at least, they are supposed to. Five months into his presidency, George Washington was shown a cartoon that depicted his decapitation. According to Thomas Jefferson, the president threw a fit that culminated in wishing he was dead.[1] Jefferson, who hired the man who published the drawing, recorded the incident in his meeting notes for historians to later find (and, occasionally, embellish).[2] James E. Pollard (1947) wrote of the incident to show that even the administration of an even-tempered president like Washington had early signs of an antagonistic relationship with the press.

Today, that antagonism is front and center. It is in the title of popular historian Harold Holzer's (2020) book *The Presidents vs. the Press: The Endless Battle between the White House and the Media*. Holzer recounts the Washington incident and many others through the Trump administration. "The press is the enemy," goes the famous line from the then-secret Nixon tapes, which the president repeats twice more for effect.[3] President Trump did not keep his feelings a secret, calling the media "the enemy of the people."[4] If you made a word cloud about presidents and the press, it would include "battle," "enemy," and maybe "death." This is what makes this chapter seem odd, at first.

Presidents have a lot to thank the press for. Battles over journalistic prying, leaks, inaccurate characterizations, and negativity mask central features of news about what presidents actually do. A lot of it—maybe even most of it—is neutral, descriptive, and, frankly, shallow. If you respond, "Well, it should be," then you are illustrating the point. Today, most journalists at least pretend to be nonpartisan, to report "just the facts." But that plays to the political advantage of the president. It produces a kind of news story that is often as good as a press release written by the White House itself. As this chapter shows, this is especially true for coverage of executive action.

If you read that last paragraph to a journalist, they might disagree or get offended. They might wheel out the greats—Carl Magee and Teapot Dome, the Pentagon Papers, Robert Redford whispering to shadows in an Arlington parking garage, or present-day reporters in press briefings. This shows, they would argue, that the press is *the* critical force in a free society, holding the line against the abuse of power. Day to day, they help hold presidents accountable for their choices. Yes, and no.

First, famous cases of press coverage that harpooned the reputation of the president are famous for a reason. Most news coverage does not do this. Seymour Hersh and Bob Woodward and Juliet Eilperin are exceptional. Deep, investigative reporting, in general, is difficult in the contemporary market for news. The scandals themselves were also exceptional. Even presidencies with the most egregious examples of public corruption are swamped—in raw frequency—by coverage of the day-to-day happenings of the president just being the president.

Second, an antagonistic press—one that goes for the scoop, exposes corruption, and sincerely believes in its role as a guardian of democracy—can still end up playing into the president's strategic interests. This is not because journalists are naive and easily duped. It is a structural feature of journalism itself. For news to be read, the story has to be short. It has to have a narrative structure. It has to be written in language an American high schooler can read. And for news to be news, it has to be novel—ideally, so novel you are the first to hear about it.

This is all good for the president, especially one interested in acting unilaterally, because, as the political scientist Stephen E. Frantzich (2019) writes, presidents are the ultimate news hook. They are famous enough that the basics of news—the who, what, where, when, and why—fall immediately from their name alone. When presidents sign a directive or take some other opaque administrative action, the natural inclination for journalists is to make them the subject. A narrative takes shape. It is the president who signed the order, demanded some bureaucrat act, or reversed the policy of the last president. It is not the bureaucrats, who actually implement the policy, and it certainly is not Congress, whose statutes the president often claims to carry out.

The other important point is that media scrutiny of presidents almost always focuses on what is new. This seems so obvious that it is not worth stating. But the attention difference matters. The modal pattern, I show, is: the president announces a policy, the press reports it for a brief time, then everyone moves on. Press coverage is asymmetric, focusing on the announcement of policy to the exclusion of its results.

Why? For one thing, reporting about outcomes is hard and risks the perception of bias. The sourcing, background knowledge, and expertise required to assess the effects of something the president has done are rare. Most often, when reporters do this kind of reporting, the results have to hit people over the head. A whistleblower leaks a legal opinion that says torture is fine. A health-care website does not work. Veterans die waiting for medical appointments. But the results of most things presidents do are rarely obvious, and reporters are not really set up to learn about them. Again, this says nothing about the will or competence of journalists. Their profession just does not incentivize this kind of reporting, and sometimes even presidents and their staff can make only an educated guess about the real consequences of their actions.

When the press covers executive action, coverage is, in effect, a symbolic win for the president. It is a clear signal. It says to the public, "The president accomplished this today"—not "The president proposed something today" or "The president has been vaguely musing about something today." It is sometimes even more than just the former. Sometimes reporters frame executive action as a response to a gridlocked Congress. This, of course, promotes the narrative I described at the beginning of this book. It plays well. Christenson and Kriner (2020) and Reeves and Rogowski (2021) show that people are sympathetic to this story. If a person is skeptical about presidential power, they tend to give the president a pass. But even when the news does not contain this story, it still redounds to the benefit of the president. Most press is good press.

This clarifies the game presidents are playing, which I laid out in chapter 2. If presidents act unilaterally, they have an audience that expects they have the power to make changes. They can expect that the way they decided to make those changes will not injure their political standing. They can anticipate that the public will assume, upon hearing the news, that the president has closed the book: the policy is enacted, done with, a success. But the audience is also not foolish, so if you tell them otherwise, many will react negatively. What media coverage of executive action reveals, however, is that the audience is most often not told about either failure or success. There are exceptions, but most of public information is about the enactment of policy, not its results. It is an inch deep because it has to be. This is critical if you are a president thinking about executive action. It tells you about the political ramifications of producing something that has little or no immediate effect on policy. This is what makes symbolic, nonsubstantive actions viable as a political strategy.

6.1 The Third Snare

It was the evening before Palm Sunday in 2003, and J. David Kuo was driving north on Rock Creek Parkway when he started violently convulsing and lost consciousness. His Mercedes sped up to eighty. A waist-high stone barrier ran between the road and the scenic tributary, twenty-five feet below, which Kuo's car would have had no trouble breaching. Before it pitched through the wall and into the water, his wife in the passenger seat awoke, grabbed the wheel, veered into oncoming traffic, then crashed into a stretch of highway safe enough to leave them both without serious injury. He was told this hours later in the hospital, after tests revealed he had a brain tumor. He was thirty-four.

For the last two years, he had helped lead a White House initiative to bring the government and people of faith together—a dream job he would now have to resign. To the dismay of his former colleagues, though, he told anyone who will listen that the president's signature campaign promise, which Kuo himself had worked for years to carry out, was a farce.

The promise was "faith-based" public programs. Though organizations like Catholic Charities and Jewish Family Services had carried out social programs for decades, Evangelical churches argued that informal rules prevented them from doing the same. They saw social welfare programs as a vast mission field. In 1995 the new Republican majority in Congress enacted "charitable choice" laws they hoped would open the doors to more faith groups partnering with government to help the poor. They were quickly disappointed. Clinton left bureaucrats to decide whether the laws were consistent with the way they already operated. Most did nothing differently.

The ambivalence left an opening for George W. Bush's campaign in 2000. The message first appeared in a speech in inner-city Indianapolis. "We will rally the armies of compassion in our communities to fight a very different war against poverty and hopelessness," Bush said, "a daily battle waged house to house and heart by heart." Bush's "compassionate conservatism" intrigued Kuo. What started as a fifteen-minute meeting with Bush on the campaign trail turned into an hours-long discussion that successfully recruited him.

Bush made similar impressions on others. John J. DiIulio Jr. studied crime and poverty in inner cities while on the faculty of Princeton, which granted him tenure after three years. The grandchild of Italian immigrants and the first of his family to attend college, DiIulio argued that the strength of religious institutions stopped disadvantaged kids from falling into criminal life. Like Kuo, he spent several unexpected hours with Bush at a campaign event in Philadelphia, where DiIulio grew up and now worked with nonprofit organizations. He came away with the belief that Bush was "a highly admirable person of enormous personal decency." Kuo felt the same way, and the belief never left either of them, even after both resigned the positions to which Bush had appointed them.

DiIulio and Kuo became the number one and two, respectively, at the White House Office of Faith-Based and Community Initiatives, created with the stroke of a pen, as one of the president's first official acts. Their mission: "to establish policies, priorities, and objectives for the Federal Government's comprehensive effort to enlist, equip, enable, empower, and expand the work of faith-based and other community organizations." In other words, they were to turn a few short lines in a campaign speech into policy—lead the "armies of compassion" and make the government more open and cooperative with religious groups.

Not everyone shared their enthusiasm. In article after article, opponents excoriated the program as a dangerous mixing of church and state. With the creation of the office, they argued, the Bush administration had shown it was a de facto arm of the religious right. It would channel federal dollars to religious organizations in the hope of choking out secular charities, and worse, it would use that money to spread religious teachings, violating the First Amendment. So they sued, early and often. That strategy, however, had only limited success. After defeating a prison program run by an Evangelical charity, the core challenges to Bush's executive actions failed, defeated by a five to four majority at the Supreme Court.

But this all came later and had little to do with whether the initiative succeeded, according to both DiIulio and Kuo. What mattered was not that the orders held up in court, or that the threat of litigation chilled participation—or any other kind of partisan combat. The problems were inside the White House, sewn in before the president added his signature to the first orders and basically invisible to the public until someone went on the record. Even then, the bad press would be nothing next to the fanfare when the initiative began. When DiIulio went public, he called the president's pledge for compassionate conservatism "virtually empty."

The first hint that it would turn out this way came when two transition officials, Donald Willet and Donald Eberly, began planning the initiative. It was the day after Christmas, just twenty-five days before Bush's inauguration. They could be forgiven for cutting it close. The Supreme Court had decided the Bush campaign would become the Bush administration just two weeks before. It was not much time, and it was only one of many items Willet and Eberly had in their portfolios.

For all the meetings, discussions, and speeches during the campaign, there was little on paper about how the initiative would work. They had even less time than they knew. When Karl Rove, a senior advisor to the president, determined that the president's tax proposal needed more time in the oven, he simply moved the rollout of the faith initiative up a week. The officials protested for a delay. At that time, they said, the president would have nothing to sign, because they had yet to write the executive orders. There was no office, there were no staff. There was nothing to roll out. How were they supposed to invent a program in six days? Rove replied: "I don't know. Just get me a fucking faith-based thing."

Willet and Eberly delivered, as did the signing ceremony and everything that led up to it. In fact, around the time Rove demanded final plans for the initiative, most major news outlets were running prospective pieces on the office, which did not yet exist. The signing ceremony, held on January 29, 2001, made the front page of the *Washington Post*. The photos show the president surrounded by faith leaders. He shakes hands with DiIulio. Everyone is smiling, all as the news carries well beyond the *Post*: New York, Charleston, Pittsburgh, Philadelphia, Los Angeles, Chicago, Austin, Boston, and of course, any paper that relied on the Associated Press for its national coverage. The president "launched a broad governmental effort [. . .] to invigorate religious charities and nonprofit organizations in the battle against the nation's social problems," the *Post* announced. The first mention of objections from opponents appears eight paragraphs in, on page A8, buried after bipartisan endorsements and quotes from administration officials.

But the problems kept coming. The office needed twenty-five people, its leaders said. They got seven. Satellite offices in departments outside the White House had trouble keeping the few people they had. The main problem, researchers would conclude later, was neglect. According to DiIulio and Kuo, there were fundamental differences between them and political advisors about what exactly the office was good for. DiIulio, a self-described "old, Madison-minded American government professor," wanted a performance audit that would precede serious policy change. He claimed he had to beg to get that provision added to the order. Even after it carried the president's signature, the audit "got less staff help on it than went into any two [public-relations] events."

DiIulio resigned after six months, a time line quite welcome for all involved. The occasion spotlit what mattered to the initiative's main audience, best summarized by the Baptist televangelist Jerry Falwell. Asked about the departure, he told a reporter that DiIulio had gotten "into trouble the first day in office because he didn't know the clientele." DiIulio penned a 2750-word resignation letter the following year alleging that the administration had few left working there who were "worried at all about policy substance." DiIulio was out, replaced by a lawyer who had worked for Mother Teresa.

Kuo stayed on but faced the same problem. How could he keep senior officials interested in the follow-through? In a White House dealing with tax cuts, education reform, and the new global war on terror, this became "a matter of survival," he later said. His answer relied on the political experience he had acquired before he met Bush. The midterm elections loomed.

Republicans had a slim majority in the House and lost control of the Senate after Jim Jeffords of Vermont switched parties. To make the program relevant again, Kuo went to the political affairs office, offering to hold events for Republicans in close races, in an attempt to mobilize Evangelicals. The office was ecstatic, quickly producing a list of about twenty names.

Meanwhile, the initiative touted awards granted to faith-based organizations. Billions of dollars had gone to faith-based groups, thanks to the president, or so it claimed. In sworn testimony, Kuo later claimed he asked satellite offices to come up with those figures to provide cover for the president. The grant figures were fungible, and a report by the GAO explained why. The White House was not collecting the information it needed to track its own progress. There was no definition of what counted as a "faith" organization and no lawful way of forcing applicants to disclose. So they guessed, in ways that produced figures showing a 20 percent increase in funding for faith groups. The figures still showed that the increase was a function of an uptick in applications, not a change in the way grants were awarded.

As it turns out, there were changes—even important ones—but they flew well below the press's radar. The satellite centers, in response to the audit DiIulio ordered, helped revise the way some departments awarded grants and contracts, making it clear to faith groups what was and was not prohibited. The changes Republicans had hoped for in 1996 were largely obtained through opaque bureaucratic procedures, far afield from efforts by anyone at or near the center of power at the White House.

By 2003 Kuo had gone all in to reinforce the opposite impression, orchestrating press events and meetings, while beginning to question his role. Then came the crash and the cancer diagnosis. It meant he would leave the White House without prying questions from reporters. He went quietly, for a time. But then he read the news. He listened to the White House touting the president's accomplishments and heard it rebrand existing programs as a new win for compassionate conservatism. So he wrote op-eds, testified before Congress, talked to *60 Minutes*, and wrote a book.

He had a warning. Despite the essential goodness of the man elected president by voters, the presidency contorted his own faith for a "political throne." The Christian right was not in charge, he wrote, it was just another constituency. He quoted Charles W. Colson, who first introduced him to politics decades before: "[O]f all the groups I dealt with, [. . .] I found religious leaders most naive about politics. Maybe that is because so many come from sheltered backgrounds, or perhaps it is the result of a mistaken perception of the demands of Christian charity." Or, he went on, "they may simply like to be around power."

6.2 Covering Executive Action

Let's say you were paying attention to politics during Bush's faith initiative. What would you be in a position to know? What would the news tell you President Bush had done? This, of course, depended on timing and on how closely you were watching. Hundreds of articles mentioned the initiative, and dozens were written before the president officially took office—before it was clear what the initiative was. It was reported as the fulfillment of a major campaign promise. In that sense, it is exceptional, because most executive action does not get that much press. But it is quite typical in other ways.

Despite hundreds of articles by dozens of different reporters, most mentions of the initiative read as if from the same script. The president made a promise, and he delivered by signing an order. He did so very early on, before a major push for a faith-based initiatives bill in Congress. Most of the coverage of his executive action is about the January 29 announcement, which tells us a lot. For one, most of that press coverage was positive. It describes the president apparently following through on a promise less than two weeks into his presidency.

The date itself also tells us something. January 29 was not some externally mandated deadline. It was not ordered up by a court or part of the legislative calendar. It came from the White House, and in this case, directly from Karl Rove, a senior advisor to the president. There was coverage of the president signing the order on that particular date because of a conscious choice, one that was up to the president and his trusted aides. In this case, the timing was significant. They decided they needed more time on the president's tax proposal, so they moved the faith initiative up. This was zero-sum, in a sense. They had less time to set up the initiative before it was announced. Bush signed tax-cut legislation, once in 2001 and again in 2003. He never got a faith-based initiatives bill. A week probably would not have solved the problems DiIulio, Kuo, and others later complained about. But the example is revealing of their motives. Bush and Rove made a judgment call about when to roll out this executive action. The timing was strategic and based in part on how they expected the press to react.

There is also nothing unique about *how* the press reacted. They tell the reader a simple story. Here is a new president who said he would do something, and now he is doing it, all by himself. Many people liked this—just take a look at them smiling in the photo. A few paragraphs later, if readers even get that far, they may be informed that some oppose this move, or that the move will take a long time to be carried out, or that it is only a partial step. Contingency is buried, as is token opposition. What is front and center is the story that the president is in charge, doing what he said he would. This illustrates the symbolic component of policy.

Of course, that does not mean that the faith initiative got no bad press, or that all coverage was of its announcement. There was bad press, and there was coverage of results. The negative headlines ran, however, because both DiIulio and Kuo grew disaffected and resigned. DiIulio was a Democrat and an academic. Telling the truth did not cost him what cost others. Had Kuo not developed a terminal illness, we would not know about the program's other issues. This is all to say: the fact that the public got reporting on the results of the initiative was exceptional. It took dramatic resignations from people willing to go on record. Something has to go seriously awry for that to happen. Even when things go wrong, most of the time, the president does not hire the kind of people who yak to reporters.

When people do decide to talk, the negative press that resignations generate is minor, relative to the positive press generated at the signing ceremony. The former went out in fewer outlets, in fewer cities, with shorter articles, placed deeper into the newspapers. It is easy to explain why. DiIulio and Kuo were not household names. Write a piece on them and you have to explain who they are, what they were doing, why they resigned, and why it matters. It is a more complicated, nuanced story, one the White House will dispute.[5] There were also complicated stories about the results of the initiative that were positive. The satellite offices in various departments did eventually secure changes to their procedures that came close to what Evangelical Christian organizations wanted. This rarely, if ever, came up. How could it? It was inside baseball. It is even more complicated than a resignation story, and it took years to happen.

Rove and others like him knew all of this, either implicitly or explicitly. They knew that news coverage was shallow, that headlines and ledes matter, and that the president can drive coverage by acting—even if only for a short time. They knew that kind of press would make the president look as if he were accomplishing something. For them, it was important to keep a steady stream of this kind of press flowing.

The faith initiative also illustrates what this knowledge can do to policy. It warped its design in damning ways. Days—and even hours—before announcing the program, there was no plan, nor any people to carry it out. The GAO report, which I referenced in the story, was produced because members of Congress wanted third parties to assess whether the action was consistent with the law (Government Accountability Office 2006). What the GAO found instead was that the boasts were based on dubious reporting procedures, and that even the office itself was not collecting the information it would need to assess the program's impact.

Planning, personnel, design—these were choices the White House made. This was not an act of God, a lack of time, or incompetence. In fact, it demonstrated competence! Only it shows competency in symbolic governance, in squeezing a political win from the office of the presidency, not in changing the status quo. This is another way of saying that the good press seemed to be as much a goal as effective governance, with results that are not shocking, at least in retrospect.

But all this is conjecture based on one case. Is any of this true in general? To get an answer means collecting news coverage of executive action, something Benjamin Goehring and I have done.[6] This is a lot more difficult than it sounds, and worth describing in some detail. If you are not interested in this detail, you can safely skip to section 6.3.

There are a lot of ways to collect news coverage of presidents and executive action. One is to take a list of actions, then look for their appearance in a newspaper of record such as the *New York Times* or the *Washington Post*. This is what Howell (2003) did for executive orders. These papers have huge circulations and large staffs, and it can be argued that if something about the president appears anywhere, it will at least appear there. Likewise, they might be important and influential for other news organizations. Another approach is to start from the papers themselves and work backward using search terms like "executive action" or "executive order." Count those mentions, and you get a rough sketch of coverage over time. This is what Christenson and Kriner (2020) did. The advantage is that no predetermined list constrains their picture of coverage. Presidents act in many ways, so starting from the coverage itself might be a better approach.

But there are obvious downsides to either method. The Howell approach will miss anything outside the list, or anything in other publications. As I will show later, it is quite common for regionally significant outlets to mention an executive action that the *New York Times* ignores. The other approach, based on key words, may pull in articles that do not cover executive action. Nor can we tie a particular article to a particular action. Executive action provokes diverse reactions. Perhaps some are consistent with the story I have told about the faith initiative. Others may not be. That variation can teach us something, so we need to link the action to its press. Most important, when researchers collect press coverage, they are not doing so to study the press itself. They are trying to count executive action or rate its significance. They said only that something had been covered, but almost nothing about the *way* it was covered.

This creates a blueprint for the kind of data needed. It must be broad enough to capture the diversity of executive action and the variety of news outlets that report on it. But it goes beyond mere mentions to the actual content of the coverage itself. This is what Goehring and I did. We started with the list of executive actions I described in chapter 3, capturing executive action in its many forms. We then created another list of newspapers to capture the regional variation we suspected would be there.

Let's say the president declares that part of your state is now a national monument. If your state is someplace like Kansas or North Dakota, it is possible that esteemed newspaper of record on Eighth Avenue in New York City may find this news worth ignoring. And it should. There are only so many pages of print. It can't cover everything. That is the point, and the reason more sources are generally better.

The complete list of news outlets contains fifty-one newspapers, from forty-six states and DC. The states left out are Alaska, Arkansas, Oklahoma, and Rhode Island.[7] A few states are represented by more than one paper. They are, by and large, the most populous ones: California, Florida, Michigan, New York, and Pennsylvania. For the most part, our list is papers with the largest circulation in their respective state. It includes the *New York Times*, the *Wall Street Journal*, and the *Washington Post*. But it also includes the *Minneapolis Star-Tribune*, the *Las Vegas Review-Journal*, the *Burlington Free Press*, and the *Arizona Republic*, each of which accounted for more than 40 percent of the newspaper circulation of papers in their respective states from 1988 to 2004 (Gentzkow, Shapiro, and Sinkinson 2011, 2014a, 2014b). Thus, we have large papers that focus mostly on what is national news and medium-sized papers that pay special attention to what goes on in their state.

Collecting this coverage has to be done manually, one executive action at a time. Every executive action on the list is unique, so each had a specialized search syntax based on action type, president, and policy topic. Then a researcher or research assistant went through the results, which sometimes numbered in the thousands, and determined whether the news article mentioned the particular executive action in question. If so, it was added to our data. Finally, we collected the full text of every article in the dataset. There were quality checks built into every step to ensure that everyone was performing this task in the same way. If you are interested in that, more detail is available in the study I cited (see also Goehring, forthcoming).

Most important is that this process ends with a large dataset of news articles produced by news outlets from a geographically representative sample of the United States. It accounts for a significant proportion of all the news available about executive action during this period (i.e., early 1988 to early

2021). In short, it is the best snapshot of how the press reports on the presidency, and more specifically on executive action.

6.3 Executive Action in the News

A broad sweep of published news reveals important facts about executive action in the press. Our search for coverage included a random sample of 1174 from the list of 1647 executive actions described in chapter 3.[8] The news dataset contains, in total, 13,419 instances of coverage of executive action. There are 12,256 unique articles, since some articles mention more than one action. This is a bit of an overestimate, because some articles are reprinted in multiple outlets. On average, there are about 400 mentions per year, but as I will show, this number masks important changes over the period 1989–2021.

Two initial facts are worth noting—one obvious, the other surprising. First, the most frequent number of mentions any executive action gets is zero. This meshes with what others have found. Howell (2003) shows that the *New York Times* mentioned only 284, or about 17 percent, of executive orders issued between 1969 and 1998. More recently, Christenson and Kriner (2020) find fewer than fifteen mentions in the *Times* per year between 2001 and 2016. On the other hand, though the mode of mentions is zero, *a slight majority—51.3 percent of actions—are covered at least once.* This brings up three important points. Adding in more newspapers did what we hoped it would: it increased our coverage of things big papers like the *Times* will likely exclude. But remember, my list of executive actions is curated beyond the complete list of executive orders. I have left out many mundane, administrative things that are not really executive action. I expected the rate of coverage for what is left would be higher.[9]

Lastly, times are changing. Our coverage window is, roughly, 1989–2021. For presidents H. W. Bush, Clinton, and W. Bush, the probability that an executive action was mentioned at least once in the news was flat, at about 45 percent. For Obama, that figure was 55 percent, and for Trump it was 65 percent. Recall that figure 3.2 showed local upward trends in the frequency of executive action for Obama and Trump. So there were more actions during this period, and they were more likely to get press coverage. There are many explanations for this, none of them exclusive of any others. Perhaps the profession of journalism decided executive action was more important for their readers. After all, Charlie Savage won a Pulitzer Prize for covering Bush-era executive actions in 2007, right around the time coverage rates were rising.

Perhaps inactivity in Congress meant there was simply more attention paid to the presidency. Maybe it was just Trump. Perhaps newspapers increased their White House coverage in response to Trump's election.

But there is also an explanation consistent with the kind of presidential power I describe in this book. Actions under Obama and Trump were more effectively designed to attract coverage. The Obama and Trump administrations wrote up their orders—and indeed, announced and rolled them out—in ways that made writing a news story about them easier.

Whatever the explanation, it is clear that executive action is in the news more than ever. It is a regular part of our politics—or, to use an overused and pedantic word, it has been "normalized." This also makes clear where the common impression that executive action is skyrocketing comes from. It is no different than the effect of reporting about crime on misperceptions of crime. People think crime is on the rise when more stories of crime appear, regardless of the true significance of any instance of crime (e.g., Lowry, Ching, Nio, and Leitner 2003).

That is not the only variation that might skew a person's perceptions. As it turns out, information about any individual action may depend on where you live. Most executive actions have regional peculiarities. Figure 6.1 plots four illustrative cases. At the end of the Clinton administration, the president created a series of national monuments, mostly in the west and southwest. As panel (a) shows, this is precisely where much of the coverage of those actions occurs. Likewise, W. Bush's steel tariffs were widely written about where steel is an important industry. Trump's executive order on historically Black colleges and universities was most publicized in Mississippi, Alabama, Georgia, and Virginia, where most of these institutions are located. News about DACA, in contrast, is more national, even if it is tilted toward states with more undocumented immigrants (i.e., Texas, California, New York, Florida, and Illinois).

These basic facts help clarify the symbolic value of executive action. Relative to other ways of making policy, it has attained a status in the popular press unthinkable a few decades ago. It is in the news all the time. Moreover, national policies have regional implications, and their press coverage reflects that. If the president wants to get his position to the public—and in particular, the slice of the public that will care—an executive action is a great way to do that. Suppose the president wants to send a message to people who support and are involved in HBCUs. Executive action provides the headline, and the American media landscape will pipe it to where it matters.

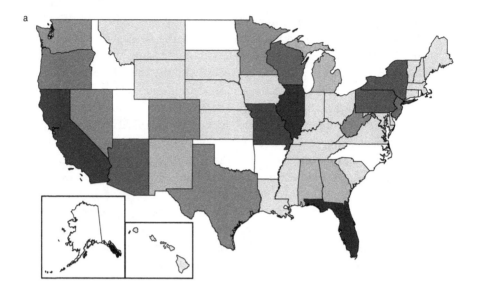

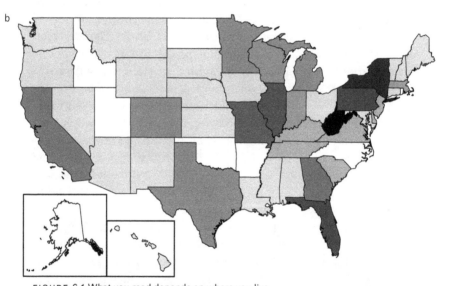

FIGURE 6.1 What you read depends on where you live

The figure plots news mentions (per publication) of executive actions by state: (a) national monuments by Clinton, (b) steel tariffs by W. Bush, (c) the DACA program created by Obama, and (d) Trump's executive order on historically Black colleges and universities. Darker shading indicates more news articles.

c

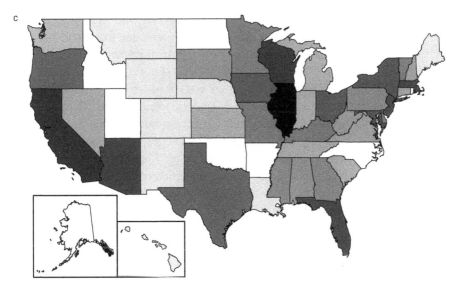

d

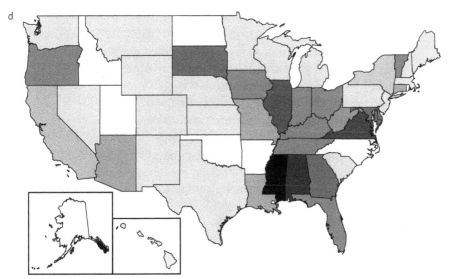

FIGURE 6.1 (continued)

6.4 Slanted News

In the United States, talking about ways the news is "slanted" is a favorite pastime. Usually this means slanted ideologically—in either a conservative or a liberal direction. This is what presidents themselves focus on—that some side is treating them unfairly. But that is not as important for them as the nonideological ways news is slanted. That slant has less to do with opinions than it does the business models of news organizations and the profession of journalism more generally. The slant is over which actions get covered, when they are covered, and how. As it turns out, a very small number of executive actions get most of the coverage. The distribution is also skewed by time. Most of the coverage occurs early on, even before the president acts. This has nothing to do with political bias, outright falsehoods, or the fact that journalists tend to be liberals. The press covers executive action the way the president's advisors might write a press release. They give the president credit for making some policy change, they are light on detail, and they bury most questions about what happens next and who might oppose it.

These are not idle musings, they are general facts about the news data we collected. Most often, if an executive action is mentioned at all, it is mentioned once. Among actions that are mentioned, the median number of articles referencing the action is six. But the average is much higher because of a handful of high-profile actions, which, by definition, you will have heard of: Obama's Race to the Top Initiative (775 articles), Trump's "sanctuary cities" executive order (559 articles), Obama's DACA program (379 articles), Trump's assassination of an Iranian general (373 articles), and Trump's exit from the Paris climate agreement (351 articles). The top ten most covered actions account for 28.7 percent of all news mentions of executive actions.[10]

The skew tells us something. For anyone trying to understand executive action and the American presidency, scholars included, the most accessible examples are extreme. It is no wonder the public has the impression that the president can make substantive changes to the status quo. Most information out there is about them doing big, dramatic things. Even for scholars, it is easy to think up theories for exceptions. But the central tendencies tell us something more general and illuminating. When something is covered, it is usually covered by a handful of articles. They are directives about employing more adults with disabilities, reducing the risk of contaminated food, creating minor national monuments, or reducing energy consumption by federal agencies.

Counting news articles can only tell us so much. You could argue this shows us nothing that would advantage the president. The skew could simply reflect that reporters focus on what matters most to readers and reveal all kinds of negative facts that makes for healthy accountability between the president and an audience.

The timing of this coverage starts to disabuse us of this idea. Figure 6.2 plots two ways to describe the timing. For each president, we ended our news period when they left office. This means actions taken later in the term were less likely to be covered and received less coverage overall. To deal with that, first I set aside actions that were issued in the final two years of a presidency. Then I looked at the median number of days that passed between the enactment of a policy, and its news coverage. This is what the left panel shows. Fifty percent of George W. Bush's actions, for example, had most of their coverage occurring within 0.8 month, or within the first twenty-five days. You may notice many actions are covered negative days before enactment; these are leaks and policy rollouts that occur before the president has signed anything. Another way to look at time is to scale the number of days elapsed by how much time is left until a transition. This allows us to include actions that occur late in the presidential term. This is what the right panel shows. A majority of the executive actions of Bill Clinton were covered with 99 percent or more of the term to go. Timing-wise, this looks a lot like the first wave of our panel survey from chapter 4.

The exceptions are useful. What kinds of actions get later press? The extreme cases I have already mentioned, which attract sustained coverage because the story keeps changing. Race to the Top, for example, had several competitive rounds of waivers that various states applied for and were granted. That kept it in the news and also gave it the regional significance that inflates its news relevance. Sometimes an action stays relevant because it is challenged in court—and the court's decision produces a fresh report. More rare are cases when the executive action appeared in the news months or years after enactment. Some of these were secret at the time, like George W. Bush's torture and extraordinary rendition programs. The point, again, is that these scenarios is rare.

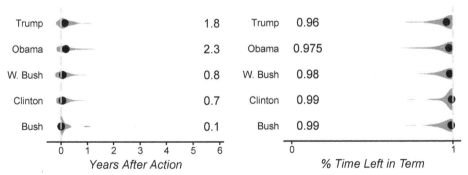

FIGURE 6.2 Most coverage occurs at the announcement of new actions

The figure plots the timing of coverage by president. The left panel drops actions in the last two years, then shows the distribution of the median amounts of time (in months, within action) at which articles appeared. The margin digits show the median number of months by president. The right panel includes all actions but shows the percentage of time left in the term for the median article to appear, again within action. The margin digits report the median percentage.

The coverage and time patterns, though, present a potential problem for a key idea of this book, which is that presidents take executive action to acquire symbolic, political wins. If most actions get little or no press and that press is quick, does this demonstrate that executive action does not tend to pay off the way I say it should? No. Presidents have a portfolio. Theirs is a game of hundreds (or thousands), and the benefit their agenda produces as a whole. More important, the content of coverage further reveals the political benefits of executive action.

To be a credit-claiming opportunity, coverage needs to make two distinct but important points. Policy changed and the president did it. This was not some half measure or an idea bandied about at Camp David. The status quo has changed. We have some indication that press looks like this because of the timing. It is hard to report anything but the fact that policy changed if you are only reporting right at the start. Results take years to materialize. Second, the article has to attribute that change to the president. We can learn this by reading what journalists have written and looking for patterns in language.

But there are tens of thousands, so instead I tried to summarize the key thing we are interested in. To explain how, it helps to walk through the first lines of a typical story about executive action. It appeared on September 22, 2016, in the *Chicago Tribune* and reads: "President Barack Obama signed a presidential memorandum Wednesday establishing that the effect of climate change must be factored into the development of all national security–related doctrine, policies and plans. The move signals Obama's determination to exercise his executive authority during his final months in office to elevate the issue of climate in federal decision-making."[11] There is no ambiguity. The president, alone, enacted an order about climate change. How do we know? Words such as "signed," "establishing," "determination," and "exercise" are used.[12] These attribute credit to Obama. A reasonable approach, then, is to look for the occurrence of words like this near mentions of the president. Another approach is to look for the opposite language. Take, for instance, another article, this time from the February 5, 1993 issue of the *Tribune*: "Earlier, the Senate rejected a Republican-led effort to ban homosexuals from the armed forces. With Vice President Al Gore presiding for the first time, the Senate, in a 62–37 vote, blocked the GOP effort to write into law a strict anti-gay policy that the military practiced before Clinton. The president's compromise plan last week ordered the Pentagon to take steps that would end the practice."[13] Here, instead, the *Tribune* writers supply negative words— like "reject" and "block"—to indicate policy stoppage rather than progress. (They appear alongside other words that give the president credit—"plan" and "ordered.") To put all this more generally, some words assign credit for change (I refer to these as "attribution" words), while others describe the lack thereof (which I call "gridlock" words). As both *Tribune* articles suggest, even the simple exercise of looking for these words as they appear near the president or Congress can be informative.

I did this at scale for the rest of the news data. I put together lists of attribution and gridlock words, 334 and 166 terms, respectively.[14] For attribution, they are words such as "achieve," "act," "ban," "boost," "craft," "implement," "impose," "push," "suspend," "unveil," and "win." Gridlock is instead marked by such terms as "balk," "block," "collapse," "defeat," "fizzle," "paralyze," "rebuff," "stall," "stymie," and "wavered." I then compute the prevalence of these words, especially near mentions of the president or Congress.[15]

It would be easy enough to show that these kinds of words appear in executive action articles regularly. But to be most useful, we need something to compare this coverage, too. Presidents get press for all kinds of reasons: they attend events, go on trips abroad, negotiate with Congress, and golf. What is needed, then, is some sweep of news that features the president, but not any kind of executive action. This is one way to take stock of how the press presidents can expect from executive action differs from other kinds of press. To do this, I followed a procedure similar to the one used to collect executive-action coverage. They had to mention the president in office, had to be published by one of our newspapers, and had to appear during their term. The main difference is that these articles could not mention executive action. This comparison sample of coverage included 7950 articles, compared to the executive-action sample's 12,100.[16]

This news illustrates key differences in how press for unilateral action differs from other press presidents receive. First, and most obviously, there is more evidence of credit or attribution to the president in articles on executive action (14.3 words, relative to 10.1; $p < 0.000$). The simple difference in typical attribution words near mentions of the president holds regardless of how it is estimated. You can control for president, newspaper, and article length.[17]

A lack of difference is also illuminating. There is no evidence executive-action articles are more or less likely to contain gridlock words that appear near the president. This is especially important, because the main reason for the difference in attribution is that executive-action articles include more mentions of the president, period. That means even though these articles put the president front and center, they are no more likely to associate the president with words that have a clear, negative valence in American politics.

What about the president's credit relative to Congress? For each article, I took the simple difference between the two, so positive values indicate there were more words assigning credit to the president, and negative values indicate more assigned to the Congress. Figure 6.3 makes the main point gleaned from these differences. For executive-action articles (dark bars), most attribution is to the president, while for other news (light bars), most of it falls to Congress. This is true for every president, though the Trump administration seems to be an exceptional case.

Figure 6.3 also shows that the patterns I have mentioned so far are there, whether you look at the full article or just the lede. The first few lines of an article are, of course, the most important. Many readers do not read beyond them. On average, the first paragraph of our news articles is sixty-eight words long.[18] Within those openings, the same patterns hold: more attribution to the president in executive action relative to non-executive action, and more to the president relative to Congress. For the lede, there is some weak evidence of differences in gridlock language associated with presidents, but the differences are very small, uncertain, and not robust to different ways of estimating them.[19]

Maybe none of this surprises you, whoever you are. When the press covers executive action, the president becomes the center of attention and gets the credit. Congress is upstaged. And relative to other kinds of press, it is less negative. All of this is important, but all it does is underscore descriptive differences across media coverage of the president.

But the most important pattern in this coverage has nothing to do with difference across types of coverage. It is in how coverage of executive action

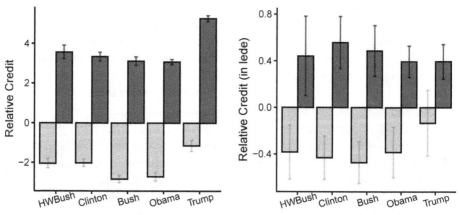

FIGURE 6.3 Press about executive action assigns more credit to the president relative to Congress and relative to other political news
The figure plots means and 95 percent confidence intervals, by president, for attribution words near mentions of the president minus attribution words near mentions of Congress, for both non-executive action articles that mention the president (light bars) and executive action articles (dark bars). Average counts were obtained by repeating the co-occurrence analysis for every combination of lede lengths (65–71 words) and definitions of "near" (within 3–7 words).

changes (or does not change) over time. Figure 6.2 showed that executive-action coverage tends to bunch near the announcement, with little or no follow-up. But perhaps the media, with its persistent bias toward negative news, only reports on executive action if something bad happens. The Bush faith initiative is a case in point. Perhaps it only reappeared in the news once high-profile resignations put its failures into the press. This could facilitate some accountability for the president, placing them at risk for exposure when their initiatives fail or are empty.

As it turns out, this is not generally true. Some initiatives do follow a path of negative press—with more gridlock words appearing near the president—but most do not. I looked within executive actions, estimating the effect of publication date on the presence of gridlock words.[20] If press gets more negative for the president over time, the publication date should have a positive effect on the co-occurrence of the president and gridlock words.[21] It is not there, though, either for the full article or lede.

What is there, however, is a consistent downward trend in *attribution* to the president. So articles that mention the action months or even years after tend to assign less credit to the president, even if they mention him. A simple and reasonable explanation is that when executive actions are mentioned later, they are usually there to provide context for contemporary news. This cuts against the idea that the later-term news in the dataset represents some kind of check on the president. More likely, references to executive action down the line give little new information about what that executive action has done.

6.5 The Impression of Power

In *The Impression of Influence* (2014), Grimmer, Westwood, and Messing hand members of Congress a charge. Members retain office by effectively marketing their influence over policy, playing into the idea that they have the power to get things done and signaling that they have used it. Presidents are not as different as we might like to think. They do the same kind of thing even if it differs in degree. We have to rethink received wisdom about the kind of thing an executive action is. Legally, they are administrative moves that direct executive-branch agencies to take some action. Politics reifies them with the reactions of audiences and the press.

What that process does *not* do is important. It does not, in general, facilitate a clean scenario that makes it easy for people to judge the success or failure of a policy. It does not, in general, lead some large swath of the public to turn against the president for acting beyond the bounds of the Constitution. It does not, in general, spark careful media scrutiny from a well-informed press corps. These are just stories we tell. They may be reassuring for those uncomfortable with the idea of rule by decree in a modern democracy, but they are just stories. The point of empirical investigations, though often tedious, is to replace these stories with ones that are more accurate.

Lurking behind this evidence is a gigantic, loud caveat. Most press may well be good press, this lurker might say, but I have defined "press" in an old-school, even antiquated way. I have looked at newspaper articles—and who reads those, anymore? Few people, relative to the violent ocean of disembodied voices on social networks like Facebook, X, Instagram, YouTube, and TikTok. Many—or maybe even most—people now get their news through funhouse mirrors. Is it possible the stylized facts I present about the political value of executive action are simply wrong? It is hard to know without evidence, but I don't think so.

Traditional news probably offers the rosiest opportunity for healthy information flows between the president and the public. Everything supposed to make the media a "responsible" intermediary between elected officials—their professionalism, commitment to fact-checking, attempted nonpartisanship—vanishes on Internet-based social networks. It seems difficult to argue that these networks incentivize the kind of deep-dive, muckraking investigations that might expose the efficacy of the president's actions. So, if anything, I think social media exacerbates all the patterns I say contribute to the shallowness of information available to the public.

News on social media, for the most part, leeches off of traditional press. These networks do not usually produce a separate stream of information about the behavior of the president of the United States, and when they do, it is picked up by traditional press. News stories that circulate on these networks are mostly just the decapitated headline of an article produced by a traditional journalist. There are no tweets, likes, or posts in this chapter, but the evidence I have presented is mostly upstream of that behavior. In short, I doubt that social media holds presidents more accountable for their executive action.

At first, executive actions are symbolic. Regardless of their impact on policy, they grab headlines. They send a clear signal about the president's position. They tell the public the president has accomplished something. They brand the president. Unlike the actions of members of Congress, the expectations of the presidency feed into the presumption that the president's actions are effectual. Politically speaking, executive actions are much more important than press releases about some new fire station in Waco, Texas. The president has control over when they are released. The media have strong incentives to closely monitor the actions of the president and produce the kind of reporting that reinforces the narrative that the president is responsible and in charge.

The symbolic value might disappear if, for instance, members of the public overwhelmingly punished the president for failing to move the dial—and if moving the dial was possible to observe. There is some evidence that, in an idealized scenario, they might punish the president. There are also plenty of presidential actions that draw bad press long after their initial announcement. And there are other actions that have, for example, resulted in legal defeats, which explicitly tie the president to failure. But most information out there about executive action has nothing to do with its consequences.

This all supports two other assertions from chapter 2. The symbolic component of executive action is short-lived, and substantive policymaking involves subsequent risks. The attention and headlines are there for a surprising number of executive actions, but they quickly disappear, only to reappear if the story changes in a way that involves some kind of entertaining political intrigue. The situations inviting that intrigue usually involve legal proceedings, personnel changes, and scandal. Actions with less substantive weight are unlikely to get mixed up in any of that. That is by design.

7: HELP WITH WHAT?

"The president needs help" is the most quoted line in the history of reforming the presidency. Written by three political scientists appointed by President Franklin Roosevelt, their goal was to help him control the bureaucracy, then rapidly expanding because of the New Deal. That is what presidents are supposed to need help with: control.

Roosevelt was only modestly impactful at the time, but he set off a dramatic expansion of what is often called the "presidential branch"—the collection of offices and bureaucrats in the White House and the EOP. It got bigger, acquired new roles, and became more presidential. Presidents' moves to expand, shuffle, or reorganize were interpreted as a key sign of the modern presidency. Presidents, overburdened with the expectations of their office, were trying to cope by getting help they needed. They created structures to drive policy from the top down. These were supposed to bring, as Moe (1985) writes, "existing structures making up the institutional presidency" into congruence "with the incentives and resources of the president" (238).

The reforms worked. Aides directly responsive to the president got involved in writing and implementing policy in the rest of the executive branch. Bureaucrats grew more used to—and even tolerant of—intervention from the White House. In short, presidents politicized the presidential branch. Presidents want to change policy, so they organize their presidencies to get more of what they want. They do not want neutral competence or even efficiency for its own sake. They want to move the dial in the direction they prefer, and the structures they set up reflect that. This argument is simple, powerful, and contested by virtually no one.

But it is incomplete. That is because modern presidents structure the offices and staff nearest to them in ways orthogonal to the goal of controlling bureaucrats. They make institutional choices that are not designed to help them control policy. Like a lot of other arguments in this book, this one is inspired by a simple observation about the way things actually are. If I described the recent history of the "presidential branch" to you, and you had in mind that the president's goal was to use that branch to control the bureaucracy, some of their choices would seem subpar.

You do not need to visit a presidential library to get a sense of this. Read the list of offices filling up the White House and the EOP these days. There are still institutions created decades ago—like the National Security Council or the OMB—that have legally defined policymaking roles. But right alongside (or inside) them, there are also offices and councils for women and girls, on climate, for AIDS, for rural America, for innovative America, for faith communities, for indigenous peoples, or for historically Black higher education. They meet regularly, hold conferences, and put out reports. For every office, you can look at portraits of presidential appointees, and read how the White House describes their jobs. Are these officials, and the offices they fill, there to help the president drive policy from the top? Absolutely not.

This is not the same as saying those offices and staff do nothing. Like most at the White House, they work nonstop and could be making more money elsewhere. The question is whether they make the president more effective, in the sense that it enhances their control of the administrative state.

But the way they spend their time often has little to do with steering the ship of state. Their efforts are overt and public facing. They issue public reports, convene gatherings, and write press releases. They brand what the government is already doing. They co-opt interest groups. When they intervene in governing, it is to help produce symbolic policy, or to strategically time initiatives for political purposes. They are political instruments, not governing ones.

The conventional wisdom about these kinds of White House players is they tend to do more harm than good—at least in terms of producing good policy. One reason is that they give particular interests a platform that can bias policymaking against the president. Another is that they muddy lines of communication and water down the authority of cabinet-level administrators. In other words, they can make it harder for presidents to get what they want.

Or do they? What do presidents want help with, exactly? This is the key point of this chapter. It applies the argument of this book to the way presidents organize their presidency. Much of the structure of the presidential branch is peculiar, if maximizing policy control is all the president wants. But this is a narrow view of presidents' goals and strategies. The presidential branch is marked by a history of attempts to get hold of bureaucratic policymaking. But alongside that is a history of empowering presidents to enhance the symbolic dimension of their actions. Strictly speaking, this does not need to have anything to do with political control of the administrative state. Like symbolic executive actions, these efforts can complement more substantive policymaking and serve their broader goals of retaining office, which is why presidents do both. But they also take up finite time and resources, which can frustrate the production of good policy.

Most of the history in this chapter took place after Moe and others had argued that the presidential branch was designed to make the president more effective at controlling policy. Many of the new offices and institutions that most enhance the messaging capabilities of the president were either created or expanded during or after the H. W. Bush administration. This is telling. When FDR commissioned the Brownlow Report, the president of the United States had fewer people officially working for him than the night shift at a McDonald's. From a reformer's perspective, expansion of the presidential branch was low-hanging fruit. A lot could be gained by controlling the budget, reviewing new regulations, and providing a place where policy changes could be formulated and parceled out to implementing agencies. But, these strategies can only take a president so far, and there is only so much Congress has been willing to tolerate. Enhancing the immediate resources and information available to the president is sometimes controversial.

But Congress was notably silent when many of the aforementioned offices were created. In the past three decades, rarely have they protested the creation of a new White House office. When they have, that just meant individual members denounced the move without taking action to stop it. There were plenty of members of Congress who disliked George W. Bush's faith-based initiatives office, or Biden's climate-change office. But abolition has never been on the table. It is tempting to say, by way of explanation, that Congress is too dysfunctional to do anything. There is a simpler reason. There is no need to abolish these offices because they do not meaningfully enhance the president's power over policy. All the juice has already been already been squeezed by other organizational moves, like the creation of the Office of Information and Regulatory Affairs (OIRA) and the politicization of the OMB.

What do these new kinds of offices and staff give the president? They are expressions of preferences. They clarify the president's position. Liberal (conservative) presidents invent offices that express liberal (conservative) priorities. Oftentimes they co-opt activist elements of the president's political base by giving them something to do. Many of these aides have little experience in government and know next to nothing about the actual bureaucratic structures presidents purport to control by appointing them. What they are best at is enhancing the symbolic component of policymaking by producing the kinds of public-facing documents and events that grab headlines and show the president is taking action. They list accomplishments. They create talking points. They are often de facto branches of the political and communications arms of the White House. They may have little or no influence on what the rest of the government does, but that is not what the president needs their help with, anyway.

7.1 Carrot

On a Monday morning, Secret Service agents led eighty-eight presidents on the five-minute walk from the Eisenhower Building to the West Wing. They were leaders of historically Black colleges and universities, and of associations that lobby on their behalf. For months, White House staff, led by Omarosa Manigault-Newman, worked to bring the leaders to Washington for the signing of an executive order. For Manigault-Newman, the number of university leaders was no accident. Past administrations brought a few dozen, mostly from the largest and most prestigious schools, so she wanted to go bigger—by going smaller. Invitations went to every president of every HBCU, including colleges smaller than a typical suburban high school, universities with endowments the size of an upper-middle-class 401k, and even the two HBCUs whose students are mostly white.

The morning listening session lasted fifteen minutes before the unexpected call-over came from the president's son-in-law and senior advisor, Jared Kushner. To Manigault-Newman's surprise, Kushner said the president would see the group, but not in the large EOP conference room where aides had planned for each president to take turns speaking to senior staff. He wanted them in the Oval Office, now.

The Oval Office is about 750 square feet, less the furnishings that are not for standing on. It was quickly crowded. The president shook hands and signaled his photographer, who climbed a ladder to get shots wide enough to include all the guests willing to pose. The photos ran in every major newspaper. President Trump stood out, smiling behind the Resolute Desk, surrounded by the guests. Almost all were persons of color. The next day, back at the Eisenhower Building, the presidents nearest Trump in the photos had high praise for him. One said, "Who knew it would take President Trump" to have "more African Americans in the Oval Office than ever before in [U.S.] history?" Many shared his sentiment and gladly stepped in front of the camera.

This did not include Wayne A. I. Frederick. Born in Trinidad forty-five years before, Frederick had a prodigious medical career, earning an MD at twenty-two and rising in academic oncology over the next two decades to become the seventeenth president of Howard University. At the time, Howard—which depended on the U.S. Congress for 40 percent of its yearly operating budget—had trouble paying to heat its buildings in the winter. Over the last forty years, the share of Black students attending HBCUs dropped from one in five to less than one in ten. With their declining enrollments and budget pressures, HBCU presidents and advocates lobbied the federal government for funding. Since the Carter administration they had done so with the backing of both Democrats and Republicans in the White House.

Though this brought Frederick to the Eisenhower Building, and even into the Oval Office, he did not stand beside President Trump for a photo. By this time he had hosted officials from the Trump administration and grown cautious. Hours after her Senate confirmation, assistants called to set up a campus visit for Betsy DeVos, the new secretary of education. DeVos blundered during the visit by calling HBCUs, which were founded by former slaves barred from college after the Civil War, "pioneers of school choice." Earlier that month, President Trump had described Frederick Douglass, dead since 1895, as "an example of somebody who's done an amazing job and is being recognized more and more." Wayne Frederick avoided the executive-order signing ceremony and the later press conference.

If he hoped the lower profile would make a difference this time, he was disappointed. The next day at Howard, hallways and sidewalks were chalked and painted with personal attacks on Frederick. On the main lawn, letters in blue spray paint labeled Frederick a "plantation overseer" for the Trump administration. Student groups issued statements that endorsed the "spirit" of the vandalism. There were speculations about Frederick's resignation or firing, and classmates taunted his twelve-year-old son at school. It was the start of a difficult period, which culminated in a vote of no confidence by the Howard faculty the next year. Fortunately for Frederick, the vote was symbolic, as Howard, like most universities, does not trust academics with management decisions.

But the rest of the Trump administration put Frederick in a tight spot—courting politicians whose policies and rhetoric were openly despised by the university community he served. Later, in the *New Yorker*, he summed up his predicament: "'People think we're doing God's work, on God's time, with God's money, [. . .] we don't have access to the latter two.'"

The time in the Oval Office bought Frederick and the other college presidents an executive order—applauded as a "home run" by one, something many of them "thought would never happen in their lifetime." The order's function: to move the White House Initiative on HBCUs, normally housed in the Department of Education, into the White House Office itself. This was a change for organizational charts and a physical relocation from the LBJ Building, a brutalist eyesore one block south of the National Mall, to the more ornate Eisenhower Building, next to the White House.

The move was part of a trend in HBCU executive orders, issued now by every president for almost forty years. Carter created the initiative. H. W. Bush renamed it a "White House" initiative. Obama added a preamble extolling the virtues of HBCUs. Trump doubled that preamble and made the White House more than just part of the name. (For the next president, the order's preamble would span a full page.) With this decision, those willing to speak at the press conference reasoned publicly, the current president had made the initiative "more real."

It was not real for everyone. But the people willing to say so did not feel as strongly as the presidents, who were happy to stay for the closing press conference and heap praise on President Trump. Instead, the others became "skeptics" or "critics," buried beyond the lede in news stories, who called the order symbolic and unnecessary. A few posted in private blogs or just stayed quiet—a wait-and-see approach for those unwilling to burn a bridge so early in the term. Perhaps, they thought, the new home at the White House would bring more focus, more people, and ultimately more money.

Initial signs were not favorable. On paper, the initiative was now in the White House, but it was headless for more than seven months. A finalist asked the administration to give the director purview over recent problems with the HBCU loan program. With no clear answer, he withdrew from consideration. Eventually, the White House appointed Johnathan Holifield, a motivational speaker and former NFL player who had not attended an HBCU. It took another six months to find someone to chair the president's advisory board.

After that, the apparent wins started coming. Funding for the colleges increased, Pell grants could now be used year round, a ban on funding faith-based HBCUs was lifted, and then, in 2019, the funding program became permanent, ending the annual trips to DC and the cycle of lobbying for a share of the budget. It was these wins President Trump would list during his 2020 reelection bid, proclaiming his administration had "saved" HBCUs. It had all begun with that first meeting just weeks into his presidency.

But of course, that narrative was a stretch. The funding increases all came from Congress. Supporters of the president gave him credit for not requesting cuts to HBCU funding, but every year Congress approved more funding than the president requested. Pell grant extensions were also popular and bipartisan. The decision to make HBCU funding permanent came from Congress, too. Alma Adams, a Democratic congresswoman from North Carolina who had attended an HBCU, cosponsored the legislation and had been lobbying for the change for years. "The only words the president contributed were his signature," she said.

Then there was lifting the "ban" on funding for religious HBCUs, a move that generated headlines linking the change to Trump himself and touted as a clear accomplishment of the initiative. It came via a determination memo of the Department of Justice, occasioned by a Supreme Court decision that had declared religious exclusions in grant programs unconstitutional. Now that the Court had said the rule was void, the Department of Education could fund the roughly 40 percent of HBCUs with declared religious roots, the memo seemed to say. But for years before, money had gone to those same "religious affiliated" colleges—to institutions of higher learning founded by Baptists, Methodists, Episcopalians, and Presbyterians. In President Obama's second term alone, $334 million in loans went to the colleges Justice Department officials were now claiming to make eligible. The only de facto ineligible HBCU, apparently, had been a seminary in Florida with about 230 students.

None of these facts would prevent the administration from announcing the success the following month at a conference for HBCUs, held annually for decades. It was the chief task of the White House initiative. Johnathan Holifield would travel frequently to meet with presidents on campus and organize regional discussions. Manigault-Newman would do the same, up until her firing. But if the White House initiative had nothing to do with any of the major changes for HBCUs during the Trump administration, what did it do?

Over the years Holifield developed a long answer, which filled the first ten to fifteen minutes of his presentations. He used a series of metaphors. The first metaphor: "We're a conditions creating function. We steward no grants. We steward no programs. We steward no contracts." The second metaphor: they were a "skunkworks operation," an innovation program outside a regular corporate structure. The third metaphor: they were like Newton's second law of motion "an accelerating intervening force [. . .] needed to move a resting mass into action." The fourth metaphor: the initiative was like a trim tab, "a small, high leverage rudder for the rudder" of an ocean liner. The final metaphor: a carrot. "I often describe us," he said, "as all carrot and no stick. In other words, we're all opportunity and no ability to make anyone do anything."

7.2 Showrunning

When Trump moved the HBCU initiative into the White House, he took a particular kind of action. He reshaped the presidential branch. He made a decision about how his presidency would be organized: there would now be a group called the White House Initiative on Historically Black Colleges and Universities working right next door to the West Wing.[1] They operated there for the next four years. Every president makes decisions like this, and they are the kind that can be understood, in part, using the argument of this book.

Start with the strategic problem the president faces. Recalling what Moe (1985) says, it has something to do with bringing the presidential branch "into congruence" with the president's incentives. This is a good guidepost. Presidents direct a mini-branch of government below them, and they decide how to set it up. Some setups will be better than others, given their goals. So in what ways is the presidential branch deficient, given those goals?

The classic answer is that the presidential branch falls short of presidents' desire to control policy. The political context that birthed this argument is itself instructive. Moe wrote "The Politicized Presidency" during the Reagan administration, which scholars agree aggressively sought control over the administrative state. As Matthew Dickinson (2005) wrote later, Reagan's OMB, in particular, "moved from privately advising the president to serving as a presidential spokesperson to other political advisors. [. . .] Rather than experienced administrators [. . .] presidents have looked for individuals who shared their political goals" (152). This fact puzzled (or maybe just annoyed) "good-government" types, who saw these trends as a mistake that made the public worse off.

Filling places such as the OMB with people who shared the president's preferences and would be committed to effectuating them was far from the original design. The OMB's predecessor, the Bureau of the Budget, started out staffed by career personnel with expertise in public finance. The Brownlow Commission endorsed FDR's model for an impartial and apolitical budget office (Dickinson 2005, 140). Early directors took this very seriously. Director Charles Dawes declared his neutrality in the first budget sent to Congress: "[W]e have nothing to do with policy. Much as we love the President, if Congress [. . .] passed a law that garbage should be put on the White House steps, it would be our regrettable duty, as a bureau, in an impartial, nonpolitical and nonpartisan way[,] to advise the Executive and Congress as to how the largest amount of garbage could be spread in the most expeditious and economical manner."[2] Mick Mulvaney empties bag after bag of refuse on the steps of the White House. OMB directors today are not neutral administrators. They would reprogram funds from this fiscal year's trashscaping account and put it to some other purpose. They might even help the White House dump trash on the steps of the Capitol instead.

These directors are important agents of the president's policy agenda. What Moe captures best is the fact that this kind of decision—to make a neutral office more politically responsive—is no accident or mistake. A nonpolitical presidential branch would make decisions that make the president worse off, plain and simple. So presidents have structured it, in part, to help them control the rest of the executive branch and bring about policy changes that otherwise would not occur. These include structures such as the National

Security Council and the OMB—and within it, the OIRA, which serves as a centralized clearinghouse for regulation.

But alongside these structures there are hundreds of jobs in the presidential branch that exist for reasons that have less to do with taking hold of government policy and effectively implementing presidents' preferences. Nor are they appendages of the "neutral competence" so desired by early reformers in public administration. They are there, quite simply, to help the president show that he is the president, that he cares about some constituency, that his administration is focused on some goal. This behavior is not the product of some strategic miscalculation or incompetence. To see that, you need different ideas about what presidents can do to get what they want.

Presidents use their immediate offices to get control policy—but that is not all they do, because they are also understand the feedback loop between their actions and goals. Again, according to Moe (1985), the president's "chances for reelection, [. . .] standing with opinion leaders and the public, and [. . .] historical legacy all depend on [. . .] perceived success as the generalized leader of government. [. . .] Whatever his particular policy objectives, whatever his personality and style, the modern president is driven by these formidable expectations to seek control over the structures and processes of government" (239). What matters is the "perception" of success. Some management decisions help foster this perception more than others.

Presidents organize their presidency under a special kind of uncertainty. The impacts of organizational structures in the White House or the EOP are more complicated than something like DACA or forgiving HBCU debt. For the latter, it might take a while to track their true impacts. But managerial decisions are a step removed. Offices take hundreds or even thousands of actions. They develop cultures. They alter decision-making processes. They bring in new or different information. They give voice to organized interests. All of that makes it difficult know for certain whether it is best to have one kind of office over another, or to arrange those offices in a particular order.

Scholars are well aware of this uncertainty. Peri Arnold's (1998) classic account of presidential reform concludes: "The plain fact is that no modern president has fully managed the executive branch. [. . .] [P]residents fail as managers because they seem to have little appetite for the task, and their interests lie elsewhere" (361–62). As Moe (1985) writes, "[N]o systematic body of knowledge is available to presidents—or anyone else–for confidently linking alternative institutional designs to alternative sets of consequences" (242). Stephen Hess and James Pfiffner (2021), after decades and several volumes of studying how each president organized his presidency, conclude only that "a presidency needs to be organized. There is no one best way. Good organization does not guarantee wise decisions" (204). This makes clear why alternative considerations inform the folk wisdom of advisors and sometimes prevail. If you focus only on control of the administrative state, there's no guarantee it will work.

Presidents have almost complete autonomy in how the White House is organized. This is not simply because of their advantages as a first mover, their ability to veto legislation, or the fact Congress has trouble acting collectively to curtail presidential power. As Sean Gailmard and John Patty (2013) convincingly show, there are "supply-side" considerations as well. In other words, Congress itself has incentives to give presidents resources and access to private information. That way, when presidents inevitably use the authority they have, their decisions are well informed and make *Congress* better off.

So Congress gives presidents personnel and resources, then largely leaves them to run the presidential branch. What people actually do with their time, who reports to whom, and so on are all up to presidents. This is the way presidents have always wanted it. The Brownlow commissioners originally wanted advisors under the president to have prespecified duties, but FDR apparently wrote back in disapproval, so the recommendation was not included in the final report (Arnold 1998, 105).

Given this latitude, presidents set up an organization designed for a mix of both substantive policymaking and symbolic governance. I call the latter "showrunning." Done well, it conveys the idea that president is solving major problems, either by packaging what the government is already doing or by developing and executing new initiatives. When presidents organize their immediate offices with these goals in mind, they are building up a capacity to go symbolic. What structures enhance presidents' ability to do the latter?

You know the traditional showrunners because if they stopped talking, they would not be doing their jobs. They are the press people, communications specialists, and speechwriters. They hold briefings with the media, release lists of the president's accomplishments, and insult members of Congress on social media. They rise to their positions because they are adept at political messaging. One way to track whether presidents are bringing their branch "into congruence," then, is to track the prevalence of these positions. How many of them are there? What is their rank? How much are they paid? How important are they in decision-making? These are similar to questions Lee (2016) asked about Congress. She concludes that the desire to draw contrasts between the parties for audiences has led Congress, as a whole, to hollow out its own capacity for policy development. The reason is that individual members see more benefit in placing resources toward communications rather than policy. The simple version of this chapter is: presidents often see it that way, too.

There are structures and personnel unique to the White House less obviously designed for messaging but perhaps more important for showrunning. There are groups and offices dedicated to conveying a commitment to some policy area. Of course, they are not described this way by presidents themselves, and certainly not by the staff who work there. One longtime White House staffer, Bradley H. Patterson Jr. (2000), is worth quoting on this point: "If a president wants [...] to dramatize his personal commitment [...] he will be pressed to create new organizational forms to support this efforts. [...] To alter his executive branch would take months (and may never happen), but he has an appealing and facile alternative: [...] he can create a new presidential assistant—and do it in an hour" (263–64). Typically, they label their duties as "coordinating" the efforts of other agencies in the executive branch, or as pushing some agenda item forward. But they have no special authority to do so. They mostly end up packaging and describing what has been done, without having any material impact on it. Often they focus on the producing vague policy ideas, usually in the form of reports or initiatives. Sometimes these ideas become executive actions. The kind I showed in chapter 4 tend to be timed for election cycles and go away during lame-duck periods.

Trump's HBCU initiative qualifies. In a moment of clarity, its head said bluntly that they had "no ability to make anyone do anything." How did the people working in this office spend their time, then? They held events. They traveled. They talked to members of Congress. They wrote up mission statements and produced reports. These reports did not highlight what the initiative was doing, but instead pointed to grants HBCUs had received from other government agencies, or new monies Congress had provided. They wrote the president's reelection campaign with a list of accomplishments he could toss into debate sound bites. And he did.

This was not the centralization of policymaking. It was not an attempt to control the administrative state. Centralized control of HBCU policy was possible. Suppose the White House initiative ran the HBCU loan program or worked through OIRA to prescribe regulatory changes to its repayment plan. They did not. They also did not dictate which HBCUs received grants, and they did not decide who qualified as an HBCU. They did not even have a role in the legislative changes to the program that came in 2019.

These were all conscious choices by the Trump administration, ones that cannot be written off as evidence that Trump did not care about HBCUs. Creating an office like the HBCU initiative, or the faith-based initiative in the Bush administration, or the Y2K office in the Clinton administration, is a strategy. It is not like investing explicitly in people who write speeches and talk to the press. Instead, it is an investment in the kind of organization that will, on a regular basis, create the impression the president is changing policy, getting things done, and directing things from the top down.

The HBCU initiative also highlights an additional function of some of the more specialized offices. In this case, the White House HBCU Initiative might be best described as an administrative home for an interest group. The interest group is made up of people, mostly college administrators and alumni, with a vested interest in the financial well-being of HBCUs. It is inescapable that for the presidents who came to the Trump White House in February 2017, the finances of their institution impacted their take-home pay. Laudable as their mission is, they also had vested interests in a particular government program. Members of their association, the group that lobbies on their behalf, were eventually appointed to jobs and board seats in the initiative. The initiative gave them an administrative home. This also allowed the association to claim to its membership it was working on their behalf. After all, they were now a stone's throw away from the West Wing.

This brings up the answer to an important question, which is how an attentive interest group could apparently be "fooled" by executive actions with little substantive backing. Surely organizations created for the purpose of lobbying policy, who are thought of as informed fire-alarm pullers, will demand real policy change—and when they do not get it, the president will pay a price. Several facts in the case of HBCUs, and the faith-based initiatives for that matter, are very instructive. First, there were naysayers who said both offices were symbolic and not living up to their mandates. Plenty of HBCU proponents were eventually willing to dunk on the Trump White House. But they competed with voices that sang the administration's praises, and their naysaying came only later. The wait-and-see approach of some in the community meant that whatever their opinions of the administration, they would be buried or unpublicized by virtue of the time they chose to voice them.

Second, these kinds of actions exploit a classic problem for nonprofits. Like any organization, their leaders are imperfect agents of their members. The success of the leaders of the organization and the successes wanted by members are not always the same thing. In fact, if the members get every change they want, the need for the organization dies. It is no accident these White House offices often draw their staff from the very interest groups that motivate their creation. This can compromise their willingness to pull the fire alarm. It makes exit and protest less viable. This is why, I argue, interest groups are often the loudest proponents of executive actions with symbolic effects, and why they see even the meager actions of a president as a win. The symbolic component of executive action is valuable for them, too.

It is also worth repeating that what I describe as a "function" of these offices—accommodating interest groups—is mostly described as a downside by scholars of the presidential branch. They explicitly advise presidents against it. Why? Because it does not, in general, help them reach the goal of good management, good policy, or policy control. It becomes unclear who reports to whom. People end up duplicating functions. On net, the resources they soak up could be used elsewhere—more legal counsel, more budget or regulatory experts—and presidents might even be better off, at least with respect to policy control, if they did not exist at all.

Offices that enhance the president's symbolic capacity are not always tailored to some named interest or goal. There are generalist offices, which include the Office of Public Liaison, the Office of Strategic Initiatives, and the Office of Political Affairs. They provide the president with political advice—with information about support for initiatives, demands from constituent groups, and when it would be good time to act. They are as concerned about optics as traditional communications staff, but their jobs often impact the planning and execution of policy. They think about political implications. Presidents did not always have staff and whole offices dedicated to this, so the rise of this kind of advice is part of the story.

This brings us to the last way presidents foster their own capacity for going symbolic, which has to do with the kind of people they use to fill positions in the presidential branch. This, incidentally, is another source of annoyance for academics who study the presidency. The top dogs aside, most of the people who end up working in the White House are not very experienced, in a very specific way. They have plenty of experience in advocacy organizations, or in working for political campaigns, or in being communications staff for some member of Congress. This is why, when a student tells me they want to work in the White House, I suggest they get involved in political campaigns, not get a degree in public administration. The quickest route is to be a political adept and an administrative charlatan. It is not that these staffers are inexperienced. They have a particular kind of experience, the kind that helps politicians package and promote their actions.

That makes three types of strategies for fostering the symbolic capacity of the presidential branch: growing traditional communications apparatus, creating offices to accommodate (general or specific) political interests, and staffing up for political (rather than policy) combat. The question is, when will presidents deploy these strategies to bring the presidential branch in line with their goals?

There are two primary answers that come from the argument in chapter 2. Presidents tend to create structures that bolster the symbolic component of policymaking when their discretion is constrained. This is the same dynamic that leads presidents to produce orders with minimal direct effects when they have little legal power. Both expectations are about the policy areas that see more substantive action. In this case, responding to expectations, presidents should shape the portions of their administrations dealing with these low-authority areas to instead communicate their position.

Second, this kind of investment should come in response to political competition, the same variety seen impacting the behavior of parties in Congress. Remember that changing the status quo becomes more costly as this competition increases. This is because elements in Congress and elsewhere can easily sabotage the bureaucrats who actually carry out the president's policies. This increases presidents' need to highlight symbolic victories. This has implications for the timing of investment in symbolism and is the reason my argument matters for the modern era, which is defined by fiercely competitive elections for filling the legislative and executive branches. The three strategies I have highlighted have always existed, but there is a difference in the degree to which presidents rely on them over time.

This brings up a caveat, which is that reshaping the presidential branch is not like other executive actions. Hiring and reorganizing is a heavy lift that takes more time and effort. It is also cyclical. Usually presidents set up their organization at the start and then make modular adjustments over the course of the term. For this reason, we cannot expect presidents to reshape their organizations in the same reactive way they take executive action. It happens gradually, the same way institutional changes designed to control the administrative state do. Presidents also learn from one another, as people who work in Democratic and Republican administrations hopscotch from one to the next.

That means these hypotheses are best tested by looking at the history of the presidential branch. This is a different kind of evidence, relative to the previous chapters. I rely mostly on secondary sources to make a broader point about the presidential branch. That makes this evidence less final and persuasive, in my view. The point of assembling it is to show what is already out there while generating ideas for how this argument could be evaluated further.

7.3 Symbolic Capacity

The recent history of the presidential branch is not like the fifty-year period after the Brownlow Commission. Two basic facts appear for interpretation. First, the "traditional" mechanisms of policy control identified by scholars have slower growth. Second, over the same period, presidents have invested in the kinds of people and organizations that are not primarily designed to help them control the administrative state. The major changes on this front kick off during the Clinton administration, after the "Gingrich Revolution" in 1994. Jointly, these facts imply that institutional resources in the presidential branch have shifted from substance and toward symbolism. This does not mean that there have been no innovations in political control of the bureaucracy, or that presidents do not care about having the capacity for substantive policymaking. As always, these stylized facts are central tendencies. As presidents have inched forward in bureaucratic control, their ability to convey that control has been dramatically enhanced.

The OMB helps illustrate the first fact. Again, in the political environment of the 1980s, the OMB looked like the ascendant instrument of presidential control. And in many ways it is. But in some ways, the OMB has had the growth of its influence slowed since the 1970s. That time coincides with a dramatic expansion of mandatory spending (Pfiffner 2020). Mandatory spending is "automatic" or "permanent" in the budget—these are supposed to be entitlements, like Social Security. But members of Congress know that the way to lock in a program is to designate it mandatory (Clarke and Lowande 2016). Then there is no yearly fight over how much Congress should dole out that year. That is why designating the HBCU fund mandatory was a win. In 1985 the budget was about 50–50 mandatory and discretionary. But in 2022 mandatory spending took up 73 percent of the budget. Only 14 percent of the budget is non-defense discretionary spending. The central political function of the OMB is to give presidents influence over that remaining piece of the pie. The pie has shrunk and continues to shrink—and with it, this avenue of policy influence. Of course, this is *relative* influence, not absolute. As, at the same time, the amount of discretionary spending has gone up in absolute terms. So the influence has not gone down. But it also has not expanded at the rate it did before.

Another important fact is that OMB staff may have peaked in 1974 at 694.[3] Today, by its a recent budget request, it has 516 full-time equivalent employees (Executive Office of the President 2021). If you look at the president's budget request, you will find 636 "OMB Contributors" listed who helped prepare the budget, so it is difficult to say that the actual number of people in and out of those offices has dropped off all that much (Government Printing Office 2022). What is clear, however, is that the number of people has not increased. If anything, it has gone down, and modestly faster than the White House Office. At the OMB's peak in 1974, the White House Office had 547. In 2023 the White House had 522 staffers listed in its annual report to Congress.

This does not mean that the OMB has diminished in power; it continues to invent more brazen accounting tricks meant to effectuate presidents' preferences. Eloise Pasachoff (2021), for example, details a few episodes of the Trump administration's creative reuse of funds, most notably to find money to construct the promised "border wall." Other important expansions of the OMB's influence over the administrative state are instructive. Geovette E. Washington and Thomas E. Hitter, former general counsels at the OMB, highlight two important developments (Washington and Hitter 2020). First, the frequency of government shutdowns has created episodes of heightened influence, because the OMB approves shutdown plans. What functions of government are so essential they cannot be discontinued? Who will go to work when the money runs out? Questions left to American presidents by way of the OMB. Notably, though, this power has not emerged as a result of presidents' conscious choices to invest in the OMB. It is a side effect of heated budget battles in Congress.

What has emerged as a function of presidential initiative, on the other hand, is enhanced control over regulation. Within the OMB, the OIRA has become, since its creation in 1980, a central clearinghouse and driver of regulatory action across the federal government. Its role has expanded in recent years owing mostly to innovations in the Obama and Trump administrations. As Washington and Hitter (2020) note, the Trump administration managed to bring Treasury Department regulations into the regulatory review process, even though, like "independent" agencies, their proposed rules had been exempted (215). They conclude, "[A]n OMB employee hired in 1970 would most likely be struck by how the agency is now called on to actively set policy both across the executive branch and within an agency [. . .] through a comprehensive regulatory review" (216). However, also notable are quite different developments in the procedures for reviewing polices issued by the White House. The Legislative Proposals Division (LPD) at the OMB handles bills sent to Congress as well as the preclearance of executive actions. Andrew Rudalevige (2020) reports a few changes at LPD. The Division issued annual reports on the status of the presidents' legislative proposals, to track the progress of these priorities. This ended in around 2012 (Rudalevige 2020, 125).

In addition, according to Rudalevige, the preclearance process for executive actions has been subject to political considerations. To get to the president's desk, the standard protocol is for implementing agencies to review and comment on executive orders and other directives. OMB officials say this process is sometimes "gamed" by White House personnel concerned with the timing of an executive action. They want the signing to coincide with some event or political theme. As one exasperated former lawyer for OMB told Rudalevige, the Division personnel thought to themselves: "'Can't you just pretend you're signing something?'" (2020, 132).

Few things better illustrate the balancing of substantive and symbolic policymaking. In these instances, the people carrying out the executive order might have information valuable to a president who wants to change policy. They are not rogue agents, either. They serve at the pleasure of the president. Nor are their comments binding, or even capable of derailing an order entirely. The tension is between a process that would likely produce a better policy, and the desire to fill the president's schedule with the kind of activity that will benefit them politically.

As OMB has seen some of its policymaking power co-opted by showrunners, presidents have built up their capacity for the symbolic in the ways outlined earlier. Unlike the OMB, the NSC, and even the Council of Economic Advisors—all created by Congress—these are organizations created and sustained by presidents alone. These innovations have origins that precede the late 1980s, when most of the analysis in this book begins. Stephen Hess (1976) wrote decades ago of the Nixon administration: "Each successive president added other representatives, until under Nixon there were White House assistants for the aged, youth, women, blacks, Jews, labor, Hispanic Americans, the business community, governors and mayors, artists, and citizens of the District of Columbia, as well as such concerns as drug abuse, energy, environment, physical fitness, volunteerism, telecommunications, and national goals" (5). The specialized, showrunning offices have grown out of what used to be a few staff representatives. From these kinds of representatives, Hess and Pfiffner (2021) conclude, "the modern presidency has moved toward creating all policy at the White House" (6). Of course, creating policy (or better yet, *describing* it) and effectuating it are different things. The offices presidents create, often beneath the Domestic Policy Council, mostly do the former and not the latter.

I described two such offices in detail: the Office of Community and Faith-Based Initiatives, and the White House Initiative on HBCUs. In general, it is difficult to imagine either group existing prior to the modern era. The conventional view among public-management experts is that offices such as these are bad for the business of governing. According to Hess and Pfiffner (2021), "[S]pecial White House offices create unreasonable expectations for constituencies that previously lacked a White House contact." (171). Implicit in this assertion is, of course, that one can expect little in the way of substantive results from them.

The longer history of the HBCU initiative shows this. Every president since Carter has issued an executive order on the HBCU initiative. Each has innovated, but usually on a dimension unrelated to controlling policy from the White House. George H. W. Bush added an advisory board, which only accommodated the interest group with regular formal meetings.[4] Bill Clinton placed the initiative under OMB oversight and required agencies to produce annual reports describing their compliance.[5] George W. Bush moved the office from its more parochial location in the Office of Postsecondary Education to the Office of the Secretary of Education.[6] Trump's order moved it again, this time physically into the White House.[7] This was not the centralization of policymaking by the president. With the possible exception of Clinton's innovations, these moves were about ensuring that the initiative was more closely associated with the president, signaling each successive president's commitment, and ensuring that the initiative's work could be coordinated with the political strategy of the president.

Another example is the Office for Women's Initiatives and Outreach in the Clinton administration. Even a cursory look an office like this reveals it was not designed to allow Clinton to secure more policy wins for women's groups. It did not pretend, either. Here is language from its archived, late-1990s web page: "The President created the White House Office for Women's Initiatives and Outreach in June of 1995 to better serve and listen to his constituents. The office serves as a liaison between the White House and women's organizations, listening to women's concerns and proposals and bringing these ideas to the President and others in the Administration. [. . .] The office schedules events and speeches for White House officials and presidential appointees and holds events and roundtables."[8] Lauren Supina, its director, described her job as "promoting" the president's policies and "outreach" to stakeholders. Before becoming director, Supina had no prior experience in government. Her expertise was in political organizing—as the past director of the Democratic National Committee's Women's Leadership Forum.[9] Detailees working under Supina were on loan from the press shops at the Department of Defense and Department of Agriculture. This office was designed not for substantive policy but for special events, speechwriting, and press releases. Creating this office in 1995, following major electoral defeats in Congress, was an investment in symbolic governance. This office, and others like it, are examples of presidents shaping their organization to hone a specific political message.

Beyond these specialized units, presidents have leaned into generalists who help serve some of the same symbolic functions. They coordinate the political strategy of the president beyond any single area of focus. Modern presidents are careful to integrate their campaign and party organizations into the management of the presidential branch (Milkis 1993). George H. W. Bush hired his campaign manager to run his Office of Political Affairs. Clinton elevated the political affairs director to the rank of presidential assistant, which made them part of the circle of senior staff (Patterson 2000, 206–7).

But it was George W. Bush, more than any other during this period, who was an innovator on this front. His willingness to consult political strategists was not new. All of his predecessors had political strategists working for them. President Clinton, especially, was known for relying independent consultants and bringing them into policy discussions. The contrast lies in the degree to which their roles were institutionalized and brought into the policymaking process.

President Bush created the Office of Strategic Initiatives (OSI), run by Karl Rove. According to Hess and Pfiffner (2021), the OSI "was established to allow staff to think ahead and devise long-term political strategy" (170). It was from this office that Rove delivered his profane demand for a faith-based initiative. The anecdote is indicative of what "many observers" thought, according to Dickinson (2005)—"that Rove dominated the policy process during Bush's first term" (154). Dickinson concluded, "[I]t clearly signaled Bush's intent to make certain that policy development remained integrated with political strategy."

This is what distinguishes the OSI from offices that existed in earlier administrations. President Reagan, for example, created the Office of Planning and Evaluation, headed by Richard Beal, and the Office of Political Affairs, run by Lyn Nofziger. In both cases, these operations were separate from the policy process, providing information about retrospective and prospective constituent responses to the president's moves. Before his death in 1984, Beal was an information-technology expert who helped run the White House's polling operations.[10] Nofziger collected and replied to correspondence, organized visits to the White House, and delivered this feedback up the chain of command. Both offices, and the voices they amplified, surely had an influence on Reagan's decisions. James Druckman and Lawrence Jacobs (2015) write about how this works and what its implications are for democracy. But the important thing is that this influence was indirect. When a draft executive order was passed around for comment, Beal and Nofziger were not on the circulation list. Rove was at the top.

The growth of political affairs and public liaison operations runs contrary to the recommendations of experts and some practitioners. Hess, for example, wrote a memo to Jimmy Carter's transition team in 1976 in which he says of Nixon's Office of Public Liaison, "From the standpoint of good government, this operation should be abolished."[11] Patterson (2000) quotes former staffers who refer to these operations at various points as "gratuitous," "dysfunctional," and "manipulative," and one who refers to the polling operations, specifically, as people who should be "put out to pasture" (217). The three presidents since George W. Bush have all continued or expanded these institutions. The people directing these offices are always in the elite group of highest-paid assistants to the president, alongside senior lawyers and chiefs of staff.

Another, related development in organizing the presidential branch cannot be ignored: czars. The imperial-sounding title appoints some individual to the job of coordinating the federal government's response to a particular issue. Czars received the most media attention during the Obama administration, because of talking points from the opposition party that attacked them as unaccountable or unconstitutional.[12] Obama may have appointed more than any other president. Not surprisingly, simply counting czars is difficult because there is no legal or agreed-upon definition. It is just a colloquial term for a White House official who coordinates the government's response to something. The relevant question is how this choice serves the substantive and symbolic dimensions of policy.

The conventional view before President Obama was that czars did not enhance the president's control of policy. Hess (1976) writes that past czars "cluttered the chain of command. The cabinet people resented the dilution of their policymaking authority; the czars, without control of budgets or appointments, resented lacking authority to carry out their responsibilities" (184). Even Justin Vaughn and Jose D. Villalobos (2015), who authored a volume outlining circumstances in which czars *are* efficacious, concede that the concerns of critics are somewhat justified by the evidence they present, and that czars themselves are most effective when they provide voluntary, noncoercive coordination that taps into an coalition already on board with policy change.

Why, then, do modern presidents appoint them? Why have more recent presidents doubled down on them? As Patterson (1988) writes, "[T]he very fact of the czar's appointment will help rebut the political attack that the beleaguered chief executive is 'doing nothing about' the problem at hand" (272). Years later he wrote, "[D]on't mention that the problem the czar is poised to tackle may not be curable by means of administrative fixes anyway. The title of assistant to the president conveys a sense of action" (Patterson 2000, 264). Czars might pay dividends in presidents' quest to control policy, or they might be self-defeating. But their outward, symbolic benefit is comparatively certain. The president has put someone in charge of the problem. He is on the case. He cares.

The kind of people recent presidents have brought into the White House is also revealing of their motives. Contrary to what the typical American might expect, the White House is not primarily a place for expert policymaking officials at the peak of their careers. Again, as Hess (1976) writes, White House staff "consist largely of those who surrounded the president during the campaign [. . .] Their primary interest, however, will usually have been the art of politics, not governance" (12). The stories I have already told illustrate some of this. J. David Kuo was not an expert in federal grants or procurement, which would have allowed him to better monitor and effectuate President Bush's executive actions on faith-based initiatives.

One interpretation of personnel decisions like these is that presidents are trading away administrative know-how for loyalty to the agenda. There is a large, well-done body of academic literature on the subject, mostly dealing with the selection of cabinet and other positions outside the White House.[13] Officials like Kuo and other young campaign assistants may well be more loyal to the president and less competent. But it is important to reiterate that people like Kuo have other competencies. Kuo would have known next to nothing about procurement rules, but he knew how to write speeches and talking points. These are real skills, and not everyone has them. Plenty of expert administrators are blundering neophytes when they get involved in political controversy.

When presidents trade away one kind of expertise, they often get another. Political acumen is valued because symbolic politics is important for presidents' future. The hiring of White House officials inexperienced in governing is not a by-product of presidents' decision to prioritize loyalty. They also invest in a capacity to do something other than control policy.

The tendency to hire inexperienced White House staffers may be accelerating. Hess and Pfiffner, for example, write that "of 450 initial White House assistants" in the Clinton administration, "sixty-three were twenty-three years old or younger and many others were under thirty" (2021, 160). Again, it is not that these staffers had no expertise; it is that their expertise is in political messaging and strategy. Their raw number and prominence, of course, obscures where they are located and what impacts they have on what the White House produces. Even within offices that have a specific policy mandate, room is made for officials whose primary functions are packaging the activities of the administration for publicity purposes.

President Biden, for example, created a White House Office of Domestic Climate Policy, headed by Gina McCarthy, who had run the EPA under President Obama.[14] By early media accounts, this office enhanced the president's influence on climate change–related policies throughout the federal government. But it is notable that below McCarthy, the highest-paid ring of deputies included a communications specialist, who formally worked for Al Gore,[15] along with a press specialist on loan from the National Oceanic and Atmospheric Administration. There were thirteen other officials in the office as of 2022. This kind of capacity paid off. Alongside accounts that the office centralized policymaking in the White House are some that it intervened in political strategy. It timed the release of oil and gas leases to coincide with the Thanksgiving holiday, and it delayed the release of EPA rules to aid the negotiation of a climate bill in Congress.[16]

People in the press office are not the only ones concerned about appearances. These officials and their expertise are embedded throughout the presidential branch. In this modern era, they are not dying out. Presidents have recognized their importance and invested in them, just as they moved beyond "neutral competence" and politicized control over policymaking.

7.4 Councils, Foreign and Domestic

The presidential branch has changed, and those changes reveal motives beyond just good government and policy control. But it is also difficult to understand the changes without a reference point. The whole government could have changed over this period. Perhaps there was some anthropological change after the new millennium—driven by the acceleration of the information age with the Internet, smartphones, and social media. Now, this thesis might assert, modern presidents had no choice but to concern themselves with packaging and publicizing their accomplishments. In that case, the development of a symbolic infrastructure in the presidential branch is not some strategic response, any more than was the replacement of telegraph with beepers.

This kind of epoch-based, developmental hypothesis is less persuasive once you consider units of the presidential branch that were *not* restructured for symbolic politics during this period. The best example is the National Security Council (NSC) and its staff. It is a natural comparison case for its younger sibling, the Domestic Policy Council (DPC). The councils are thought of as "whole-of-government" coordinators of foreign and domestic policy. They are to identify problems, develop proposals, and monitor their implementation. These are canonical roles of a presidential branch attempting to insert the president's policy preferences in government.

But what these councils do, and how they have been structured are very different. The NSC was built to ensure that the president has the advice he needs to make foreign-policy decisions and the capacity to oversee their implementation. The DPC has done the same for domestic policy, but only in fits and starts. To an outside observer reading the DPC's description of its role, it is performing the same coordinating function as the NSC. The DPC oversees other offices that emphasize the policy priorities of the president and follows through on the implementation of executive action. In practice, however, its role is less comprehensive, its staff less experienced, and its jurisdiction beset by rivals with competing mandates.

The NSC became a means of foreign-policy control mostly by presidential design. In its original incarnation, there is nothing to hint that this cabinet-level, interagency committee should be a creature of the White House and the EOP. As early as 1950, President Truman developed it into "a presidential instrument" within the EOP, with an executive secretary serving at the pleasure of the president as head of its staff (Nelson 1985, 361). This is owed in part to its vague mandate, described by the National Security Act of 1947 as "to advise the President with respect to the integration of domestic, foreign, and military politics relating to the national security" (Sec. 101[a]). The president could assign additional functions, and future presidents did.

Over time, it expanded beyond its advisory capacity to include monitoring policy. Much of this is thought to have occurred during the Nixon administration as a result of the prominence of Henry Kissinger. But Clinton expanded the membership of the NSC and created working groups to coordinate the implementation of the president's foreign-policy decisions.[17] President Obama, too, reorganized the role of the NSC to emphasize monitoring and implementation.[18]

Its staff reflects these changes in function. During this modern period, the NSC staff has grown dramatically, from around fifty people during the first Bush administration, to between three hundred and four hundred at the end of George W. Bush's second administration.[19] Funding from Congress has not gone up at a comparable pace, suggesting that most staff expansions come from detailees working in national security–related agencies. According to a recent CRS Report, "[A] substantial number of NSC staff members over the years have been career military or civil servants with backgrounds in foreign policy and defense" (Best 2011, 24). This has been a source of criticism from Congress, whose members sometimes complain the president is deflating the number of White House personnel by borrowing career civil servants. In the modern era, the NSC has always included a communications office. But it has remained one of several dozen NSC offices with no significant growth.

What do these staffers prioritize? Advisors to the Clinton administration are particularly instructive cases. Anthony Lake, President Clinton's first National Security Advisor, later described the Clinton White House and its orientation toward the NSC: "Frankly, a lot of the people who came in with him on the political side of the house still saw foreign policy as something you don't talk about. [. . .] It was very hard to fight through a lot of the opposition from the schedulers and others when trying to set up meetings with foreign leaders, phone calls, et cetera. They saw it as a diversion from the main agenda."[20] The administration saw little value in injecting political considerations in policy areas they saw as "distractions," even arguing that it was wrong for President Clinton to keep pace with his predecessors on time spent on foreign policy. It did not remain that way. Lake's replacement, Samuel R. Berger, reportedly inserted concerns about domestic political backlash in the administration's Kosovo policy. One contemporary account said Berger sought "to shape subjects as diverse as what gets said at State Department briefings to the Pentagon's planning for a Kosovo peacekeeping force, to be deployed after an eventual settlement."[21] These are products from the mold of the politicized presidency. Presidential aides injected presidents' preferences into policymaking, leveraging both their own expertise and the president's unique statutory and constitutional authority over foreign affairs.

The NSC, in summary, has become the critical example of White House policy influence: "its combination of skill and size is a measure of the ascendency of the White House in executive branch policy development and policy coordination" (Patterson 2000, 72).

Today's DPC has historical precedents that go back to the Nixon administration. President Nixon created a "Domestic Council" by executive order.[22] Its goals were broad: to define the nation's goals, develop proposals for reaching them, then monitor those policies after the president had decided on them. President Clinton created the modern incarnation of the Domestic Policy Council, also by executive order.[23] It carried the same broad mandate— nothing less than to "coordinate the domestic policy-making process," to "ensure that domestic policy decisions and programs are consistent with the president's stated goals," and to "monitor implementation" of those goals.[24] The DPC itself was a goal of advocates of administrative reform, who saw the sprawling, informal, and unstructured system of presidential aides competing for the president's attention as inefficient.

Not surprisingly, the DPC was to be a creature of the president, with no congressional intrusion into its staff or committee structure. But unlike the NSC staff, the DPC staff did not become the temporary home of expert detailees from agencies. Today the DPC staff is often where campaign workers find jobs in the administration. Most instructive, however, has been the DPC's place in the presidential branch relative to the NSC. The NSC has maintained consistent hierarchical structure, overseeing various directorates beneath the main committees, which correspond to areas of U.S. foreign policy and NSC functions. But the DPC and its subordinate offices shift dramatically with every administration. Most important, the DPC has never established consistent control over the offices presidents used to emphasize their commitment to one policy area or another. At the beginning of the Biden administration, only the remnants of the faith initiative and the new climate office reported to it, whereas offices for HBCU policy, women's policy, gender policy, and COVID-19 had reporting status equivalent to the DPC.[25]

According to Arnold, the reforms that created the DPC "were failures. [. . .] [The] Domestic Council never quite fulfilled [. . .] expectations [. . .]. Far from becoming a mechanism for policy formulation, the Domestic Council became a large staff for presidential errands, admittedly increasing presidential reach but providing little analytic or formulaic capacity over policy. [. . .] [R]ather than constituting a mechanism for the regulation of the executive branch, the Executive Office reforms were overwhelmed by the President's short term demands" (298). In a comparative assessment, Hess (1976) writes that "the domestic and economic councils never had reached the level of institutional coherence of the National Security Council" (150).

What explains the contrast? Presidents' legal authority in foreign policy, relative to domestic, has resulted in very different incentives for institution building. The NSC is built for policy control and staffed with experts who known how to follow through. Often, they know because they currently work in the agencies that conduct actual operations. The DPC has far less coherence, less experienced staff, and less formal authority over other offices within the White House. It is only one of many competing organizations where domestic policy is developed, chosen, and monitored. That does not mean the DPC and those other offices are inactive—quite the opposite. Presidents simply see value in elevating components of their domestic policy within the structure of the White House. Domestic policy can remain less rigid and hierarchical *because* the president has less discretion to make changes. A sprawling and decentralized domestic-policy apparatus is a liability only if the actions it takes are wholly substantive. But this chaotic administrative structure helps presidents balance the substantive and symbolic dimensions of policy.

Presidents make important management decisions and are closely watched by pundits and experts alike. In some imagined world, these decisions might reflect apolitical concerns about the public welfare. The president would assemble a team of noted administrative experts who neutrally execute the will of the people. It is well-known, however, that the presidential branch is not neutral. Presidents have policy preferences that they attempt to impose, using these immediate resources, on the rest of the government. Both neutral competence and politicized semicompetence exist in the presidential branch. The White House and EOP are staffed with dedicated public servants who care about doing a good job and carrying out the president's policy agenda.

But that is not all they are doing. In some offices, it is not even most of what they do. Modern presidents have fostered their administrative capacity to go symbolic, alongside the substantive capacity to govern. During this recent history, presidents have dedicated whole offices and personnel to demonstrate that they are in charge and fixing problems. Presidents have some leeway, but the total number of full-time employees in the White House is relatively fixed. This means that in building capacity for one function, they may be leaving something on the table. This is one of the possibilities I turn to in the last chapter of this book.

8: EXECUTIVE POWER IN DEMOCRACY

What is it, exactly, that makes presidents powerful? The day they take executive action comes because of built-in advantages. They sign their name and need no one else's. Once set in motion, it's up to someone else to stop it. Their primary antagonist up the street is too polarized and dysfunctional to mount an effective challenge. So presidents often succeed, and today, almost nothing in American politics and policy seems outside the scope of this basic story.

But changing policy is not everything. We do not typically see or feel the effects of what the president does, so we rely on symbols to judge them. This is what the modern presidency is best situated to generate. A lot of tiring effort awaits anyone who wants to change the status quo. But presidents are uniquely suited to showing everyone they have done something. The product may or may not lead to actual change. But, more than likely, it improves the odds the president will retain their office and bolsters their historical legacy. That makes the presidency uniquely powerful among unequal branches of government. But this also leads to a potential danger, which is the subject of this last chapter.

At the time of this writing, danger seems to be on the mind of everyone who watches American politics. Steven Levitsky and Daniel Ziblatt, in *How Democracies Die* (2018), describe how events around the Trump presidency looked like the late stages of other democracies, ones that slid into dictatorship. William Howell and Terry Moe (2020) open their recent book by writing that whether the United States will remain a democracy "is very much in question" (1). Jacob Grumbach (2022) calls out the Republican Party as the lone horseman of democratic decline in the states. Read these books, and many others like them, and it will be difficult to escape some basic impressions. Democracy is weakening. It is failing tests. It is flashing warning signs, going backward, and up in the air. Everyone should be concerned.

There is nothing new about these feelings, even if the political conditions and people voicing concerns are different. There is certainly no shortage of this sentiment in writing about the presidency. Read the antifederalists.[1] The presidency would be the death knell of republican government, they told us, two and a half centuries ago—it will be the same as a king, it will mean rule by martial law. In the last century, the Pulitzer Prize–winning historian Arthur Schlesinger Jr. coined the term "imperial presidency" to describe the dominance of presidents in foreign affairs, something he said could lead to rule by decree in all other affairs (Schlesinger 2004).

This book started with a popular story about the presidency that sets aside these fears. Congress is broken, but the American people demand solutions to problems. Our government does not provide them. America's aged Constitution sets up too many veto points and warps representation of the people. The American president is the only nationally elected politician and is endowed with vast resources and discretionary powers. But this is actually a danger, according to the many who talk of democratic decline. It incentivizes and empowers presidents, forcing them to change the status quo by breaking through procedural barriers, to erode democratic norms by acting alone, and ultimately to whip up popular support for the rule of one.

The argument of this book suggests that the dangers aren't so obvious. It says presidents are not doing as much as they claim in press releases. Presidents often create the impression they are making changes. They get away with this because all the accountability mechanisms in American government—the public, the media, parties, interest groups, elections—are insufficient to force presidents to be effective. Nor do these mechanisms regularly expose or render irrelevant a symbolic action when they see it. More often than not, these mechanisms play into the president's hands. Presidents steer the ship of state and use it to credit-claim, either because there is no alternative or because it is more convenient than actually governing.

This complicates the standard diagnosis of president's role in the ills of American democracy. Maybe there is some relief, as the president's executive actions appear more contingent and less unilateral than previously thought. On the other hand, things could be worse than they seem. This is what needs to be sorted out. There is no shortage of arguments about what the presidency means for the long-term health of democracy in America. They are all based, at least implicitly, on some idea about how the presidency works. This book is one such idea. The president is at the center of American politics, and you cannot separate developments in the office from developments in the system. But it is important to be clear about how these developments implicate the health of American democracy—to describe where the real dangers lie, and where they do not.

I need to establish a few ground rules before answering those questions. This ending contains no prescriptions or recommendations. There will be no five-point plans, no proposed solutions or even suggestions. It is difficult to alter the way people govern themselves. Even if you manage to, changes to complicated systems have unintended and unpredictable consequences. Political scientists and others who write about American politics spend much more time trying to understand how things work than they do thinking through reforms. This is probably why many scholars I know skip the concluding chapters of books written by their own colleagues.

Though the book contains no prescriptions for reform, it does engage in speculation. This is unavoidable, because, as I write in a later section, most of what you would need to know to support the arguments I am going to make is difficult to know or just has not been investigated. So I engage in some data-free speculation. The best I can do, for now, is be up-front about it. With those caveats in mind, I argue that this turn in the presidency is bad for democracy. Presidents' incentives lead them to undermine trust in government, expand the rule of one, and set examples for other leaders to do the same.

8.1 Symbolic Politics and Democratic Decline

Even when modern presidents use their power for symbolic effect, they damage democracy. To understand why, we should dispel a few claims about the use of executive power in American government. First and foremost, the frequency of executive action is not evidence that democracy is in trouble. Many make this error. Take, for example, Levitsky and Ziblatt's (2018) description of the power of President Franklin Roosevelt: "His use of executive orders——more than 3,000 during his presidency, averaging more than 300 a year—was unmatched at the time or since" (158). They go on to call the "We Can't Wait" initiative of the Obama administration an instance of "norm breaking" (163). For them, the exercise of decree authority seems itself a demonstration of dictatorship.

This is a misunderstanding. Roosevelt's figure is high because back then, presidents made lots of routine and boring decisions. He issued a huge number of orders because he had to effectuate democracy-killing acts such as lowering the speed limit for cars in the Panama Canal Zone. Plenty of executive actions are ministerial. Miss this, and you will come under the false impression recent presidents are just doing what all presidents have done—or are maybe less rambunctious, because the number of presidential directives peaked seventy-five years ago. The "We Can't Wait" campaign may well have broken norms, but not because of the number of actions President Obama took, or because those actions were effective at changing the status quo. Today's threats are unique and are, by design, not easily counted.

Others suggest the precise opposite: executive action is great for democracy. In fact, they argue, it might be sign of a *healthy* one. For those opinions, we have to check back in with our friends at the law school. Recall that some espouse the theory of the unitary executive. Take, for example, Steven G. Calabresi, co-chairman of the Federalist Society, who writes: "It is vital some mechanism be available to fulfill the 'promise' of the constitutional text that we will have one, and only one, president, able in theory to direct all matters that involve policy discretion" (Calabresi 1995, 58). Translation: presidents should control policy from the top down. It is the finest way of governing in a democracy, he goes on, relative to rule by congressional committees in Congress, or the judicial system. This is a good thing, for reasons summed by in one word: accountability. The president is "the only official who is accountable to a national voting electorate and no one else," Calabresi tells us (59). He goes on to write that "[t]he President of the United States and his subordinates are the conscious agents of just such a national majority coalition. If that coalition will, by its very nature, be likely to be moderate, temperate, and just, so too will its agent be likely to be moderate, temperate, and just" (67).

This is a tidy, romantic picture of presidents and their incentives. Set aside whether there is any evidence at all that presidents are uniquely temperate. The fact is, the accountability mechanism Calabresi's argument relies on is actually generic, weak, and inconsistent. This is what makes symbolic governance viable for the president. The "national constituency" of the president does not hold the line the way these normative arguments demand—at least not to the extent that unilateral policymaking by the president becomes a boon to democracy. This is like saying submachine-gun ownership follows nontrivially from the right of self-defense.

How, then, does executive action damage democracy in practice? Three ways. It sets up would-be dictators by damaging trust in government. It creates incentives for U.S. presidents to take risky actions, which then set precedents that expand the president's power over time. And most important, it encourages other chief executives to deploy the same tactics.

Nonsubstantive actions can have short-term benefits for democracy, but they also have a longer-term, corrosive effect. To illustrate the benefits, recall the 1776 Commission and the anti-antifa immigration orders—both from the last year of the Trump administration. Both had little to no substantive effect on what the government did, but both were all over the news. In the short term, these posed no direct threat to democracy. They were feckless decrees, the last gasps of an administration on its way out. They were meant to shore up the president's brand as a politician fighting the Left's rewrite of American history and its promotion of "lawlessness" in cities. But, of course, there is an alternative worse than a branding exercise. Suppose the president actually had labeled all protestors terrorists, rounded them up, and deported them. Suppose the president actually could impose a civics lesson on grade-school children, censoring all alternative viewpoints. Sometimes the only thing worse than symbolic policymaking is actual changes to policy.

In this way, symbolic politics is occasionally a release valve for popular demands that run counter to the general welfare or the rule of law. There is a lot of writing in political science about circumstances like these.[2] If presidents kowtow to popular desires that run counter to the people's interest, they are "pandering," this area of research says. A president who issues a mostly symbolic order can pander without damaging the interests of the public, because those actions do not have the substantive effects they promise.

But there is also a more important, long-term disease to consider. Executive action might acclimate democratic publics to rule by one person. There are hints in the empirical facts presented in this book that this is happening now. Remember that executive action is now a regular part of the news cycle. It wasn't twenty years ago. Remember that the public has ideas about where presidents have the most latitude to act alone, even if they are mistaken and less certain about this than experts. Many of the areas they view as most presidential are ones presidents have acted on recently. They see DACA, they see the border wall. They see drone strikes on American citizens. It is a small step to conclude that, with each executive action, presidents are helping to generate expectations about their own power. But symbolic moves have the same public face, without the substantive effect. This is what makes them uniquely insidious. They create the short-term impression that the president is governing and getting things done. They do not address the underlying problem. This is the kind of dynamic that damages the reputation of public institutions.

In the United States, the reputations of public institutions, with the exception of the military, are already in the basement. The political scientist Amy Lerman has written about it in a book titled *Good Enough for Government Work* (2019). Most people associate government-run programs and institutions with inefficiency and ineffectiveness. Trust can be restored by honestly describing problems, communicating what is being done to fix them, and setting expectations about results. These are lessons from the corporate world Lerman thinks would be useful for public bureaucracies. None of them are on display when presidents act for symbolic purposes. Billing these minor policy moves as grand demonstrations that the president is not waiting for Congress to get things done displays none of the humility implicit in the standard operating procedures for improving public reputations. In fact, it works in the opposite direction.

But this is not like getting people to eat at Chipotle again, or even to sign up for Obamacare. The reputation on the line is that of the office of the presidency. The president is an elected politician in possession of vast powers over life and property. It is a gaping hole in American democracy that could be exploited by would-be dictators at the gates. What Howell and Moe, as well as Levitsky and Ziblatt, get absolutely right is that would-be demagogues use the erosion of trust in public institutions to aggrandize their own authority. The demagogues tell a compelling story. Those other presidents lied to you, and I alone can help. This is the opportunity presidents help generate when they focus on creating the impression of governance without actually governing. It is a concern that has grown over time as people have become used to presidents' ways of promoting themselves. But it presents a game-ending risk, something far more damaging than a few bad policies.

Of course, it might not be so bad. The argument that I just made is supported mostly by reasoned speculation. It is difficult to measure trust in government or the degree to which you think dictatorship is fine—let alone understand causal associations between things presidents do and those public beliefs. If this sounds like waffling, that's because it is. When the risk is great, it's important to say so, even when there is significant uncertainty. If you go to the Food and Drug Administration's web page right now, they will tell you that toast might cause cancer, and also that it might not.[3]

Watchers of American democracy increasingly voice concern over local election administrators, county sheriffs, and conspiracy-minded congressional candidates. All of these are important and worth overseeing. The thesis that democracy declines gradually over time makes sense and is probably correct. But again, this is a central tendency. There is also the tail-end risk to consider, one getting far less attention in contemporary politics. The presidency is *the* institution that introduces the risk of total ruin for American democracy. It is what happens when so much power is concentrated in a single office. But this also means changes in circumstances that affect the presidency ripple through the system as a whole.

A second problem is that some executive actions the president expects to fail might instead succeed. I argued in chapter 2 that presidents sometimes take an executive action because the symbolic benefits outweigh the time and resources they expect to waste. But occasionally, by chance, their move will work. It will dramatically change policy. When it does, a new precedent has been set, to be used by the next president. This argument is not that different from the concerns others voice about the president in a democracy. What this book does is offer an explanation for that gradual aggrandizement. The problem is that presidents have so much to gain politically from such actions, even when they are unsuccessful.

There are others who learn from the president. The American presidency sets trends for chief executives in the United States and also abroad. In state governments today, more governors are adopting the strategies deployed by U.S. presidents. Governors take bold, headline-grabbing executive actions—some that lack substance, others serious and boundary pushing. They do so in part because they see the political success presidents have had deploying similar strategies. They have political ambitions of their own, and these are served by leveraging the same political narrative. They are not waiting for the legislature; they are in charge, getting things done. If this undermines government at the federal level, it might do the same elsewhere. I return to this point at the end.

Someone might defend symbolic executive action, even with these consequences in mind. They might disagree with my speculation about its effects on trust or about the likelihood governors and other chief executives will learn from the U.S. president. Then, they might ask: what is the harm? Presidents have a role to play as symbolic political leaders, and these actions are the fulfillment of that role. When executive action does nothing to change policy, it may still be important, because people need collective symbols to rally around.

What these kinds of arguments ignore is that the president of the United States is not a celebrity or a public intellectual, a person whose time and energy we can afford to waste. Presidents have a real job. Dedicating time to creating collective symbols for their political base means taking time away from something else. Many good ideas to improve the way the federal government works are hopelessly boring to the typical person. Let's say the president would like to announce a plan for more agencies to share core administrative functions, eliminating waste and duplication across government. Or maybe the next president decides to try to enforce the law that says agencies need to disclose the number of contractors they hire, so that the American public understands how much of its own government it is outsourcing (Potter 2023). In terms of public attention, these initiatives, and others like them, have no shot against the 1776 Commission.

We know this because presidents have done things like this. President George W. Bush created a centralized, color-coded performance rating tool for government programs.[4] President Barack Obama did more than any president to promote "open government," putting government data and records online in a timely, transparent, and usable fashion.[5] Almost no one cared. These nonpartisan, managerial wins were ignored during their reelection campaigns. Both initiatives were discarded by their successors.

Defenders of symbolic politics also tend to assume its results are neutral or benign. Sometimes it is not. Recall the story of Neil Troppman and the

National Tracing Center. There is a strong case, in my view, that the president's incentives for symbolic governance actually damaged a core function of the ATF. It goes beyond this one case. The morass of task forces, commissions, advisory groups, interagency committees, czars, initiatives, and offices created by presidents to demonstrate that they are fixing America's problems most often layer atop existing organizations. This can make agencies worse at their jobs. Presidents' dirty secret is that their most tried-and-true solution to bureaucracy is often . . . more bureaucracy.

8.2 How Things Could Change

A fourth of the White House staff wake up tomorrow and learn they are out of the job. They leave DC and put their skills to use as marketing professionals—or become something in short supply in the United States, such as electricians or plumbers. The president's showrunners are demoted, hived off from serious policy production, notified last about decisions. Former campaign staffers are replaced with people who know about administration and care about public service. The president revamps the clearance process for executive actions. Agencies will be consulted. Implementation plans are in place before signage. The creation of new organizations and groups requires extra scrutiny to avoid overburdening the already scarce time of public officials. The president carefully avoids novel uses of legal discretion. In public, they never lambast Congress for its lack of productivity and refrain from taking actions similar to those Congress is considering. The Justice Department and Office of Legal Counsel are emptied of anyone who read Calabresi (1995) in law school and felt a warm glow. Signing ceremonies are banned, as are the words "blue ribbon" and "initiative." Turkeys are spatchcocked and roasted without the insult of false salvation. The presidency becomes boring.

This is all nonsense—not because none of these things are good ideas, but because the logic of this book dismisses them as pipe dreams. Presidents and their agents are strategic. They act on incentives induced by their goals and the rules of the game. They will never read this book, and if they did, the problems it identifies could not be resolved by its persuasive charisma. I have already talked about their likely reaction to many of the arguments and assertions in this book. They will say that what is called symbolic is actually transformative and catalyzing. They will fiercely defend the work of their colleagues and assert that it is indeed substantive. They will certainly not do any of the things imagined in the paragraph above, because those things would be contrary to their interests and the interests of the president. They would foresee the inevitable revolt of party operatives, the frustrations of tying one's own hands, the inevitable critiques that the president is weak, not doing enough, inactive, and asleep at the wheel. "President Biden Refuses to Pardon, Lets Thanksgiving Turkey Die," the Fox News headline would read. Presidents and their advisors would see reforms like these as political self-harm, and they would be absolutely right. It is the core frustration of any attempt to reform political institutions: the people who have the power to change them are typically wedded to the status quo.

But the question remains: are there incentive-compatible actions that might change the game? Yes, but they would happen slowly. These are not reforms to be legislated. They are potential changes to the way professions operate. The first has to do with the media. In principle, I see no reason why news organizations could not change the way they report executive action. There are plenty of presidential actions journalists downplay or ignore entirely, things that were novel long ago but today are so routine they rarely make a blip. It was major news in the 1860s when President Andrew Johnson traveled around the country, drunkenly stumping against Congress. Speeches today only make headlines if the president says something outlandish. It was major news then, as well, if the president took a position on some pending action of Congress. Today their positions are just context in a broader story. The subject shifted. The president's actions faded into the background, as filler alongside other items now considered newsworthy.

It is not hard to imagine the same dynamic happening to executive action over time. Virtually every elite voice today, including those of presidents themselves, their staff, and scholars, is telling newsrooms executive action is a big deal—something they should report on, something that should be the lede. They give executive actions the benefit of the doubt. That could change. News staff could subject executive action to higher scrutiny. They could ignore more actions, or bury them beyond the lede. Alternatively, they could emphasize a different and more interesting story, one that is more skeptical of the effects of such actions. The skepticism is already there in commentary and follow-up pieces. It just appears later, and as a result is downplayed or politically irrelevant. Changes in journalistic norms and practices happen slowly, but they do happen, and often they are a function of realizations about how politicians take advantage of the news. Journalists want to get it right, and they do not like the idea that they are being duped. In theory, this would alter the political calculations of the president and their advisors. If executive action is not the safe public-relations win that it has been, presidents will use the tool differently.

The other audience with an interest in identifying symbolic actions for what they are is interest groups. Heads of nonprofits could adopt the same kind of awareness of executive actions' limitations and avoid being taken advantage of for symbolic politics. Their most valuable resource in these scenarios is their public endorsement. For organizations favorably disposed to an action, they often provide the equivalent of the blurb on a book jacket, and even when they append these statements with caveats—such as "now the real work begins"—those contingencies are buried.

This difference in standard operating procedures might be all the more potent because it is asymmetric. For organizations opposed to the action, their explicit denunciation signals to observers that the president has done something important that they dislike. When the president issues symbolic actions on firearm regulation, for example, the National Rifle Association always has an incentive to portray it as a terrible abuse of authority, something that is effectual. On the other hand, if proponents of gun control withhold endorsements, the White House is left with nothing but negative voices, changing the political value of the action itself.

I see these changes in professional practices as realistic because they may already be happening. Executive action has been routine in American politics for a relatively short time. It takes time for elite audiences to adjust and develop expectations about new political phenomena, or to adopt a heuristic that guides responses. This book has dealt with a period of American politics in which conditions are stable enough to allow systematic analysis. But even in that period, things have changed a lot. Journalists and nonprofit advocates gradually learned and adopted one set of procedures for reacting to what presidents do. These procedures are not locked in by incentives, and therefore, they offer the most realistic prospects for an alternative to the status quo.

What these kind of changes require, of course, is better and more accurate understandings of the limits of executive action. They require a careful inventory of the results these actions do and do not produce, and a better set of stylized facts to be communicated outside of the narrow group of experts who study presidential administration. The problem is, we do not have that.

8.3 I Don't Know

Suppose someone wanted to decide, for themselves, whether the use of unilateral power was a good idea. This could be journalists and interest groups—or maybe even White House staffers. What would they have to help them make that call? A collection of anecdotes—things such as DACA, the border wall, the "sanctuary cities" order, and Race to the Top. This book added other anecdotes—firearm tracing, bans on transgender military personnel, faith-based initiatives, American heritage rivers, and HBCUs. They each complicate the story those other actions tell by raising doubts about the efficacy of this way of governing. But this is still a war of anecdotes, one the stories cannot settle. What we do not have is a general sense of how effective executive action actually is.

In this context, the study of effectiveness really means two things: implementation and results. Implementation turns presidential directives into more than paper. We do not know how many executive actions are ignored, not complied with, or half-heartedly carried out. How many regulations requested are never written? How many reports required are never received? How often do both happen, but with some delay? How often are things implemented that contradict or moderate what the president actually wanted?

There are no good answers to these questions, for obvious reasons.[6] Compliance is not easily studied because there is no prospect for passive data collection, which social scientists these days rely on. Agencies do not announce they are ignoring an executive order. The White House does not announce it is behind schedule in carrying out the president's orders. These are internal management documents of the executive branch. There is no national registry, no national status report, nothing produced that would quickly reveal the answers we need. Nor will there ever be, because that kind of transparency goes against presidents' and bureaucrats' incentives.

Studying results is harder. Presidents and their supporters care that the orders achieve some outcome or result—improving educational attainment for Black students, reducing gun violence, curbing greenhouse emissions, increasing domestic oil production, and reducing illegal border crossings. Do executive actions move any of the benchmarks that motivate their issuance? Under what circumstances do they succeed or fail to reach those goalposts? Do third parties—namely, businesses, interest groups, and state and local governments—mitigate or enhance these effects? Even when orders are *not* successfully implemented, can they still have secondary effects on these outcomes? Again, there are no good, systematic answers, because there is no quick-kill way to get them.

As this book has shown, objective results are not the only thing worth measuring. Executive action has symbolic political value—another kind of result that can be studied. Plenty of actions are mundane and unimportant. Plenty of actions muddy their political intent by the way they are written, while others make special efforts to do the opposite. Which actions send a clearer signal to voters and interest groups? Does the issue-framing of an action matter for public support? What kinds of heuristics induce skepticism among the president's audience? These are all questions for opinion polls and experiments, eminently answerable but seldom asked. This book has cited plenty of surveys about executive action, but none takes stock of such action's symbolic value.

These gaps demand a research agenda with two fronts. The first takes a single executive action or series of related ones, then follows through from its implementation to the outcomes it is supposed to have impacted. The second collects many of the former, standardizes the answers they provide, weights their reliability, and decides if there are any reasonable generalizations to be drawn from it. This is a way of producing knowledge that will be familiar to anyone in medical research and in some social sciences. But there are no meta-analyses of presidents' interventions in American life.

There are also obvious, nonpractitioner reasons for such a research agenda. Politicians are strategic and credit-claim, but they also care about getting things done. If that is the case, whether an action is objectively efficacious matters, as do the contextual factors that contribute to efficacy. Likewise, whether an executive action turns into a symbolic win, and under what circumstances, is critical. Presidents and their advisors make choices about executive action with a lot of uncertainty about how effective it is. To the extent that wishful thinking guides their behavior, better knowledge about effectiveness couldn't hurt.

This is all about the American presidency, but the problems of executive power are everywhere people try to govern themselves. It is no coincidence that the study of unilateral action in the United States really begins with the comparative study of decree authority, in a volume organized by John Carey and Matthew Shugart (1998). Today the study of performative governance is mostly confined to that of Chinese bureaucracies (Ding 2022). Executives everywhere have the same basic need to demonstrate to some audience that they are solving problems. The office of the presidency is still occupied by one administration at a time, and the inherent limitations that imposes on research are not going to change. But this does not, in itself, imply that the right comparative frontier is at some cross-national level.

On the contrary, the most driving questions are subnational. If symbolic politics is really about attaining some messaging win, those incentives should actually be *weakest* at the top. It is the lower-tier politicians, ones ambitious enough to seek higher office, who have the strongest incentives to attract attention and build their brand. That is why the most compelling case of looking beyond presidents in the U.S. federal government is that of state governors. The United States has fifty of them—fifty chief executives, who themselves issue decrees. Increasingly, they seem to behave like minipresidents. They send the state national guard to the U.S.-Mexico border.[7]

They create gubernatorial honorifics and initiatives. They sue their own governments.[8] They put immigrants on planes and send them to other states.[9] They ban guns in the capital city.[10] They do so with the same kind of fanfare awarded to presidents. Their actions are not dramatic usurpations of popular will or the exercise of executive power despite the constraints other branches. They are not really trying to change the status quo. They are auditioning.

8.4 All the Way Down

Lieutenant Governor Janice McGeachin appears about twenty seconds into the video. The others film themselves wearing plainclothes in their backyards. McGeachin leans out of the driver's seat of an olive-drab camper with an American flag draped over the side. The video lists freedoms Idahoans have lost since the pandemic, ones McGeachin and the state legislators joining her ask the audience to fight for. As she adds "pursuing happiness and security" to the list, she reaches in the center console and produces a two-toned Glock 19, then lays it flat on a Bible.

The video was posted to YouTube on October 27, 2020. By this time, about twenty Idahoans were dying and another seventy more were entering intensive-care wards every day. Governments had closed businesses, restricted travel, mandated masks, and launched health screenings. In the United States, trillions had been spent on relief programs, medical research, and mitigation efforts. New proposals were floated constantly as states and localities issued mandatory orders for people to stay in their homes.

Things had been different in Idaho. Following others, Governor Brad Little closed the state for business, extended the closure, released emergency funds, and deployed the National Guard. But after an initial peak of a few dozen infections per day that April, the curve sank to a handful per day. In June they reopened offices, restaurants, gyms, and movie theaters. To outsiders on the coasts, Little was another Republican governor acting irresponsibly based on flawed beliefs about the severity of the disease.

To McGeachin and others in the YouTube video, though, Little was something different. After he extended the first three-week closure, they demanded immediate reopening. McGeachin headlined a protest at the statehouse, where she presided over the state senate. At the rally were antivaccine activists, some of whom were later arrested for refusing to leave outdoor playgrounds. A week after the protest, McGeachin was invited to the illegal reopening of a brewery. The brewery's owner compared life under Little to living in Nazi Germany. McGeachin had "more stones than the governor," she told reporters. "Brad Little has acted like a Democrat through this whole thing, and the people know it."

McGeachin got to that point with a sense for political opportunities. To become first woman to serve as lieutenant governor, she bested the chair of the Idaho Republican Party. In 2016 McGeachin threw in with Trump early in the primary, eventually becoming the number 2 in his state campaign. She acted with the same boldness now, writing op-eds, attending other events, and declining the weekly phone calls staff had arranged for her and Little since they both took office. By October 2020 she had assembled a coalition of like-minded state legislators who opposed rule by local health authorities and then posted the public declaration to YouTube, attracting the online ridicule of anyone outside her core constituency. Asked about the public feud, Little said it did not make running the state harder, but "it doesn't make it easier" either. By then he had spent over twenty years in Idaho politics, and he responded with co-partisan diplomacy.

That ended the next May. Little would travel each spring to meet with other Republican governors. As he left the stage at the JW Marriott in Nashville, his phone rang. On the other end was the secretary of state, who informed him that he had received and validated an executive order issued by the governor's office. This was how Little learned that McGeachin, acting as governor, had repealed one of his executive orders and replaced it with a new one. It is odd news, for two reasons.

Article IV, Section 12 of the Idaho constitution says: "In the case of [. . .] absence from the state [. . .] the powers, duties, and emoluments of the office [. . .] shall devolve upon the lieutenant governor." No lieutenant governor before McGeachin had used this obscure provision. Besides the public demonstrations, McGeachin spent little time in the state capitol, keeping half-day office hours twice a week while the state senate was in session. That any lieutenant governor, let alone McGeachin, would begin issuing executive orders while the governor was out of town was surprising. But the fact that this order repealed Little's mask mandate was more confusing, because he never issued one.

Little had left mask orders to local health authorities, drawing criticism from hospital associations who demanded a statewide mask mandate. McGeachin went the other way, attempting to prevent any health district from imposing a mandate. Few, including Little, believed the governor had the power to order such a ban. Little flew back to Boise and rescinded the order within twenty-four hours. "I do not like political stunts over the rule of law," he said—knowing that exactly one week before, McGeachin had announced she was running for governor.

The public rebuke from Little did nothing to discourage McGeachin, who kept the headlines coming. A month later, with Little out of town once more, she issued a letter to the director of the Department of Health and Welfare requesting that it look into reports hospitals were requiring vaccinations for employees. In September her campaign claimed vaccinated persons were more likely to die from COVID-19. By then Little knew the challenge from the right McGeachin presented and so arranged to be among the set of governors who would send troops to the U.S.-Mexico border, a different kind of stunt intended to highlight the ineffectiveness of the Biden administration's immigration policies.

But, to do that, he had to leave Idaho again—this time going as far as Mission, Texas, a border town on the Rio Grande where Texas Governor Greg Abbott first mobilized his own National Guard. McGeachin issued an order banning vaccine mandates by businesses and schools and sent another letter, this time to a different state official. "My constitutional authority as Governor," the letter read, "affords me the power of activating the Idaho National Guard." It was a ploy to retake the spotlight on the immigration issue.

But the order was so ambiguous that its recipient, Major General Michael J. Garshak, rebuffed it, stating he was not aware of any circumstances that required mobilization. The letter came as no surprise to Little. Before McGeachin announced her letter to Garshak, Little issued a press release: "I am in Texas [. . .] I have not authorized the Lt. Governor to act on my behalf. I will be rescinding and reversing any actions taken by the Lt. Governor when I return."

He did not wait that long. By rescinding the order from afar, he seemed to be provoking a lawsuit to force the state supreme court to declare, once and for all, whether Article IV, Section 12 endowed the lieutenant governor with the authority she had used twice before. It is not an easy question to answer. Looking beyond the state, some high courts working under similar constitutions seemed to side with McGeachin, others with Little. But no lawsuit ever came. Instead, the state's attorney general drafted an opinion interpreting the provision in Little's favor.

Little went further. For staff in McGeachin's office, after that October, Little's schedule went dark. McGeachin could not act in his absence if she learned of his absence too late, and if he did what Americans now did regularly as a result of the pandemic: work remotely. Little, now less tolerant of McGeachin's actions, had whittled her capacity to act down to nothing.

That ended it. Under Little, state troopers would be sent to the U.S.-Mexico border. McGeachin got the "full and complete endorsement" of Donald Trump. She managed a headline from time to time in the lead-up to the Republican primary in May 2022—administering oaths to members of a militia group on the anniversary of the Oklahoma City bombing and demanding that Little order child protective services to return the abused child of the militant Ammon Bundy. But none of these things drew the national attention the dueling orders among political rivals had. McGeachin lost the primary by thirty percentage points, as Little's actions in office drew the vast majority of Trump's supporters. Even after the primary, Little kept his travel schedule hidden from McGeachin.

For the past two years, McGeachin had tipped her hand. As far back as the op-ed that first spring of the pandemic, she announced her ambition: "I am one heartbeat away from the governor's chair."

Chapters 1, 3, and 5–8 of this book include sections with historical narratives. These are not case studies. They are dramatic renderings of historical events. I present them without in-text references or footnotes to discourage people from thinking of them as the former. No facts are invented, and no arrangement of facts is intended to mislead or confuse what actually occurred. A separate bibliography for each vignette follows for anyone who would find it useful.

The presidency has always been a subject dominated by stories and storytellers. This is still true, even though the last few decades of scholarship includes rigorous theorizing, data collection, and analysis. I agree with others that this is good. But I also wonder if it has missed an opportunity. Scholars avoided stories altogether, when they could have been telling *better* ones: stories that were more accurate, more focused on the mechanics of governing, that illustrated the explanations proposed and used by social scientists. Few people learn through tables and figures, and even those people have to be educated and professionalized into it. So this book tries to do both. The reader can decide whether they compromise or enrich each other.

ACKNOWLEDGMENTS

Walker Percy said that to start a book, you have to be angry about something. If you have read this far, you know a lot bothers me about the way we talk about the presidency. The book is me explaining why. It took a long time. The first words were written in January 2021, these last words in December 2023. I found out writing a book is a lot easier than trying to write a good one. Over that period, and before, a lot of people have given me their time and support, even when they had no particular reason to. I tried to honor that by listening to them and doing my best to write something worth reading.

I am thankful every day for the unpredictable string of events that gave me a job and my family a home in Ann Arbor. Otherwise I'd be working at a Chuy's somewhere, and this book would have never been written. So thanks are due first to the political science department at Washington University in St. Louis, especially Justin Fox and Andrew Reeves; and then to the Center for the Study of Democratic Politics at Princeton, especially Brandice Canes-Wrone and Nolan McCarty; and finally to the political science department at the University of Michigan, especially Rick Hall and Chuck Shipan.

Whatever weaknesses remain in the book are my responsibility alone. However, I owe thanks to a long list of people who helped the project along, in ways large and small. For helping me use their materials, I thank the archivists at the George H. W. Bush, William J. Clinton, and George W. Bush presidential libraries. For answering questions from someone they'd never heard of, I thank Mark Breederland, Bryan Caplan, Juliet Eilperin, John Hartig, Jeh Johnson, Erik Longnecker, Denis McDonough, and Robert Wolcott. Thanks are also due to people outside academia who gave comments that helped keep the book grounded: Matt Chervenak, Sara Freelove, Gregory Korte, and Curtis Phelps. For helping me with research, I thank Adam Bressler, Cory Dubin, Skyler Edinburg, Sarah Fernandes, Justin Fortney, Sebastian Leder Macek, Ben McGraw, Sunayna Patel, Andres Ramos, Zeina Reda, Emily Schmitt, Pulak Taneja, and Madelyn Yake. For reminding me how much fun work can be, I thank Ayse Eldes.

For feedback on different sections of the project, I thank audiences at American University, the University of California, Berkeley, the University of Michigan Law School, New York University, and the Sunwater Institute, along with Andy Ballard, Matt Beckmann, Andrew Clarke, Nathan Gibson, Doug Kriner, Tim LaPira, David Miller, Brendan Nyhan, Rachel Potter, Brandon Rottinghaus, Eric Schickler, and Craig Volden. For giving me a sunny place to jump-start writing post-pandemic, I thank Jeff Jenkins. For encouraging me to stay subversive, I thank Terry Moe. Many colleagues at Michigan rooted for me, gave advice, asked critical questions, and protected me from university nonsense. Jenna Bednar, Deborah Beim, Ted Brader, Charlotte Cavaille, Rob Franzese, Rick Hall, John Jackson, Don Kinder, Ken Kollman, Barb Koremenos, Walter Mebane, Nina Mendelson, Rob Mickey, Iain Osgood, Scotte Page, Yuki Shiraito, George Tsebelis, Nick Valentino, and Mariah Zeisberg—thank you for making being at Michigan so rewarding.

For reading the whole thing and sitting for hours discussing it in Philadelphia, I thank Tony Bertelli and Andrew Rudalevige. For constructive comments that brought me to the last draft, I thank Jon Rogowski and an anonymous reviewer. For meeting in Ann Arbor, suffering through the long first draft, and then helping me figure out what to do with it, I thank Christian Fong, Sean Gailmard, Will Howell, George Krause, Dave Lewis, and Chuck Shipan. For getting the book in print and trying to get humans to actually read it, I thank Sara Doskow and Frances Lee.

The years spent on the book were infinitely richer because of family and friends. For their kindness and friendship, I thank Josie and Denny Barnard, Jessica and Jowei Chen, Bob Dascola, Chris Fariss, Jessica and Christian Fong, Nora and Harrison Frye, Daniel Houston, Brittany Limes, Toni Nogalski, Mike Poznansky, Andrew and Hannah Roberts, and Melissa Ross and Ben Goehring. For nudging me to find rest, I thank Jeff and Mary Freelove. For always being on my team, I thank my brothers, Cameron and Connor. For freely giving the love and support I try always to copy, I thank my parents, Keith and Cathleen. For the gift of seeing the world like new, I thank my sons, Hudson and Everett.

Most of all, I thank my wife, Claire, to whom this book is dedicated. Her strength and love are daily blessings in my life, but I don't usually do public displays. So here it is, my dear—your tree carving, a message anyone can read, scanned and indexed forever by book-crawling algorithms, shelved away in the basement of some university library, to be rediscovered by strangers long after we both are gone: I love you.

NOTES

Chapter 1

1. The presidential oath of office demands presidents swear to "preserve, protect, and defend the Constitution" to the best of their ability. Abraham Lincoln interpreted this as enabling "all indispensable means" of policymaking. Abraham Lincoln, Letter to Albert G. Hodges, at Gerhard Peters and John T. Woolley, *The American Presidency Project*, https://www.presidency.ucsb.edu/node/305029.

2. It eventually was in 2020, after several acts of Congress. A report on the Consolidated Appropriations Act of 2018 (P.L. 115–41) had to clarify that funds could be used for gun violence research, then Congress had to appropriate funds for that purpose (P.L. 116–94). This is a theme: most concrete and effectual policy change requires changes to statutes.

3. At Carl Sandberg College in 1995, Clinton said: "Being a president's just like running a cemetery, you've got a lot of people under you and nobody's listening." He claimed he was quoting a college president, so the quip is not as cynical as it sounds out of context. William J. Clinton, "Remarks at Carl Sandburg Community College in Galesburg, Illinois," at Gerhard Peters and John T. Woolley, *The American Presidency Project*, https://www.presidency.ucsb.edu/node/221289.

4. "Remarks of Senator John F. Kennedy at National Conference for Constitutional Rights and American Freedom," New York, October 12, 1960, https://www.jfklibrary.org/archives/other-resources/john-f-kennedy-speeches/constitutional-rights-conference-nyc-19601012.

5. See Juliet Eilperin and Darla Cameron, "How Trump Is Rolling Back Obama's Legacy," *Washington Post*, updated January 20, 2018, https://www.washingtonpost.com/graphics/politics/trump-rolling-back-obama-rules/.

6. See, e.g., Joseph Zeballos-Roig, "Here's How a Biden Administration Could Still Make Significant Progress on Liberal Goals with a Republican-Held Senate," *Business Insider*, November 8, 2020.

7. The signing statements he writes about are more like professed wishes than orders to administrators.

8. See Hansi Lo Wang, "John Lennon's Deportation Fight Paved Way for Obama's Deferred Action Policy," NPR, August 23, 2016, https://www.npr.org/2016/08/23/490957803/john-lennons-deportation-fight-paved-way-to-obamas-deferred-action-policy.

9. Harry S. Truman, "Executive Order 9981: Desegregation of the Armed Forces," July 26, 1948; General Records of the United States Government, Record Group 11, National Archives.

10. Dwight D. Eisenhower, "Executive Order 10730: Desegregation of Central High School," September 23, 1957 (Little Rock Crisis); General Records of the United States Government, Record Group 11, National Archives.

11. Jeh Johnson, interview with the author, January 17, 2023.

12. Joseph R. Biden, "Establishment of the Presidential Commission on the Supreme Court," Executive Order 14023, April 9, 2021, *Federal Register* 86, no. 70: 19569.

13. Douglas MacMillan, Heather Kelly, Elizabeth Dwoskin and Josh Dawsey, "Trump Announced Google Was Building a Virus Screening Tool. Then Someone Had to Build It," *Washington Post*, March 16, 2020.

14. Sacha Pfeiffer and Tim Mak, "Trump's Plan For Drive-Up COVID-19 Tests at Stores Yields Few Results," NPR News, June 1, 2020.

15. Barack Obama, "Tracing of Firearms in Connection with Criminal Investigations: Memorandum for the Heads of Executive Departments and Agencies," January 16, 2013, *Federal Register* 78, no. 14: 4301–2.

16. James Buchanan died sick, depressed, and alone while dedicating his short post-presidency to defending his decision to do nothing in response to the 1860–61 secession crisis.

17. See https://doi.org/10.7910/DVN/JMBGLE.

18. For example, see Edwards (1989); Cohen (1999); Moe (1985); Cameron (2000); Howell (2003); Lewis (2004); Canes-Wrone (2006).

19. Moe announced this within a collection of review essays, but others disagreed, mostly on the basis that his characterization of earlier work was unfair; see *Presidential Studies Quarterly* 39(4).

Chapter 2

1. For a review of "production-related" diseases in turkeys, see Greger (2011). This cold open is borrowed from the ending of a *Politico* piece by Matthew Choi (2020).

2. According to ProQuest, President Trump's "covfefe" tweet from May of 2017 generated over 1,800 news articles. His emergency declaration for Puerto Rico after Hurricane Maria drew one-sixth of covfefe's coverage.

3. Since the video is eighteen seconds long, this means roughly 1,300 years of human life have been used up watching this content.

4. He did so in an interview with *60 Minutes* that aired on September 21, 2022.

5. "Gov. Perry Responds to President Obama's Executive Actions," KTLV News, January 16, 2013, https://www.kltv.com/story/20603601/gov-perry-responds-to/.

6. In a press release, Rep. Markwayne Mullin (R-OK) wrote that "President Obama's executive orders on gun control are in violation of the Constitution and Bill of Rights. [. . .] In President Obama's first term he has issued 144 total executive orders. Today's total signifies a nearly 15% increase in the total number of executive orders for his term on this one issue."

7. Rubio made this argument in a video posted to Twitter; https://twitter.com/marcorubio/status/1352600933365112832.

8. "Proclamation 7392—Boundary Enlargement and Modifications of the Buck Island Reef National Monument," *Compilation of Presidential Documents*, January 17, 2001.

Chapter 3

1. Barack Obama, "Remarks by the President on the Economy—Austin, TX," White House, Office of the Press Secretary, July 10, 2014, https://obamawhitehouse.archives.gov/the-press-office/2014/07/10/remarks-president-economy-austin-tx.

2. Josh Earnest, "Press Briefing by the Press Secretary Josh Earnest," White House, Office of the Press Secretary, December 18, 2014. https://obamawhitehouse.archives.gov/the-press-office/2014/12/18/press-briefing-press-secretary-josh-earnest-121814.

3. This does not mean one type of directive, known as a "proclamation," does not count because it does something similar. The most famous of these, the Emancipation Proclamation, did simply declare that all enslaved persons in territory not occupied by the Union would be free. But in it the president cited his authority as commander in chief, detailed the policy and where it would be applicable, and described an effective date. He also followed up the proclamation with relevant orders to the military. So this famous case does count.

4. Donald J. Trump, "Military Service by Transgender Individuals: Memorandum for the Secretary of Defense [and] the Secretary of Homeland Security," August 25, 2017, *Federal Register* 82, no. 167: 41319–20.

5. Donald J. Trump, "Military Service by Transgender Individuals: Memorandum for the Secretary of Defense [and] the Secretary of Homeland Security," March 23, 2018, *Federal Register* 83, no. 60: 13367–68.

6. The final order was "Directive-Type Memorandum (DTM)-19-004—Military Service by Transgender Persons and Persons with Gender Dysphoria," Office of the Deputy Secretary for Defense, March 12, 2019. For one briefing, see "Policy on the Military Service of Transgender Soldiers Training Module Tier 3: Units and Soldiers" (September 16, 2016), a U.S. Army presentation prepared during the Obama-era changes.

7. This is the second version of a dataset I developed in Lowande (2021b).

8. This total is consolidated. Some policy areas, such as "Defense," were initially broken down into more specific categories, such as "Defense Space" and "Armed Forces Retention." After the search procedure, these were collapsed.

9. See their active web page, https://justfacts.votesmart.org/about/political-courage-test/.

10. Some orders, of course, fell into more than one category. I am counting each only once in this total.

11. Brian Dirck, "Abraham Lincoln, Woodrow Wilson, and Dying for One's Country," in *Wars Civil and Great: The American Experience in the Civil War and World War I*, ed. David J. Silbey and Kanisorn Wongsrichanalai, 45–70 (Lawrence: University Press of Kansas, 2023), https://doi.org/10.2307/jj.10405506.7.

12. I first read one hundred orders and identified their preambles. I then wrote an algorithm that identified common phrases indicating the "start" and "stop" of rhetorical preambles. Some of these are more straightforward to identify than others. For example, some orders have the first section labeled "preamble" or "background" or "objective." Others have rhetorical language embedded throughout substantive directives. For this reason, the code was typically only able to identify three out of four of uses of symbolic language. I know because I went through the remaining four hundred orders it missed and fixed the errors by hand.

13. Theodore Roosevelt, Executive Order, November 15, 1901, at Gerhard Peters and John T. Woolley, *The American Presidency Project*, https://www.presidency.ucsb.edu/node/206926.

Chapter 4

1. Gregory Korte, "White House Posts Wrong Versions of Trump's Orders on Its Website," *USA Today*, February 14, 2017, https://www.usatoday.com/story/news/politics/2017/02/14/white-house-posts-wrong-versions-trumps-orders-its-website/97845888/.

2. Charles S. Clark, "Trump Continues to Set Records for Agency Vacancies," *Government Executive*, January 16, 2018, https://www.govexec.com/oversight/2018/01/trump-continues-set-records-agency-vacancies/145218/.

3. There are exceptions. See, e.g., Howell and Magazinnik (2017 and 2020) on President Obama's Race to the Top initiative, or my own work on the 1033 program (Lowande 2021a).

4. William J. Clinton, "Memorandum on the Mexico City Policy," Administration of William J. Clinton, January 22, 1993, https://www.govinfo.gov/content/pkg/WCPD-1993-01-25/pdf/WCPD-1993-01-25-Pg88-2.pdf.

5. See "Proclamation on the Birthday of Founding Father Caesar Rodney," October 6, 2020, https://trumpwhitehouse.archives.gov/presidential-actions/proclamation-birthday-founding-father-caesar-rodney/.

6. Donald J. Trump, "Establishing the President's Advisory 1776 Commission," Executive Order 13958, November 2, 2020, *Federal Register* 85, no. 215: 70951–54.

7. "The 1776 Report," President's Advisory 1776 Commission, January 2021, 1–45, https://trumpwhitehouse.archives.gov/wp-content/uploads/2021/01/The-Presidents-Advisory-1776-Commission-Final-Report.pdf.

8. William Clinton, "Executive Order on Federal Actions to Address Environmental Justice in Minority Populations and Low-Income Populations," February 11, 1994. https://www.ncbi.nlm.nih.gov/books/NBK100855/.

9. William J. Clinton, "Increasing Seat Belt Use in the United States," Executive Order 13043, April 6, 1997, *Federal Register* 62, no. 75: 19217–18.

10. George W. Bush, "Establishing the Global War on Terrorism Medals," Executive Order 13289, March 12, 2003, *Federal Register* 68, no. 50: 12567–68.

11. Richard Feynman, "Cargo Cult Science," 1974, http://calteches.library.caltech.edu/51/2/CargoCult.pdf.

12. All of these orders, naturally, were date-blinded. A small proportion of orders were coded based on title because their title is all we have. They remain classified. There were thirteen of these, and excluding them makes no difference in the analyses that follow. None were coded as having minimal direct effects.

13. Recording this information is itself another check, since I can determine whether the findings and inferences later are supported, regardless of date-blinding. Even this is not perfect, of course, since the cases are not blinded at random.

14. The analysis in chap. 3 measured these preambles using the word count or the proportion of the order they constituted. Because the full text of these orders is informative only for the directives, and the full sample includes nondirective orders, I chose to use this dichotomous coding for the main analyses. Naturally, the measures are highly correlated. For every increase of ten percentage points in the proportion of an order that is rhetorical, there is an increase of ten percentage points in the likelihood that it has minimal direct effects ($p < 0.0001$).

15. These were both implemented using the MCMCirtKd() command of MCMCpack. In general, the six-item model required more iterations to converge owing to more problematic items—specifically, whether the order was deemed primarily a request for information or peremptory. These more subjective indicators exhibited more autocorrelation between chains.

16. This point estimate is the marginal effect of a logistic regression with standard errors clustered by policy topic.

17. Barack Obama, "Presidential Memorandum—Climate Change and National Security," White House, Office of the Press Secretary, September 21, 2016, https://obamawhitehouse.archives.gov/the-press-office/2016/09/21/presidential-memorandum-climate-change-and-national-security.

18. This assumes these estimates of a latent concept (discretion) are actually data measured without error. A better approach would be to propagate the uncertainty in these measures into any subsequent analysis. The results of this slightly more complicated approach yield the same basic findings.

19. This point estimate is the marginal effect estimated with a bivariate logistic regression with standard errors clustered by policy topic.

20. For the latter changes, see P.L.111–52, Title II.

21. See 20 U.S.C. 7241 and 20 U.S.C. 7861 of P.L. 107–10. January 8, 2002.

22. William J. Clinton, "Memorandum on Helping Schools End Social Promotions," February 23, 1998, at Gerhard Peters and John T. Woolley, *The American Presidency Project*, https://www.presidency.ucsb.edu/node/225454.

23. U.S. Department of Education, *Taking Responsibility for Ending Social Promotion: A Guide for Educators and State and Local Leaders* (Washington, DC: May 1999).

24. These estimates come from an analysis at the Congress level ($p = 0.19$).

25. This comes from a logistic regression with divided government predicting minimal direct effects, standard errors clustered at the Congress level.

26. This story is the same if you move from examining divided government to a more nuanced measure of opposition. Examining the relationship monthly, I take the proportion of total seats held by the opposition party (average across the House and

Senate). The virtue of this measure is that it takes into account the fact that within Congress, there is some modest variation owing to vacancies and party switching. But this is not enough. The 95-percent confidence interval for the effect of a typical change in opposition strength is between +0.08 and -0.14 performative executive actions. The direction of effect is unclear, but it is also exceedingly small.

27. According to King (2020), only three of the fourteen pundits surveyed by the *Washington Post* correctly predicted the swing.

28. Keith Schneider, "Clinton Relies on Voluntary Guidelines to Protect Environment in Arkansas," *New York Times*, April 4, 1992, https://www.nytimes.com/1992/04/04/us/1992-campaign-candidate-s-record-clinton-relies-voluntary-guidelines-protect.html.

29. "Bush vs. Clinton: What Is an Environmental President?" *Los Angeles Times*, September 27, 1992, https://www.latimes.com/archives/la-xpm-1992-09-27-op-488-story.html.

30. "Gone Fishing," *New Yorker*, August 10, 1992.

31. Stories ran in the *Orange County Register*, the *San Francisco Chronicle*, the *St. Louis Post-Dispatch*, the *Oregonian*, the *Seattle Post*, the *Tulsa World*, and the *Boston Globe*, to name a few.

32. "Proclamation 6457: Giant Sequoia in National Forests," July 14, 1992, 106 Stat. 5381.

33. Julie E. McDonald, "The Sequoia Forest Plan Settlement Agreement as It Affects *Sequoiadendron giganteum*: A Giant Step in the Right Direction," USDA Forest Service Gen. Tech. Rep.PSW-151 (1994.).

34. Dana Wilkie, "Bush Extends Safety for Sequoias, Defends Environmental Record," *San Diego Union-Tribune*, July 15, 1992.

35. The president arrived by helicopter the day of the event.

36. For example, there is evidence that the first President Bush attempted to intervene in meat-labeling regulations, but it is only through later accounts by FDA officials that we learned of the attempt, and therefore we do not know the exact date of the attempted intervention.

37. George W. Bush, "Facilitation of Hunting Heritage and Wildlife Conservation," Executive Order 13443, August 16, 2007, *Federal Register* 72, no. 160: 46537–38.

38. "Facilitation of Hunting Heritage and Wildlife Conservation: The Recreational Hunting and Wildlife Conservation Plan as Directed by Executive Order 13443," December 14, 2008, https://www.fs.usda.gov/biology/resources/pubs/wildlife/rec_hunting_action_plan_2008.pdf.

39. I find unexpected patterns somewhat reassuring. Suppose figure 4.2 was flat until reelection, shot up, then dipped its top after election day. Patterns that are too perfect should arouse skepticism.

40. This is a logistic regression with minimal direct effects as the outcome, and dummy variables for lame-duck and presidential-election year, along with the discretion measure discussed in section 6.2.

41. These figures are deflated if you add many intercept shifts for things that might plausibly impact the outcome, as many do. If you add dummy variables for each president and policy topic, the effects are halved. I do not, because I am not interested

in within-president, within-policy-area comparisons. I do not even know what that means.

42. Barack Obama, "Job-Driven Training for Workers," January 20, 2014, https:// obamawhitehouse.archives.gov/sites/default/files/docs/skills_report.pdf.

43. "Obama Signs New Job-Training Law," *New York Times*, July 23, 2014, https://www .nytimes.com/2014/07/23/us/obama-signs-new-job-training-law.html.

44. Donald J. Trump, "Memorandum on Inadmissibility of Persons Affiliated with Antifa Based on Organized Criminal Activity," January 5, 2021, https://trumpwhitehouse .archives.gov/presidential-actions/memorandum-inadmissibility-persons -affiliated-antifa-based-organized-criminal-activity/.

45. Eric Tucker and Ben Fox, "FBI Director Says Antifa Is an Ideology, Not an Organiza- tion," AP News, September 17, 2020, https://apnews.com/article/donald-trump-ap -top-news-elections-james-comey-politics-bdd3b6078e9efadcfcd0be4b65f2362e.

46. William J. Clinton, "Memorandum on Reducing Teenage Driving under the Influence of Illicit Drugs," October 19, 1996, at Gerhard Peters and John T. Woolley, *The Ameri- can Presidency Project*, https://www.presidency.ucsb.edu/documents/memorandum -reducing-teenage-driving-under-the-influence-illicit-drugs. William J. Clinton, "Memorandum on the Manual on School Uniforms," February 24, 1996, at Gerhard Peters and John T. Woolley, *The American Presidency Project*, https://www.presidency .ucsb.edu/node/222116.

47. George W. Bush, "Executive Order 13352—Facilitation of Cooperative Conserva- tion," August 26, 2004, at Gerhard Peters and John T. Woolley, *The American Pres- idency Project*, https://www.presidency.ucsb.edu/node/217423. From a public letter written by an attendee: "The entire event reminded me of a huge pep rally—all who attended left feeling energized and in anticipation of the next steps. It has now been 13 years since the conference, and I, as well as the other 2,000-plus who attended, are still waiting for the next steps" (Messmer 2018).

48. George W. Bush, "Memorandum on Potential Pearl Harbor National Monument," May 28, 2008, at Gerhard Peters and John T. Woolley, *The American Presidency Proj- ect*, https://www.presidency.ucsb.edu/node/277854.

49. Barack Obama, "United States Policy on Pre- and Post-Strike Measures to Address Civilian Casualties in U.S. Operations Involving the Use of Force," Executive Order 13732, July 1, 2016, *Federal Register* 81, no. 130: 44485–87. Only two such reports were ever released.

50. Donald J. Trump, "Memorandum on Reviewing Funding to State and Local Govern- ment Recipients That Are Permitting Anarchy, Violence, and Destruction in Ameri- can Cities," September 2, 2020, https://trumpwhitehouse.archives.gov/presidential -actions/memorandum-reviewing-funding-state-local-government-recipients -permitting-anarchy-violence-destruction-american-cities/.

Chapter 5

1. I like Lowi (1985), Tulis (1987), Bailey (2019), and, best of all, Dearborn (2021), who argues that these expectations were fostered by Congress.

2. The evidence suggests it is—though it might be getting less right over time. If it interests you, see the review of this vast literature by Donovan, Kellstedt, Key, and Lebo (2019).

3. See Lewis (2008, 141–71), who says organizational and personnel decisions negatively impacted the federal response, while demonstrating that mistakes at many levels of governance contributed to the destruction and loss of life.

4. This research was conducted as part of Lowande and Shipan (2022), to which you can refer for more details. I am responsible for any errors or leaps of interpretation contained in this book.

5. As it turns out, the specific aggregation procedure is not all that important. The task is straightforward enough that you could simply sum the number of times any given topic was selected and rank-order them; the result does not differ much from a more complicated latent variable model.

6. The accusations of the Liberty Matters PAC seem dated today. Most United Nations helicopters are white. The "black helicopter" is a symbol of conspiracy theories popular within the American militia movement in the late 1990s and early 2000s.

7. See Gallup's *Congress and the Public* page, which is regularly updated: https://news .gallup.com/poll/1600/congress-public.aspx.

8. The research in the remaining sections was conducted as part of my study with Benjamin Goehring (Goehring and Lowande, forthcoming). My coauthor is not responsible for the views I present in this chapter.

9. Each was recorded on a seven-point Likert scale, collapsed to a dichotomous "approve or disapprove" scale. These figures are simulated estimates that take into account respondent characteristics and policy areas.

10. Polls at the time indicated many were worried about water quality in rivers. One such poll indicated that 71 percent of the public were the highest level of "concerned" about clean rivers, lakes, and waterways. Other polls show large majorities with similar worries. See https://www.cnn.com/2000/NATURE/04/10/enviro.poll.enn/ index.html.

11. This is not the kind of catastrophic governing crisis people like Kamarck have in mind when they write about failure. This difference in scale should be kept in mind.

Chapter 6

1. Washington "[d]efied any man on earth to produce one single act of his since he had been in the government which was not done on the purest motives. [. . .] That by god he had rather be in his grave than in his present situation." Found in "Notes of Cabinet Meeting on Edmond Charles Genet, 2 August 1793," Founders Online, National Archives, https://founders.archives.gov/documents/Jefferson/01-26-02-0545. Original source: *The Papers of Thomas Jefferson*, vol. 26, *11 May–31 August 1793*, ed. John Catanzariti (Princeton, NJ: Princeton University Press, 1995), 601–3.

2. This is what Holzer (2020) does. He writes the president "hurled the offending cartoon on the floor" and sometimes adds in public speaking appearances that Washington "jump[ed] up and down" on the newspaper. Neither detail is recorded in

Jefferson's notes, which are the only record of the incident. See "The Presidents vs. the Press with Harold Holzer," Vermont Humanities Conference, fall 2020, https://www.youtube.com/watch?v=3DlWNj5JRRQ.

3. December 14, 1972: *The Nixon Tapes: 1971–72*, ed. and annot. Douglas Brinkley and Luke A. Nichter (Boston: Houghton Mifflin, 2014). See also https://nixontapes.org/chron52.html.

4. He first used the phrase in an October 29, 2018 post on Twitter.

5. That happened in this case. The White House denied the story that Kuo had gone to the political affairs office in order to use the initiative for the 2002 congressional races. I believe a man with terminal cancer is more reliable. Independent of Kuo, there is also a *Washington Post* article from October 2002 that suggested the White House was using the program for that purpose.

6. The research in this section is partly summarized from our working paper with Yuki Shiraito (Goehring, Lowande, and Shiraito 2023). Additional details about the data can be found there.

7. I have nothing in particular against these states, but their papers of record are not part of *ProQuest*, the commercial database we used to aggregate news coverage.

8. We sampled purely for efficiency. It is costly to collect the news coverage.

9. Existing work would say this shows that the list of executive actions is more "significant" than standard lists. Yes and no. The measurement of policy "significance" conflates two things: the importance of a policy change to a readership (most often, those who read the *New York Times*), and whether the document itself prescribed a policy change. I have decoupled the two by removing anything that did not prescribe executive action.

10. The skew here raises some questions about past efforts to gauge the "significance" of executive action. By using one or two news raters, researchers artificially flattened the distribution of "significance." Of the top ten most-covered actions, only two are executive orders. Only four are a presidential directive of any kind, which is more evidence that looking beyond directives is the right way to track this kind of policymaking.

11. "Obama Orders U.S. to Factor Climate into Defense Planning," *Chicago Tribune*, September 22, 2016.

12. The next paragraph quotes from the directive itself, which is common. The first mention of opposition comes near the end, which includes a quote from Sen. Lindsey Graham (R-SC).

13. Elaine S. Povich, "Senate Backs Clinton on Gays," *Chicago Tribune*, February 5, 1993, https://www.chicagotribune.com/news/ct-xpm-1993-02-05-9303175856-story .html; William J. Eaton, "Congress Passes Family Leave Bill," *Los Angeles Times*, February 5, 1993, https://www.latimes.com/archives/la-xpm-1993-02-05-mn-995 -story.html.

14. These figures include variations. I did not stem words because of an unacceptable false-positive rate for matches post-stemming.

15. There are many ways to refer to the president or Congress. For the latter, I allowed matches to include any uses of the terms "president," "administration," "bush,"

"obama," "trump," or "clinton." I also performed collocation analysis to identify common bigrams that refer to the president. Before the analysis, I replaced these terms with a unique presidential token. Since any definition of "near" is arbitrary, I reanalyze the articles with near defined as between three and seven words.

16. These figures are slightly lower than the initial number collected because it was not always possible to get the full text of an article within ProQuest's news database.

17. Because the dependent variable takes positive values and is highly skewed, I estimated a tobit regression, as well as a least-squares regression with a log-transformed outcome. These models included number of words, fixed effects for publication and president, and whether it was an article on executive action. For the tobit regression, the estimate for executive action is 3.1 more attribution words; for the OLS, the estimate suggests executive action results in 16 percent more attribution words.

18. As with the definitions of "near," I recounted for all definitions of "lede" between sixty-five and seventy-one words. The results I report are, therefore, based on data that averages across all thirty-five combinations of "lede" and "near" definitions.

19. In one specification—a least-squares regression with log-transformed dependent variable—executive action is associated with 0.8 percent more gridlock associations ($p = 0.07$).

20. Specifically, I estimated linear models with executive-action fixed effects, controlling for publication date and number of presidential mentions.

21. Interestingly, there is a rise in gridlock words, in general, just not ones near mentions of the president.

Chapter 7

1. As it turns out, not all ended up in that physical location. There were still four career employees who remained working at the Department of Education.

2. Charles G. Dawes, *The First Year of the Budget of the United States* (New York: Harper & Brothers, 1923), 178.

3. As of July 31, 1974, according to the table dated October 23, 1975 in Box 31, folder "White House Staff" of the Ron Nessen Papers, Gerald R. Ford Presidential Library.

4. George H. W. Bush, "Executive Order 12677—Historically Black Colleges and Universities," April 28, 1989, at Gerhard Peters and John T. Woolley, *The American Presidency Project*, https://www.presidency.ucsb.edu/node/269104.

5. William J. Clinton, "Executive Order 12876: Historically Black Colleges and Universities," November 1, 1993, *Weekly Compilation of Presidential Documents*, 2234–37.

6. George W. Bush, "Executive Order 13256—President's Board of Advisors on Historically Black Colleges and Universities," February 12, 2002, at Gerhard Peters and John T. Woolley, *The American Presidency Project*, https://www.presidency.ucsb.edu/node/216950.

7. Donald J. Trump, "White House Initiative to Promote Excellence and Innovation at Historically Black Colleges and Universities," Executive Order 13779, February 28, 2017, *Federal Register* 82, no. 41: 12499–502.

8. See https://clintonwhitehouse3.archives.gov/women/.

9. This information was pulled from her LinkedIn page in 2022.

10. Richard Pearson, "Richard Beal, Special Aide to Reagan, Dies," *Washington Post*, November 4, 1984.

11. November 22, 1976.

12. See, for example, Steve Holland, "Obama Fashions a Government of Many Czars," Reuters, May 29, 2009, https://www.reuters.com/article/us-obama-czars-analysis/obama-fashions-a-government-of-many-czars-idUSTRE54S5U120090529.

13. See, for example, Lewis (2008), Lewis (2011), or Krause and O'Connell (2015).

14. Joseph R. Biden, "Tackling the Climate Crisis at Home and Abroad," Executive Order 14008, January 27, 2021, *Federal Register* 86, no. 19 (February 1, 2021): 7619–33.

15. This was Nick Conger, a former press secretary for the EPA and communications chief for Al Gore.

16. Zach Colman, "'Slow-Walked or Watered Down': Friendly Fire Strafes Biden's Climate Office," *Politico*, June 3, 2022, https://www.politico.com/news/2022/06/03/white-house-climate-office-action-00036886.

17. William J. Clinton, "Presidential Decision Directive 2: Organization of the National Security Council," January 20, 1993, https://clinton.presidentiallibraries.us/items/show/12736.

18. Barack Obama, "Presidential Policy Directive 1: Organization of the National Security Council System," February 13, 2009, https://irp.fas.org/offdocs/ppd/ppd-1.pdf.

19. The precise number of NSC staff is difficult to determine because it does not produce public accountings. See CRS Report R44828: "The National Security Council, Background and Issues for Congress," June 3, 2021.

20. Interview with Anthony Lake conducted by Chris Bury, *Frontline*, September 2000, https://www.pbs.org/wgbh/pages/frontline/shows/clinton/interviews/lake.html.

21. John F. Harris, "Berger's Caution Has Shaped Role of U.S. in War," *Washington Post*, May 16, 1999.

22. Richard Nixon, "Executive Order 11541—Prescribing the Duties of the Office of Management and Budget and the Domestic Council in the Executive Office of the President," July 1, 1970, at Gerhard Peters and John T. Woolley, *The American Presidency Project*, https://www.presidency.ucsb.edu/node/256675.

23. William J. Clinton, "Establishment of the Domestic Policy Council," Executive Order 12859, August 16, 1993, *Federal Register* 58, no. 159 (August 19, 1993): 44101–2.

24. Ibid.

25. See White House Transition Project, "Commissioned Officers and Similarly Titled Staff, White House Office, Joe Biden," 2021, https://www.whitehousetransitionproject.org/wp-content/uploads/2021/05/WHTP2021-100-White-House-Overall-2021.pdf.

Chapter 8

1. More appropriately, read some of them. Others thought the president would be a servant of Congress. They were disorganized and contradicted one another, which is why they lost.

2. See, for example, Canes-Wrone, Herron, and Shotts (2001) or Canes-Wrone (2006).

3. When exposed to high heat, starchy foods like grains and potatoes form acrylamide, a chemical that is carcinogenic in experimental studies with rodents. It's not conclusively known whether consuming it in food increases cancer risk, but the FDA currently recommends you toast bread to a "light brown color" to limit exposure. See https://myumi.ch/4rkXA.

4. This was known as the Program Assessment Rating Tool (PART) and was eventually applied to most programs in the federal budget (see Gilmour and Lewis 2006).

5. In contrast to some White House initiatives discussed earlier in this book, the "open government" policies of the Obama administration were mostly implemented by the end of the term (see Piotrowski 2017).

6. The best attempt so far at measuring compliance is Kennedy (2015).

7. In May of 2021 the governors of Arizona, South Dakota, Iowa, Arkansas, Ohio, Nebraska, Florida, and Texas sent either National Guard troops or state law enforcement to the U.S.-Mexico border. See Jack Herrera, "Why Are Republican Governors Sending National Guard to the Border?" *Politico*, July 10, 2021. https://www.politico.com/news/magazine/2021/07/10/republican-governors-national-guard-texas-mexico-border-499040.

8. In May of 2022 the governor of Michigan sued the state, asking the state supreme court to declare a 1931 abortion law unconstitutional.

9. In September of 2022 the governor of Florida put immigrants on flights to Martha's Vineyard, Massachusetts.

10. In September of 2023 the governor of New Mexico signed an executive order to ban guns in Albuquerque. The order was deemed unenforceable by police and was quickly revised.

BIBLIOGRAPHY

Achen, Christopher, and Larry M. Bartels. 2016. *Democracy for Realists: Why Elections Do Not Produce Responsive Government*. Princeton, NJ: Princeton University Press.

"Affirmative Action: Too Hot to Handle." 1996. In *CQ Almanac 1995*, 51st ed. Washington, DC: Congressional Quarterly, 6-24–6-26. http://library.cqpress.com/cqalmanac/cqal95 1100507.

Alexander, Jeffrey C. 2010. *The Performance of Politics: Obama's Victory and the Democratic Struggle for Power*. Oxford and New York: Oxford University Press.

Alexander, Jeffrey C. 2011. *Performance and Power*. Cambridge: Polity Press.

Arnold, Peri E. 1998. *Making the Managerial Presidency: Comprehensive Reorganization Planning, 1905–1996*. 2nd ed. Lawrence: University Press of Kansas.

Barr, Stephen. 2019. "Former Congressman Paul Broun Discusses Immigration, U.S. Constitution at First 2019 ACC GOP Meeting." *Red and Black [Athens, GA]*, 14 January.

Bailey, Jeremy D. 2019. *The Idea of Presidential Representation: An Intellectual and Political History*. Lawrence: University Press of Kansas.

Beckmann, Matthew N. 2010. *Pushing the Agenda: Presidential Leadership in U.S. Lawmaking, 1953–2004*. Cambridge and New York: Cambridge University Press.

Best, Richard A., Jr. 2011. "The National Security Council: An Organizational Assessment." *Congressional Research Service* 7-5700. https://sgp.fas.org/crs/natsec/RL30840.pdf.

Bolton, Alexander, and Sharece Thrower. 2016. "Legislative Capacity and Executive Unilateralism." *American Journal of Political Science* 60, no. 3: 649–63.

Bolton, Alexander, and Sharece Thrower. 2021. *Checks in the Balance: Legislative Capacity and the Dynamics of Executive Power*. Princeton, NJ: Princeton University Press.

Bonica, Adam. 2020. "Why Are There So Many Lawyers in Congress?" *Legislative Studies Quarterly* 45, no. 2: 253–89.

Bonica, Adam, and Maya Sen. 2021. *The Judicial Tug of War: How Lawyers, Politicians, and Political Incentives Shape the American Judiciary*. Cambridge and New York: Cambridge University Press.

Brooks, Nina, Eran Bendavid, and Grant Miller. 2019. "USA Aid Policy and Induced Abortion in Sub-Saharan Africa: An Analysis of the Mexico City Policy." *Lancet Global Health* 7, no. 8: e1046–53. https://www.thelancet.com/journals/langlo/article/PIIS2214-109X(19)30267-0/fulltext.

Burlingame, Michael. 2008. *Abraham Lincoln: A Life*. Vol. 2. Baltimore, MD: Johns Hopkins University Press.

Calabresi, Steven G. 1995. "Some Normative Arguments for the Unitary Executive." *Arkansas Law Review* 48, no. 23: 23–104.

Cameron, Charles M. 2000. *Veto Bargaining: Presidents and the Politics of Negative Power*. Cambridge and New York: Cambridge University Press.

Canes-Wrone, Brandice. 2003. "Bureaucratic Decisions and the Composition of the Lower Courts." *American Journal of Political Science* 47, no. 2: 205–14.

Canes-Wrone, Brandice. 2006. *Who Leads Whom? Presidents, Policy, and the Public*. Chicago: University of Chicago Press.

Canes-Wrone, Brandice, Michael C. Herron, and Kenneth W. Shotts. 2001. "Leadership and Pandering: A Theory of Executive Policymaking." *American Journal of Political Science* 45, no. 3: 532–50.

Caplan, Bryan. 2008. *The Myth of the Rational Voter: Why Democracies Choose Bad Policies*. New ed. Princeton, NJ: Princeton University Press.

Carey, John M., and Matthew Soberg Shugart. 1998. *Executive Decree Authority*. Cambridge and New York: Cambridge University Press.

Chiou, Fang-Yi, and Lawrence S. Rothenberg. 2014. "The Elusive Search for Presidential Power." *American Journal of Political Science* 58, no. 3: 653–68.

Chiou, Fang-Yi, and Lawrence S. Rothenberg. 2017. *The Enigma of Presidential Power: Parties, Policies and Strategic Uses of Unilateral Action*. Cambridge and New York: Cambridge University Press.

Choi, Matthew. 2020. "Trump Pardons Corn the Turkey as a Finishing White House Act." *Politico*, November 24. https://www.politico.com/news/2020/11/24/trump -pardons-turkey-thanksgiving-440370.

Christenson, Dino P., and Douglas L. Kriner. 2020. *The Myth of the Imperial Presidency: How Public Opinion Checks the Unilateral Executive*. Chicago: University of Chicago Press.

Clarke, Andrew J. 2020. "Congressional Capacity and the Abolition of Legislative Service Organizations." *Journal of Public Policy* 40, no. 2: 214–35.

Clarke, Andrew J., and Kenneth Lowande. 2016. "Informal Consequences of Budget Institutions in the US Congress." *Legislative Studies Quarterly* 41, no. 4: 965–96.

Clinton, William J. 1995. "Religious Expression in Public Schools." Presidential Memorandum. July 12.

Cohen, Jeffrey E. 1999. *Presidential Responsiveness and Public Policy-Making: The Publics and the Policies that Presidents Choose*. Ann Arbor: University of Michigan Press.

Cooper, Phillip J. 2002. *By Order of the President: The Use and Abuse of Executive Direct Action*. Lawrence: University Press of Kansas.

Crosson, Jesse, Alexander Furnas, Timothy LaPira, and Casey Burgat. 2021. "Partisan Competition and the Decline in Legislative Capacity among Congressional Offices." *Legislative Studies Quarterly* 46, no. 3: 745–89.

Dearborn, John A. 2021. *Power Shifts: Congress and Presidential Representation*. Chicago: University of Chicago Press.

Dickerson, John. 2021. *The Hardest Job in the World: The American Presidency*. New York: Random House.

Dickinson, Matthew J. 2005. "The Executive Office of the President: The Paradox of Politicization." In *The Executive Branch*, edited by Joel Aberbach and Mark A. Peterson. New York: New York University Press.

Ding, Iza. 2020. "Performative Governance." *World Politics* 72, no. 4: 525–56.

Ding, Iza. 2022. *The Performative State: Public Scrutiny and Environmental Governance in China*. Ithaca, NY: Cornell University Press.

Donovan, Kathleen, Paul M. Kellstedt, Ellen M. Key, and Matthew J. Lebo. 2019. "Motivated Reasoning, Public Opinion, and Presidential Approval." *Political Behavior* 42: 1201–21.

Druckman, James N., and Lawrence R. Jacobs. 2015. *Who Governs? Presidents, Public Opinion, and Manipulation*. Chicago: University of Chicago Press.

Edelman, Murray. 1964. *The Symbolic Uses of Politics*. Champaign: University of Illinois Press.

Edwards, George C. 1989. *At the Margins: Presidential Leadership of Congress*. New Haven, CT: Yale University Press.

Edwards, George C. 2003. *On Deaf Ears: The Limits of the Bully Pulpit*. New Haven, CT: Yale University Press.

Edwards, George C. 2009. *The Strategic President: Persuasion and Opportunity in Presidential Leadership*. Princeton, NJ: Princeton University Press.

Elegant, Naomi Xu. 2021. "TikTok Banned Trump before Trump Could Ban TikTok." *Fortune*, January 11. https://fortune.com/2021/01/11/tiktok-bans-trump-before -trump-bans-tiktok/.

Executive Office of the President. 2021. *Congressional Budget Submission: Fiscal Year 2022*. https://www.whitehouse.gov/wp-content/uploads/2021/06/EOP-FY2022 -Congressional-Budget-Submission.pdf.

Farhang, Sean. 2010. *The Litigation State: Public Regulation and Private Lawsuits in the U.S.* Princeton, NJ: Princeton University Press.

Fine, Jeffrey A., and Adam L. Warber. 2012. "Circumventing Adversity: Executive Orders and Divided Government." *Presidential Studies Quarterly* 42, no. 2: 256–74.

Fong, Christian, Kenneth Lowande, and Adam Rauh. Forthcoming. "Expertise Acquisition in Congress." *American Journal of Political Science*.

Foreman, Christopher H. 2011. *The Promise and Peril of Environmental Justice*. Washington, DC: Brookings Institution.

Frantzich, Stephen E. 2018. *Presidents and the Media: The Communicator in Chief*. New York: Routledge.

Gailmard, Sean, and John W. Patty. 2007. "Slackers and Zealots: Civil Service, Policy Discretion, and Bureaucratic Expertise." *American Journal of Political Science* 51, no. 4: 873–89.

Gailmard, Sean, and John W. Patty. 2013. *Learning while Governing: Expertise and Accountability in the Executive Branch*. Chicago: University of Chicago Press.

Gentzkow, Matthew, Jesse M. Shapiro, and Michael Sinkinson. 2011. "The Effect of Newspaper Entry and Exit on Electoral Politics." *American Economic Review* 101, no. 7: 2980–3018.

Gentzkow, Matthew, Jesse M. Shapiro, and Michael Sinkinson. 2014a. "Competition and Ideological Diversity: Historical Evidence from US Newspapers." *American Economic Review* 104, no. 10: 3073–3114.

Gentzkow, Matthew, Jesse M. Shapiro, and Michael Sinkinson. 2014b. "United States Newspaper Panel, 1869–2004." Inter-University Consortium for Political and Social Research [distributor]. https://doi.org/10.3886/ICPSR30261.v6.

Gilley, Bruce. 2008. "Legitimacy and Institutional Change: The Case of China." *Comparative Political Studies* 41, no. 3: 259–84.

Gilmour, John B., and David E. Lewis. 2006. "Does Performance Budgeting Work? An Examination of the Office of Management and Budget's PART Scores." *Public Administration Review* 66, no. 5: 742–52.

Goehring, Benjamin. 2023. "Improving Content Analysis: Tools for Working with Undergraduate Research Assistants." *PS: Political Science & Politics* 57, no. 1: 57–63. https://doi.org/10.1017/S1049096523000744.

Goehring, Benjamin, and Kenneth Lowande. Forthcoming. "Public Responses to Unilateral Policymaking." *Journal of Experimental Political Science.*

Goehring, Benjamin G., Kenneth Lowande, and Yuki Shiraito. 2023. "Policy Significance: Theories and Evidence." Paper prepared for presentation at the annual meeting of the American Political Science Association.

Government Accountability Office. 2006. "Faith-Based and Community Initiative: Improvements in Monitoring Grantees and Measuring Performance Could Enhance Accountability." GAO-06-616, June 19.

Greger, Michael. 2011. "Transgenesis in Animal Agriculture: Addressing Animal Health and Welfare Concerns." *Journal of Agricultural and Environmental Ethics* 24: 451–72.

Grimmer, Justin, Sean J. Westwood, and Solomon Messing. 2014. *The Impression of Influence: Legislator Communication, Representation, and Democratic Accountability.* Princeton, NJ: Princeton University Press.

Grumbach, Jacob. 2022. *Laboratories against Democracy: How National Parties Transformed State Politics.* Princeton, NJ: Princeton University Press.

Hansen, Eric R., and Sarah Treul. 2019. "Inexperience or Anti-Washington? Voter Preferences for Congressional Candidates." Working paper, March 29.

Hartog, Chris Den, and Nathan W. Monroe. 2019. *The Jeffords Switch: Changing Majority Status and Causal Processes in the U.S. Senate.* Ann Arbor: University of Michigan Press.

Heclo, Hugh. 1977. *A Government of Strangers.* Washington, DC: Brookings Institution.

Hess, Stephen. 1976. *Organizing the Presidency.* 1st ed. Washington, DC: Brookings Institution.

Hess, Stephen, and James P. Pfiffner. 2021. *Organizing the Presidency.* 4th ed. Washington, DC: Brookings Institution.

Holmes, Steven A. 1995. "Clinton Defines Religion's Role in U.S. Schools." *New York Times*, August 25.

Holzer, Harold. 2020. *The Presidents vs. the Press: The Endless Battle between the White House and the Media—From the Founding Fathers to Fake News.* New York: Dutton.

Howell, William G. 2003. *Power without Persuasion: The Politics of Direct Presidential Action.* Princeton, NJ: Princeton University Press.

Howell, William G. 2013. *Thinking about the Presidency: The Primacy of Power.* Princeton, NJ: Princeton University Press.

Howell, William G., and Asya Magazinnik. 2017. "Presidential Prescriptions for State Policy: Obama's Race to the Top Initiative." *Journal of Policy Analysis and Management* 36, no. 3: 502–31.

Howell, William G., and Asya Magazinnik. 2020. "Financial Incentives in Vertical Diffusion: The Variable Effects of Obama's Race to the Top Initiative on State Policy Making." *State Politics & Policy Quarterly* 20, no. 2: 185–212.

Howell, William G., and Terry M. Moe. 2016. *Relic: How Our Constitution Undermines Effective Government.* New York: Basic Books.

Howell, William G., and Terry M. Moe. 2020. *Presidents, Populism, and the Crisis of Democracy.* Chicago: University of Chicago Press.

Howell, William G., Ethan Porter, and Thomas J. Wood. 2020. "Rethinking Public Appeals: Experimental Evidence on Presidential Performances." *Journal of Political Institutions and Political Economy* 1, no. 1: 137–58.

Huber, Gregory A., Seth J. Hill, and Gabriel S. Lenz. 2012. "Sources of Bias in Retrospective Decision Making: Experimental Evidence on Voters' Limitations in Controlling Incumbents." *American Political Science Review* 106, no. 4: 720–41.

Judd, Gleason. 2017. "Showing Off: Promise and Peril in Unilateral Policymaking." *Quarterly Journal of Political Science* 12: 241–68.

Kagan, Elena. 2001. "Presidential Administration." *Harvard Law Review* 114, no. 8: 2245–385.

Kamarck, Elaine C. 2016. *Why Presidents Fail and How They Can Succeed Again.* Washington, DC: Brookings Institution.

Kavakli, Kerim Can, and Valentina Rotondi. 2022. "US Foreign Aid Restrictions and Maternal and Children's Health: Evidence from the 'Mexico City Policy.'" *Proceedings of the National Academy of Sciences* 119, no. 19: e2123177119, May 2. https://doi.org/10.1073/pnas.2123177119.

Kennedy, Joshua B. 2015. "'"Do This! Do That!" And Nothing Will Happen': Executive Orders and Bureaucratic Responsiveness." *American Politics Research* 43, no. 1: 59–82.

Kernell, Samuel. 2006. *Going Public: New Strategies of Presidential Leadership.* Washington, DC: CQ Press.

King, Gary. 1993. "The Methodology of Presidential Research." In *Researching the Presidency: Vital Questions, New Approaches*, edited by George C. Edwards, Bert A. Rockman, and John H. Kessel, 387–412. Pittsburgh: University of Pittsburgh Press.

King, James D. 2020. "Bill Clinton, Republican Strategy, and the 1994 Elections: How Midterms Become Referenda on the President." *American Review of Politics* 37, no. 1: 76–99.

Korte, Gregory. 2014. "Obama Issues 'Executive Orders by Another Name.'" *USA Today*, December 16. https://www.usatoday.com/story/news/politics/2014/12/16/obama-presidential-memoranda-executive-orders/20191805/.

Krause, George A., and Anne Joseph O'Connell. 2015. "Experiential Learning and Residential Management of the U.S. Federal Bureaucracy: Logic and Evidence from Agency Leadership Appointments." *American Journal of Political Science* 60, no. 4: 914–31. https://doi.org/10.1111/ajps.12232.

Krause, George A., David E. Lewis, and James W. Douglas. 2006. "Political Appointments, Civil Service Systems, and Bureaucratic Competence: Organizational Balancing and Executive Branch Revenue Forecasts in the American States." *American Journal of Political Science* 50, no. 3: 770–87.

Kraushaar, Josh. 2021. "Mainstream Republicans Already Surrendering to Trumpism." *National Journal* (February): 1–5.

LaPira, Timothy M., Lee Drutman, and Kevin R. Kosar. 2021. *Congress Overwhelmed: The Decline in Congressional Capacity and Prospects for Reform*. Chicago: University of Chicago Press.

Lee, Frances E. 2016. *Insecure Majorities: Congress and the Perpetual Campaign*. Chicago: University of Chicago Press.

Lerman, Amy E. 2019. *Good Enough for Government Work: The Public Reputation Crisis in America (and What We Can Do to Fix It)*. Chicago: University of Chicago Press.

Levitsky, Steven, and Daniel Ziblatt. 2018. *How Democracies Die*. New York: Broadway Books.

Lewis, David E. 2004. *Presidents and the Politics of Agency Design: Political Insulation in the United States Government Bureaucracy, 1946–1997*. Stanford, CA: Stanford University Press.

Lewis, David E. 2008. *The Politics of Presidential Appointments: Political Control and Bureaucratic Performance*. Princeton, NJ: Princeton University Press.

Lewis, David E. 2011. "Presidential Appointments and Personnel." *Annual Review of Political Science* 14: 47–66.

Lowande, Kenneth. 2014. "After the Orders: Presidential Memoranda and Unilateral Action." *Presidential Studies Quarterly* 4, no. 4: 724–41.

Lowande, Kenneth. 2018. "Delegation or Unilateral Action?" *Journal of Law, Economics, and Organization* 34, no. 1: 54–78.

Lowande, Kenneth. 2019. "Politicization and Responsiveness in Executive Agencies." *Journal of Politics* 81, no. 1: 33–48.

Lowande, Kenneth. 2021a. "Police Demilitarization and Violent Crime." *Nature Human Behaviour* 5: 205–11.

Lowande, Kenneth. 2021b. "Presidents and the Status Quo." *Quarterly Journal of Political Science* 16: 1–30.

Lowande, Kenneth, and Thomas R. Gray. 2017. "Public Perception of the Presidential Toolkit." *Presidential Studies Quarterly* 47, no. 3: 432–47.

Lowande, Kenneth, and Sidney M. Milkis. 2014. "'We Can't Wait': Barack Obama, Partisan Polarization and the Administrative Presidency." *Forum* 12, no. 1: 3–27.

Lowande, Kenneth, and Michael Poznansky. 2024. "Executive Action That Lasts." *Journal of Public Policy* 44, no. 2: 344–65.

Lowande, Kenneth, and Jon C. Rogowski. 2021. "Presidential Unilateral Power." *Annual Review of Political Science* 24: 21–43.

Lowande, Kenneth, and Charles R. Shipan. 2022. "Where Is Presidential Power? Action, Expectations, and Executive Discretion." *British Journal of Political Science* 52, no. 4: 1876–90.

Lowi, Theodore J. 1985. *The Personal President: Power Invested, Promise Unfulfilled.* Ithaca, NY: Cornell University Press.

Lowry, Dennis T., Tarn Ching, Josephine Nio, and Dennis W. Leitner. 2003. "Setting the Public Fear Agenda: A Longitudinal Analysis of Network TV Crime Reporting, Public Perceptions of Crime, and FBI Crime Statistics." *Journal of Communication* 53, no. 1: 61–73.

Mayer, Kenneth R. 1999. "Executive Orders and Presidential Power." *Journal of Politics* 61, no. 2: 445–66.

Mayer, Kenneth R. 2001. *With the Stroke of a Pen: Executive Orders and Presidential Power.* Princeton, NJ: Princeton University Press.

Mayer, Kenneth R. 2009. "The Presidential Power of Unilateral Action." In *The Oxford Handbook of the American Presidency*, edited by George C. Edwards and William G. Howell. Oxford and New York: Oxford University Press.

Mayhew, David R. 1974. *Congress: The Electoral Connection.* New Haven, CT: Yale University Press.

McCarty, Nolan M. 2020. "Team Policy Production." Working paper, Princeton University. http://dx.doi.org/10.2139/ssrn.3505655.

Messmer, Terry A. 2018. "Cooperative Conservation to Enhance Human-Wildlife Interactions." *Human-Wildlife Interactions* 12, no. 2 (Fall): 157.

Milkis, Sidney M. 1993. *The President and the Parties: The Transformation of the American Party System since the New Deal.* New York: Oxford University Press.

Moe, Terry M. 1985. "The Politicized Presidency." In *The New Direction in American Politics*, edited by J. E. Chubb and P. E. Peterson. Washington, DC: Brookings Institution Press.

Moe, Terry M., and William G. Howell. 1999. "The Presidential Power of Unilateral Action." *Journal of Law, Economics, and Organization* 15, no. 1: 132–79.

Moe, Terry M., and Scott A. Wilson. 1994. "Presidents and the Politics of Structure." *Law and Contemporary Problems* 57, no. 2: 1–44.

Nelson, Anna Kasten. 1985. "President Truman and the Evolution of the National Security Council." *Journal of American History* 72, no. 2: 360–78.

Neugebauer, Randy. 2014. "2014 Questionnaires from Republican Candidates for U.S. Representative District 19." *Lubbock Avalanche-Journal*, February 22.

Neustadt, Richard E. 1960. *Presidential Power and the Modern Presidents: The Politics of Leadership from Roosevelt to Reagan.* New York: John Wiley & Sons.

Office of Management and Budget. 2022. "OMB Contributors to the 2022 Budget." In *Budget of the U.S. Government: Fiscal Year 2022*, 63–66. Washington, DC: Government Publishing Office.

Park, Ju Yeon. 2021. "When Do Politicians Grandstand? Measuring Message Politics in Committee Hearings." *Journal of Politics* 83, no. 1. https://doi.org/10.1086/709147.

Parker, Ashley. 2014. "'Imperial Presidency' Becomes a Rallying Cry for Republicans." *New York Times*, March 31.

Pasachoff, Eloise. 2021. "The President's Budget Powers in the Trump Era." In *Executive Policymaking: The Role of the OMB in the Presidency*, edited by Meena Bose and Andrew Rudalevige, 69–100. Washington, DC: Brookings Institution.

Patterson, Bradley H., Jr. 1988. *The Ring of Power: The White House Staff and Its Expanding Role in Government*. New York: Basic Books.

Patterson, Bradley H., Jr. 2000. *The White House Staff: Inside the West Wing and Beyond*. Washington, DC: Brookings Institution.

Perdue, David. 2015. "Senator Perdue Calls on President Obama to Reverse Lawless Amnesty Actions." Press *Release*, May 26.

Pfiffner, James P. 2020. "OMB, the Presidency, and the Federal Budget." In *Executive Policymaking: The Role of the OMB in the Presidency*, edited by Meena Bose and Andrew Rudalevige, 11–40. Washington, DC: Brookings Institution.

Piotrowski, Suzanne J. 2017. "The 'Open Government Reform' Movement: The Case of the Open Government Partnership and U.S. Transparency Policies." *American Review of Public Administration* 47, no. 2: 155–71.

Pollard, James E. 1947. *The Presidents and the Press*. London: Macmillan.

Potter, Rachel A. 2023. "Privatizing Personnel: Bureaucratic Outsourcing and the Administrative Presidency." Working paper, University of Virginia.

Reeves, Andrew, and Jon C. Rogowski. 2021. *No Blank Check: Why the Public Dislikes Presidential Power and What It Means for Governing*. Cambridge and New York: Cambridge University Press.

Relyea, Harold C. 2008. *The Executive Office of the President: An Historical Overview*. Vol. 1. Congressional Research Service Reports, November 26.

Rothenberg, Lawrence S. 2018. *Policy Success in an Age of Gridlock: How the Toxic Substances Control Act Was Finally Reformed*. Cambridge and New York: Cambridge University Press.

Rudalevige, Andrew. 2012. "Executive Orders and Presidential Unilateralism." *Presidential Studies Quarterly* 1, no. 1: 138–60.

Rudalevige, Andrew. 2015. "Executive Branch Management and Presidential Unilateralism: Centralization and the Issuance of Executive Orders." *Congress & the Presidency* 42, no. 3: 342–65.

Rudalevige, Andrew. 2020. "Projects Worth the Price." In *Executive Policymaking: The Role of the OMB in the Presidency*, edited by Meena Bose and Andrew Rudalevige, 117–44. Washington, DC: Brookings Institution.

Rudalevige, Andrew. 2021. *By Executive Order: Bureaucratic Politics, Presidential Management, and the Limits of Unilateralism*. Princeton, NJ: Princeton University Press.

Safdar, Khadeeja, and Lauren Weber. 2020. "White House Order against Diversity Training Generates Confusion." *Wall Street Journal*, October 7.

Schlesinger, Arthur M., Jr. 2004. *The Imperial Presidency*. New York: Mariner Books.

Sinclair, Barbara. 2006. *Party Wars: Polarization and the Politics of National Policy Making*. Julian J. Rothbaum Distinguished Lecture Series 10. Norman: University of Oklahoma Press.

Suri, Jeremy. 2017. *The Impossible Presidency: The Rise and Fall of America's Highest Office*. New York: Basic Books.

Trump, Donald J. 2020. "Combating Race and Sex Stereotyping." Executive Order 13950, September 22. *Federal Register* 85, no. 188: 60683–89.

Tulis, Jeffrey. 1987. *The Rhetorical Presidency*. Princeton, NJ: Princeton University Press.

Vaughn, Justin S., and Jose D. Villalobos. 2015. *Czars in the White House: The Rise of Policy Czars as Presidential Management Tools*. Ann Arbor: University of Michigan Press.

Washington, Geovette E., and Thomas E. Hitter. 2020. "State of the Agency." In *Executive Policymaking: The Role of the OMB in the Presidency*, edited by Meena Bose and Andrew Rudalevige, 207–32. Washington, DC: Brookings Institution.

Waterman, Richard, Carol L. Silva, and Hank Jenkins-Smith. 2014. *The Presidential Expectations Gap: Public Attitudes Concerning the Presidency*. Ann Arbor: University of Michigan Press.

Waterstone, Michael E., and Michael Ashley Stein. 2006. "Emergency Preparedness and Disability." *Mental and Physical Disability Law Reporter* 30, no. 3: 338–39.

Zhao, Dingxin. 2009. "The Mandate of Heaven and Performance Legitimation in Historical and Contemporary China." *American Behavioral Scientist* 53, no. 3: 416–33.

Zhu, Yuchao. 2011. "'Performance Legitimacy' and China's Political Adaptation Strategy." *Journal of Chinese Political Science* 16, no. 2: 123–40.

VIGNETTE BIBLIOGRAPHIES

Section 1.1: Easy as Shouting

Kelly, John F. 2017. "Rescission of November 20, 2014 Memorandum Providing for Deferred Action for Parents of Americans and Lawful Permanent Residents ('DAPA')." Memorandum, June 15.

Kerr, Paul K., and Kenneth Katzmann. 2018. "Iran Nuclear Agreement and U.S. Exit." Congressional Research Service, July 20.

O'Brien, Matt. 2014. "Immigration Shout Heard 'Round the World." *San Jose Mercury News*, November 21.

Obama, Barack. 2013. "Remarks by President Obama on Immigration Reform—San Francisco, CA." U.S. Fed News Service, Washington, DC, November 28.

Parnes, Amie. 2014. "Obama Pledges to Take Executive Actions on Immigration Reform." *The Hill*, June 30.

Parsons, Christi. 2013. "Obama: I Won't Bypass House on Immigration." *South Florida Sun-Sentinel* [Fort Lauderdale], November 26, 2013.

Rohde, David. 2012. "The Twilight of the GOP Establishment: Who Will Save Republicans, Now?" *Atlantic*, November 7.

Schmitt, Terry. "President Obama Speaks on Immigration in San Francisco, California, United States—25 Nov 2013." UPI/Shutterstock [photos].

Zernike, Kate. 2008. "She Just Might Be President Someday." *New York Times*, May 18.

Section 1.4: The Library

Aaro, Adam. 2017. "Fox 45 Exclusive: Inside the ATF National Tracing Center." *Dayton 24/7 Now*, October 30.

Wilber, Del Quentin. 2016. "ATF Gun Records Are Stuck in the 70s." *Los Angeles Times*, August 7.

Baker, Peter, and Michael D. Shear. 2013. "Obama to 'Put Everything I've Got' into Gun Control." *New York Times*, January 17.

Bureau of Alcohol, Tobacco, Firearms and Explosives. "NICS Improvement Amendments Act of 2007." https://www.atf.gov/file/155981/download.

Bureau of Alcohol, Tobacco, Firearms and Explosives. 2017. "Report of Active Firearms Licenses—License Type by State Statistics." June 10.

Dahlheimer, Zak. "Behind-the-Scenes Look at the Bureau of Alcohol, Tobacco, Firearms and Explosives National Tracing Center." WKTR, October 12, 2021.

Eilperin, Juliet, and David Nakamura. "Emotional Obama Outlines Gun Initiative." *Washington Post*, January 6, 2016.

Foley, John. 2013. "Senate Deal on Background Checks Aside, Outdated Tracing System Hurts Gun Control." Christian Science Monitor, April 10.

Goode, Erica, and Sheryl Gay Stolberg. 2012. "Legal Curbs Said To Hamper A.T.F. In Gun Inquiries." *New York Times*, December 26.

Government Accountability Office. 2016. "Firearms Purchaser Data: ATF Did Not Always Comply with the Appropriations Act Restriction and Should Better Adhere to Its Policies." GAO-16-552, June 30.

Hasselle, Della. 2016. "Louisiana Rates Second-Highest In Gun Deaths, Report Says." *Louisiana Weekly*, January 11.

Johnson, Kevin. 2015. "Millions of Gun Records Languish in Storage." *Dayton Daily News*, October 28.

Kaffer, Nancy. 2013. "Obama's Gun Reforms Help but Aren't Bold Enough." *Detroit Free Press*, January 17.

Kozlowski, Rick. 2021. "Then and Now: Martinsburg to Have Lacrosse Team for the First Time since 1970s." *Journal News*, April 8.

Longnecker, Eric. 2022. Email exchanges with Kenneth Lowande, January 31–March 4.

Macyk, Mark. 2021. "Martinsburg Lacrosse 2.0: How the Game Is Growing in West Virginia." *USA Lacrosse Magazine*, June 14.

"N.R.A. Supports New Rules on 'Bump Stock' Devices." 2017. *New York Times*, October 5.

Obama, Barack. 2013. "Tracing of Firearms in Connection with Criminal Investigations: Memorandum for the Heads of Executive Departments and Agencies." January 16. *Federal Register* 78, no. 14: 4301–2.

Rogers, Phil, and Shelby Bremer. 2021. "How Crime Guns Are Traced in the US: One Page at a Time." NBC Chicago, September 16.

Steinhauer, Jennifer. 2013. "White House Makes Moves to Promote Gun Safety." *New York Times*, June 18.

Thrush, Glenn, Danny Hakim, and Mike McIntire. 2021. "How the A.T.F., Key to Biden's Gun Plan, Became an N.R.A. 'Whipping Boy.'" *New York Times*, May 2.

Trotter, J. K. 2013. "Here are Obama's 23 Executive Actions on Gun Violence." *Atlantic*, January 16.

West, Paul, Kathleen Hennessey, and Richard Simon. 2013. "Obama Acts to Curb Guns." *Orlando Sentinel*, January 17.

"White House Statement on Executive Steps on Guns." 2016. *Boston Globe*, January 4.

Section 3.1: Reduction in Force

Ali, Idrees, and Phil Stewart. 2017. "Trump Ban on Transgender Service Members Alarms Some Military Officers." Reuters, July 27.

Bade, Rachel, and Josh Dawsey. 2017. "Inside Trump's Snap Decision to Ban Transgender Troops." *Politico*, July 26.

Bernton, Hal, and David Gutman. 2018a. "Richland Native Jim Mattis Has 'No Anger' after Trump Forces Him Out Early, Brother Says." *Seattle Times*, December 24.

Bernton, Hal, and David Gutman. 2018b. "Washington State Native James Mattis Foreshadowed Resignation as Defense Secretary in Richland Speech." *Seattle Times*, December 20.

Davis, Julie H., and Helene Cooper. 2017. "Trump Says Transgender People Will Not Be Allowed in the Military." *New York Times*, July 26.

Gersen, Jeannie S. 2017. "Trump's Tweeted Transgender Ban Is Not a Law." *New Yorker*, July 27.

Department of Defense, 2021. "In-Service Transition for Transgender Service Members (DoDI 1300.28)," April 30.

Hartzler, Representative Vicky. N.d. [Biography.] https://hartzler.house.gov/about/biography.

Kheel, Rebecca. 2017. "Joint Chiefs: No Change in Transgender Policy until Trump Sends Pentagon Direction." *The Hill*, July 27.

Kube, Courtney. 2017. "Pentagon to Pay for Surgery for Transgender Soldier." *U.S. News*, November 14.

Mattis, James N. 2018. Letter to President Donald J. Trump from the Secretary of Defense, December 20.

Moreau, Julie. 2020. "Year after Trans Military Ban, Legal Battle Rages On." NBC News, April 11.

Murphy, Patricia. 2016. "Soldiers Don't Have to Call This Transgender Officer 'Sir' Any More." *World*, January 8.

Norquist, David L. 2019. "Military Service by Transgender Persons and Persons with Gender Dysphoria (DTM-19-004)." Office of the Deputy Secretary of Defense, March 12.

Oltuski, Romy. 2017. "Badass Women: Transgender U.S. Army Captain Jennifer Peace Opens Up about Defending Her Country and Her Rights." *InStyle*, October 9.

"Recent Social Media Posts." 2018. *Harvard Law Review* 131:934–43. http: https://harvardlawreview.org/wp-content/uploads/2018/01/934-943_Online-1.pdf.

Remnick, David. 2017. "The Cruelty and Cynicism of Trump's Transgender Ban." *New Yorker*, July 26.

Rummler, Orion. 2019. "Everything You Need to Know about the Transgender Military Ban." *Axios*, April 12.

Sanders, Sarah. 2017. Press briefing. White House, July 27.

Schaefer, Agnes G., Radha Iyengar, Srikanth Kadiyala, Jennifer Kavanagh, Charles C. Engel, Kayla M. Williams, and Amii M. Kress. 2016. *Assessing the Implications of Allowing Transgender Personnel to Serve Openly*. Santa Monica, CA: Rand Corporation.

Spivak, Russell. 2017. "Trump's Transgender Tweet Isn't in Force Yet, but It's Close." *Foreign Policy*, August 2.

Transgender Service in the Military Policy: Hearings before the House Armed Services Subcommittee on Military Personnel of the Committee on Armed Services, 116th Cong. 2019a. February 27.

Transgender Service in the Military Policy: Hearings before the House Armed Services Subcommittee on Military Personnel of the Committee on Armed Services, 116th Cong. 2019b. Testimony of Captain Jennifer Peace. February 27.

Trump, Donald J. 2017. "Military Service by Transgender Individuals: Memorandum for the Secretary of Defense [and] the Secretary of Homeland Security." August 25. *Federal Register* 82, no. 167: 41319–20.

Trump, Donald J. (@realDonaldTrump). 2017. "After consultation with my Generals and military experts, please be advised that the United States Government will not accept or allow . . ." (July 26, 8:55:58 AM EDT) ". . . Transgender Individuals to serve In any capacity In the U.S. Military. Our military must be focused on decisive and over-whelming . . ." (July 26, 9:04:39 AM EDT) ". . . victory and cannot be burdened with the tremendous medical costs and disruption that transgender In the military would entail. Thank you" (July 26, 9:08:21 AM EDT).

U.S. Army. 2016. "Policy on the Military Service of Transgender Soldiers Training Module—Tier 3: Units and Soldiers," September 16.

Welna, David, and Bill Chappell. 2019. "Supreme Court Revives Trump's Ban on Trans-gender Military Personnel, for Now." NPR, January 22.

Section 5.1: The Pageant

"American Heritage Rivers." 1998. In *CQ Almanac 1997*, 53rd ed. Washington, DC: Congressional Quarterly, 4-17–4-18. http://library.cqpress.com/cqalmanac/cqal97-0000181028.

"American Heritage Rivers Initiative." 1998. *Congressional Record* 144, no. 147 (October 15): E2182–E85.

American Heritage Rivers Initiative. 1997. Hearing before the Committee on Resources on H.R. 1842, to Terminate Further Development and Implementation of the American Heritage Rivers Initiative, 105th Cong., Serial No. 105-70, September 24.

"American Heritage Rivers Keystone Project: Cuyahoga River." 1998. US EPA, *American Heritage Rivers* 1, no. 1. https://web.archive.org/web/20110514184523/http://water.epa.gov/type/watersheds/named/heritage/keyDet.cfm.

"American Heritage Rivers Keystone Project: Detroit River." 1998. US EPA, *American Heritage Rivers*. https://web.archive.org/web/20110514184523/http://water.epa.gov/type/watersheds/named/heritage/keyDet.cfm.

"American Heritage Rivers Keystone Project Proposals 2002: Table of Contents." 2002. US EPA, *American Heritage Rivers*. https://web.archive.org/web/20110514172659/http://water.epa.gov/type/watersheds/named.

Bauerlein, David. 1998. "Heritage Judges Lack Area Member." *Florida Times Union*, April 10.

Breederland, Mark. 2022. Interview by the author. March 16.

Campaign Donations from Alexander Annett to George W. Bush. 1999–2004. FEC Filing 24991096307.

Chenoweth v. Clinton. 1999. 181 F.3d 112 (Dist. of Columbia Cir. 1999).

Clinton Presidential Records. Domestic Policy Council. Bruce Reed. Subject File. OA/Box No. 21205, "Ideas [1]."

Clinton, William. 1998. Remarks by the President at Designation of the New River as an American Heritage River. White House, Office of the Press Secretary, July 30.

Designated American Heritage Rivers. 2006. US EPA, Map.

"Detroit River Remedial Action Plan—Stage 1." 1991. Michigan Department of Natural Resources, June.

Downs, Thomas C. 1999. "American Heritage Rivers Initiative: A Harbinger of Future White House Environmental Policy?" *Environmental Law Reporter*, February. https://heinonline.org/HOL/LandingPage?handle=hein.journals/elrna29&div=14&id=&page=.

Exec. Order 13061. 1997. 3 C.F.R. 1317–1320, September 11.

"Executive Summary State of the River Report." 2009. US EPA, *American Heritage Rivers*. https://web.archive.org/web/20110514172703/http://water.epa.gov/type/watersheds/named/heritage/summary.cfm.

Friedland, Bruce. 2001. "Future of American Heritage Rivers Plan Still Up in the Air: Program from Clinton Could Change under Bush." *Florida Times Union*, February 28.

FOIA No. 2006-0458-F. N.d.a. Clinton Presidential Records, Communications, Don Baer, OA/Box No. 10137, "Overall Strategy."

FOIA No. 2006-0458-F. N.d.b. Clinton Presidential Records, Communications, Don Baer, OA/Box No. 10137, "Legacy Memos."

FOIA No. 2006-0458-F. N.d.c. Clinton Presidential Records, Communications, Don Baer, OA/Box No. 13425, "Communications Director Reading [2]."

FOIA No. 2006-0469-F. N.d.a. Clinton Presidential Records, Speechwriting, Michael Waldman, OA/Box No. 14443, "State of the Union 1997—The Original Drafts, Volume 1 [Binder] [1]."

FOIA No. 2006-0469-F (2). N.d.b. Clinton Presidential Records, Speechwriting, Michael Waldman, OA/Box No. 14450, "Message Schedules, Planning 1997."

FOIA No. 2006-0470-F. N.d.a. Clinton Presidential Records, Speechwriting, Lowell Weiss, OA/Box No. 17192, "Lewis and Clark 11/9/97."

FOIA No. 2006-0470-F. N.d.b. Clinton Presidential Records, Speechwriting, Lowell Weiss, OA/Box No. 17192, "Mt. Vernon American Heritage Rivers 9/11/97."

FOIA No. 2006-0470-F. N.d.c. Clinton Presidential Records, Speechwriting, Lowell Weiss, OA/Box No. 17194, "American Heritage Rivers II 7/30/98 [1]."

FOIA No. 2006-0470-F. N.d.d. Clinton Presidential Records, Speechwriting, Lowell Weiss, OA/Box No. 17194, "American Heritage Rivers II 7/30/98 [2]."

FOIA No. 2006-0470-F. N.d.e. Clinton Presidential Records, Speechwriting, Lowell Weiss, OA/Box No. 17194, "American Heritage Rivers II 7/30/98 [3]."

FOIA No. 2012-0769-F. N.d.a. Clinton Presidential Records, Council on Environmental Policy, Kathleen McGinty, OA/Box No. 17806, "[Pacific Rivers Council Proposal] [Loose]."

FOIA No. 2012-0769-F. N.d.b. Clinton Presidential Records, Council on Environmental Policy, Kathleen McGinty, OA/Box No. 4299, "Rivers."

"Greater Detroit American Heritage River—State of the River 2001." US EPA, *American Heritage Rivers* (2001): 1–4.

Guldbrandsen, Thaddeus C., and Dorothy C. Holland. 2001. "Encounters with the Super-Citizen: Neoliberalism, Environmental Activism, and the American Heritage Rivers Initiative." *Anthropological Quarterly* 74, no. 3 (July): 124–34.

Hartig, John H. 2022. Interview with Kenneth Lowande. May 22.

Hartig, John H. 1988. "Development of Plans to Restore Degraded Areas In the Great Lakes." *Environmental Management* 12, no. 3 (May): 327–47.

Hartig, John. 2019. "Great Lakes Moment: Five Decades since the Infamous Rouge River Fire." *Great Lakes Now*, October 7.

Hartig, John H., and David Bennion. 2017. "Historical Loss and Current Rehabilitation of Shoreline Habitat along an Urban-Industrial River—Detroit River, Michigan, USA." *Sustainability* 9, no. 828: 1–20.

Hartig, John H., Gail Krantzberg, and Peter Alsip. 2020. "Thirty-five Years of Restoring Great Lakes Areas of Concern: Gradual Progress, Hopeful Future." *Journal of Great Lakes Research* 46: 429–42.

Jarvis, Craig. 2004. "Instinct, Personality Guide Burr's Rise." *Raleigh News & Observer*, October 27.

"John Hartig Biography." N.d. https://johnhartig.com/bio.

"Local Contacts: 14 American Heritage Rivers." 2003. US EPA, *American Heritage Rivers*. https://web.archive.org/web/20110514120353/http://water.epa.gov/type/watersheds/named/heritage/rivercon.cfm.

Low, Marsha. 2000. "Children Beautify Belle Isle In Nickelodeon Campaign." *Detroit Free Press*, August 7.

Manny, Bruce A., and D. Kenaga. 1991. "The Detroit River: Effects of Contaminants and Human Activities on Aquatic Plants and Animals and Their Habitats." *Hydrobiologia* 219:269–79.

Matheny, Keith. 2019. "Belle Isle Fish Habitat Project Blamed for Flooding This Summer but State Stands By It." *Detroit Free Press*, October 2.

Matheny, Keith. 2013. "Nature's Comeback." *Detroit Free Press*, June 3.

McGinty, Kathleen A. 1997. Memorandum for Bruce Reed and Jonathan Prince. "State of the Union Policy Ideas." Executive Office of the President, Council on Environmental Quality.

"Michigan Areas of Concern—Project Highlight: Detroit River." 2012–13. Blue Heron Lagoon Restoration, Michigan Office of the Great Lakes, September 2012–April 2013.

Michigan Wildlife Council. 2017. "Restoring the 'Jewel of Detroit.'" *Detroit Free Press*, July 10.

Mondry, Aaron. 2019. "A Decade of Change on the Detroit River." *Curbed Detroit*, December 17.

Kagan, Elena. 2001a. Domestic Policy Council—Policy Trading Drafts, Box 014, Folder 002, William J. Clinton Presidential Library.

Kagan, Elena. 2001b. Environment—National Heritage Rivers, Box 023, Folder 006, William J. Clinton Presidential Library.

Pearce, Jeremy. 2001. "Detroit Shore to Be Restored—Riverbank, Belle Isle Cleanup Plans Aided by Federal Money." *Detroit News*, September 28.

"Presidency; 14 'American Heritage' Rivers Named." 1998. *Dayton Daily News*, July 31.

"Rio Grande American Heritage River—State of the River 2001." 2001. US EPA, *American Heritage Rivers*: 1–6.

Rasmussen, Steve. 2002. "On the Waterfront: Did Property-Rights Paranoia Deprive Communities of Much-Needed Federal Funding?" *Mountain Express*, October 1.

Smith, Scott. 1998. "Protecting Our Rivers." *Wyoming Tribune-Eagle*, February 19.

U.S. Environmental Protection Agency. 1998. "American Heritage River News." *American Heritage Rivers* 1, no. 1 (October 5).

U.S. Environmental Protection Agency. 2004. "State of the River Report 2004—Detroit River (MI)." *American Heritage Rivers*.

"Weekend Briefing." 2000. *Detroit Free Press*, August 5.

Zinn, Jeffrey A., and Betsy Cody. 1998. "American Heritage Rivers." Report, UNT Digital Libraries, August 3. https://digital.library.unt.edu/ark:/67531/metadc809032/m1/1/.

Section 6.1: The Third Snare

Black, Amy E., Douglas L. Koopman, and David K. Ryden. 2004. *Of Little Faith: The Politics of George W. Bush's Faith-Based Initiatives*. Washington, DC: Georgetown University Press.

Bush, George W. 2001a. "Agency Responsibilities with Respect to Faith-Based and Community Initiatives." Executive Order 13198, January 29. *Federal Register* 66, no. 21: 8497–98.

Bush, George W. 2001b. "Establishment of White House Office of Faith-Based and Community Initiatives." Executive Order 13199, January 29. *Federal Register* 66, no. 21: 8499–8500.

Bush, George W. 2002a. "Equal Protection of the Laws for Faith-Based and Community Organizations." Executive Order 13279, December 12. *Federal Register* 67, no. 241: 77141–44.

Bush, George W. 2002b. "Responsibilities of the Department of Agriculture and the Agency for International Development with Respect to Faith-Based and Community Initiatives." Executive Order 13280, December 12. *Federal Register* 67, no. 241: 77145–46.

Bush, George W. 2004. "Responsibilities of the Departments of Commerce and Veterans Affairs and the Small Business Administration with Respect to Faith-Based and Community Initiatives." Executive Order 13342, June 1. *Federal Register* 69, no. 107: 31509–10.

Bush, George W. 2006. "Responsibilities of the Department of Homeland Security with Respect to Faith-Based and Community Initiatives." Executive Order 13397, March 7. *Federal Register* 71, no. 46: 12275–76.

Carlson-Thies, Stanley W. 2004. "Implementing the Faith-Based Initiative." *Public Interest* 155 (Spring): 57–74.

Carr, Rebecca. 2002. "Bush Scores Critics of Faith-Based Initiative." *Atlanta Constitution*, June 26, A3.

Dilulio, John. 2001. "Unlevel Playing Field." *Wall Street Journal*, August 16.

Dilulio, John, to Ron Suskind. 2002. Subject: Your Next Essay on the Bush Administration. Email communication, October 24.

Dilulio, John. 2010. *Godly Republic: A Centrist Blueprint for America's Faith-Based Future.* Berkeley and Los Angeles: University of California Press.

Goldenziel, Jill. 2005. "Administratively Quirky, Constitutionally Murky: The Bush Faith-Based Initiative." *New York University Journal of Legislation and Public Policy* 8, no. 2: 359–88.

Government Accountability Office. 2006. "Faith-Based and Community Initiative: Improvements in Monitoring Grantees and Measuring Performance Could Enhance Accountability." GAO-06-616, June 19.

Government Printing Office. Hearing before the Subcommittee on Criminal Justice, Drug Policy, and Human Resources of the Committee on Government Reform, House of Representatives One Hundred Ninth Congress, First Session, on H.R. 1054 to Establish the Office of Faith-Based and Community Initiatives. 2005. Serial No. 109-74, June 21.

Kuo, J. David. 2005. "Please, Keep Faith." Beliefnet.com, April. https://www.beliefnet.com/news/politics/2005/02/please-keep-faith.aspx.

Kuo, J. David. 2006. *Tempting Faith: An Inside Story of Political Seduction.* New York: Free Press.

Leonard, Mary. 2003. "Bush Presses Funding for Faith Groups." *Boston Globe*, November 30, A1.

Levin, Jeff. 2014. "Faith-Based Initiatives in Health Promotion: History, Challenges, and Current Partnerships." *American Journal of Health Promotion* 28, no. 3: 139–41.

Meyers, Mary Ann. 1997. "John Dilulio Gets Religion." *Philadelphia Gazette*, September 29.

Pew Research Center. 2003. "The Faith-Based Initiative Two Years Later: Examining Its Potential, Progress and Problems." March 5.

Pew Research Center. 2009. "Government Partnerships with Faith-Based Organizations: Looking Back, Moving Forward." June 11.

Sager, Rebecca. 2010. *Faith, Politics, and Power: The Politics of Faith-Based Initiatives.* Oxford and New York: Oxford University Press.

Schorr, Daniel. 2006. "A Loss of Faith." CBS News, October 14.

Sorin, Hillary. 2010. "Today in Texas History: GW Bush Delivers First Presidential Campaign Speech." *Chron*, July 22. https://blog.chron.com/txpotomac/2010/07/today-in-texas-history-gw-bush-delivers-first-presidential-campaign-speech/.

Tenpas, Kathryn Dunn. 2002. "Can an Office Change a Country? The White House Office of Faith-Based and Community Initiatives: A Year in Review." July. https://www.pewresearch.org/religion/2002/02/20/can-an-office-change-a-country-the-white-house-office-of-faith-based-and-community-initiatives-a-year-in-review/.

Tran, Mark. 2006. "Book Reveals White House Contempt for Religious Right." *Guardian*, October 13.

Tumulty, Karen. 2013. "J. David Kuo, Onetime Leader of Bush's Faith-Based Initiative, Dies at 44." *Washington Post*, April 6.

United States Supreme Court. 2007. Hein, Director, White House Office Of Faith-Based and Community Initiatives, et al. v. Freedom from Religion Foundation, Inc., et al. No. 06-157. Argued: February 28. Decided: June 25.

U.S. Department of Education. 2007. "An Evaluation of the Participation of Faith-Based and Community Organizations in U.S. Department of Education Discretionary Grant Programs and as Supplemental Educational Services Providers." December. https://www2.ed.gov/rschstat/eval/other/faith-based/faith-based.pdf.

Wallsten, Peter. 2006. "Book: Bush Aides Called Evangelicals 'Nuts.'" *LA Times*, October 13.

Weiner, Tim. 2012. "Charles W. Colson, Watergate Felon Who Became Evangelical Leader, Dies at 80." *New York Times*, April 21.

White House. 2001. "Unlevel Playing Field: Barriers to Participation by Faith-Based and Community Organizations in Federal Social Service Programs." https://georgewbush-whitehouse.archives.gov/news/releases/2001/08/unlevelfield.html.

White House. 2008a. "President Bush Attends Office of Faith-Based and Community Initiatives' National Conference." Office of the Press Secretary, June 26. https://georgewbush-whitehouse.archives.gov/news/releases/2008/06/20080626-20.html.

White House. 2008b. "Innovations in Compassion: The Faith-Based and Community Initiative; A Final Report to the Armies of Compassion." December. https://eric.ed.gov/?q=source%3A%22The+White+House%22&id=ED504226.

White House Counsel's Office. Brett Kavanaugh. Subject Files. Box 24. George W. Bush Presidential Library.

White House Office of Faith-Based and Community Initiatives. H. James (Jim) Towey. Subject Files. Box 1. George W. Bush Presidential Library.

Wright, David J. 2009. "Taking Stock: The Bush Faith-Based Initiative and What Lies Ahead." Roundtable on Religion and Social Welfare Policy, June 11.

Section 7.1: Carrot

Andrzejewski, Adam. 2020. "Trump's Leaner White House 2020 Payroll Saved Taxpayers $23.5 Million since 2017." *Forbes*, June 30.

Anemona Hartocollis, and Noah Weiland. 2017. "Handshakes at the White House, Hand-Wringing at Black Colleges." *New York Times*, late ed. (East Coast), March 4, A1.

Associated Press. 2019. "President Trump Lifts Funding Ban for Faith-Based Historically Black Colleges." September 11.

Biden, Joseph R. 2021. "White House Initiative on Advancing Educational Equity, Excellence, and Economic Opportunity through Historically Black Colleges and Universities." Executive Order 14041, September 3, *Federal Register* 86, no. 172: 50443–47.

Binkley, Collin. 2019. "Trump Signs Bill Restoring Funding for Black Colleges." AP News, December 19.

Bush, George H. W. 1989. "Historically Black Colleges and Universities." Executive Order 12677, April 28. https://www.presidency.ucsb.edu/documents/executive-order -12677-historically-black-colleges-and-universities.

Bush, George W. 2002. "President's Board of Advisors on Historically Black Colleges and Universities." Executive Order 13256, February 12. Code of Federal Regulations, Title 3: 200–202.

Carter, Jimmy. 1980. "Historically Black Colleges and Universities." Executive Order 12232, August 8. https://www.presidency.ucsb.edu/documents/executive-order -12232-historically-black-colleges-and-universities.

Clinton Presidential Records. Domestic Policy Council. Gaynor McCown. Subject Files. OA/Box No. 7384, "HBCUs [Historically Black Colleges and Universities]."

Clinton, William J. 1993. "Historically Black Colleges and Universities." Executive Order 12876, November 1. *Weekly Compilation of Presidential Documents*, 2234–37.

Cobb, Jelani. 2018. "Under Trump, a Hard Test for Howard University." *New Yorker*, August 15.

Cohen, Kelly. 2017. "White House Formally Names Head of Historically Black Colleges Initiative, a Non-HBCU Alumnus." *Washington [DC] Examiner*, 18 September.

Dennard, Paris. 2020. "HBCUs Have a Champion in President Trump." *Diverse*, September 24. https://www.diverseeducation.com/demographics/african-american/article/ 15107830/hbcus-have-a-champion-in-president-trump#:~:text=In%20a%20recent %20article%20in,a%20difference%20for%20America's%20HBCUs.

Douglas-Gabriel, Danielle. 2017. "Trump Moves Program on Historically Black Colleges into the White House." *Washington Post*, February 28.

Harris, Adam. 2017. "Trump Struggles to Find a Leader for White House Initiative on Black Colleges." *Chronicle of Higher Education*, July 25.

Jamerson, Joshua. 2020. "Historically Black Colleges Become Focus of Biden, Trump Outreach." *Wall Street Journal*, October 25.

Keith, Tamara. 2017. "Trump White House Staff Payroll Nearly $36 Million And Top-Heavy." NPR, June 30.

Kimbrough, Walter M. 2017. "My Statement: White House HBCU Event." *Medium*, February 27. https://hiphopprez.medium.com/my-statement-white-house-hbcu-event -bf51a619194a.

Korn, Melissa. 2017. "Loan Program for Black Colleges Struggles with Oversight, Repayment." *Wall Street Journal*, July 17.

Kreighbaum, Andrew. 2018. "Omarosa on DeVos and HBCUs." *Inside Higher Ed*, August 17. https://www.insidehighered.com/news/2018/08/17/white-house-tell-all -omarosa-manigault-newman-blasts-devos.

Kreighbaum, Andrew. 2019. "Trump Asserts New Win for Religious HBCUs." *Inside Higher Ed*, September 11. https://www.insidehighered.com/news/2019/09/11/trump -administration-acts-funding-restrictions-religious-hbcus.

Lee, Kurtis. 2017. "Historically Black Colleges View Trump Administration Warily, but Also with Some Optimism." *LA Times*, May 19.

McCarthy, Bill. 2020. "Trump's Exaggerated Claim That He 'Saved' HBCUs with 2019 Funding Bill." *Politifact*, October 27. https://www.politifact.com/factchecks/ 2020/oct/27/donald-trump/trumps-exaggerated-claim-he-saved-hbcus-2019 -fundi/.

Mervis, Jeffery. 2017. "Trump's White House Science Office Still Small and Waiting for Leadership." *Science Insider*, July 11. https://www.science.org/content/article/trump -s-white-house-science-office-still-small-and-waiting-leadership#:~:text=OSTP %20is%20not%20alone%20across,as%20the%20president's%20science%20adviser.

Obama, Barack. 2010. "Promoting Excellence, Innovation, and Sustainability at Histor- ically Black Colleges and Universities." Executive Order 13532, Office of the Press Secretary, February 26. https://obamawhitehouse.archives.gov/the-press-offi ce/ promoting-excellence-innovation-and-sustainability-historically-black-colleges- and-universities.

Reagan, Ronald. 1981. "Historically Black Colleges and Universities." Executive Order 12320, September 15. https://www.reaganlibrary.gov/archives/speech/executive -order-12320-historically-black-colleges-and-universities.

Rosenblatt, Lauren. 2017. "Trump's Promise to Black Colleges Unmet." *Chicago Tribune*, September 17.

Supreme Court of the United States, Trinity Lutheran Church of Columbia, Inc. v. Comer, Director, Missouri Department of Natural Resources, No. 15-577. 2017. Argued April 19; decided June 26.

Trump, Donald J. 2017. "White House Initiative to Promote Excellence and Innovation at Historically Black Colleges and Universities." Executive Order 13779, February 28. *Federal Register* 82, no. 41: 12499–502.

Trump, Donald J. 2017. "Remarks by President Trump at Signing of the HBCU Exec- utive Order." White House, February 28. https://trumpwhitehouse.archives.gov/ presidential-actions/remarks-president-trump-signing-hbcu-executive-order/.

Vasquez, Maegan, and Kevin Liptak. 2019. "Trump Announces Lift on Funding Ban for Faith-Based Institutions in HBCU Pitch." CNN, September 10. https://www.cnn .com/2019/09/10/politics/donald-trump-hbcu-conference/index.html.

Watson, Jamal Eric. 2019. "Holifield Works to advance Interests of HBCUs within the Trump Administration." *Diverse*, August 9. https://www.diverseeducation.com/ institutions/hbcus/article/15105225/holifield-works-to-advance-interests-of-hbcus -within-trump-administration.

Whitaker, Henry C. 2019. "Religious Restrictions on Capital Financing for Histor- ically Black Colleges and Universities." Memorandum Opinion for the Acting General Counsel Department of Education, August 15. https://www.justice.gov/ olc/file/1350166/download#:~:text=Congress%20separately%20barred%20the %20Department,§%201068e(1).

"Why Is Interest Growing in America's Black Colleges and Universities?" 2020. *Econo- mist*, September 19.

Section 8.4: All the Way Down

Associated Press. 2020. "Activist Apologizes after Refusing to Leave Playground," April 26. https://apnews.com/article/virus-outbreak-us-news-boise-arrests-id-state-wire -e33527e1cab34387c27ac287f9dc523b.

Baeza, Benito. 2021. "Acting as Idaho Governor, Lt. Gov. McGeachin Signs Executive Order on Mask Mandates." KLIX News Radio, May 27.

Blake, Aaron. 2021. "The Political Craziness in Idaho." *Washington Post*, October 6.

Boone, Rebecca. 2020. "Idaho Healthcare Leaders Plead for Coronavirus Mandate." AP News, July 15. https://apnews.com/general-news -6ad1c6878577347c19dae2eb5e9b05aa.

Constitution of the State of Idaho. 1890. Approved July 3.

Corbin, Clark. 2021. "Report: Gov. Little and Lt. Gov. McGeachin Haven't Spoken since Executive Order Flap." *Moscow-Pullman Daily News*, June 2.

Dawson, James. 2020. "Gov. Little Says He Hasn't Spoken to Lt. Gov. McGeachin in Weeks." Boise State Public Radio News, May 6.

Dawson, James. 2022. "Lt. Gov. McGeachin on Fauci: I'll 'Lock Him Up.'" Boise State Public Radio News, February 15. https://www.boisestatepublicradio.org/politics -government/2022-02-15/lt-gov-mcgeachin-on-fauci-ill-lock-him-up.

Dawson, James. 2022. "Idaho Gov. Brad Little Wins GOP Primary over Trump's Pick, Lt. Gov. Janice McGeachin." Boise State Public Radio, May 18. https://www.knkx.org/ politics/2022-05-17/idaho-gov-brad-little-wins-gop-primary-over-trumps-pick-lt -gov-janice-mcgeachin.

Druzin, Heath. 2020. "Low Turnout For COVID-19 Skeptic Rally Headlined by Idaho Lieutenant Governor." Boise State Public Radio News, August 3. https://www .boisestatepublicradio.org/politics-government/2020-08-03/low-turnout-for-covid -19-skeptic-rally-headlined-by-idaho-lieutenant-governor.

Fixler, Kevin. 2022. "Never Back Down: How Janice McGeachin Rose from Anonymity to Trump's Pick for Governor." *Idaho Statesman*, May 8.

Hassan, Carma, and Josh Campbell. 2021. "Idaho Governor and Lieutenant Governor Get into Twitter Fight over State's Executive Order." CNN, October 7. https://www .wdsu.com/article/idaho-s-governor-accuses-lieutenant-governor-of-attempting-to -deploy-national-guard-to-border-without-authorization/37883638.

Hawkins, Derek. 2021. "Idaho Lieutenant Governor Banned Mask Mandates while the Governor Was Out of Town. It Didn't Last." *Washington Post*, May 28.

Hyning, Celina Van. 2021. "Donald Trump Endorses McGeachin for Idaho Governor." CNN, November 9. https://www.ktvb.com/article/news/politics/trump-endorses -mcgeachin/277-b6db1f08-a46f-4977-ba0a-ab60478336b6.

Idaho Department of Health and Welfare. 2021. Declaration of Crisis Standards of Care, September 16. https://coronavirus.idaho.gov/wp-content/uploads/2021/09/CSC -Statewide-Declaration.pdf.

Krutzig, Sally, Alex Brizee, and Ryan Suppe. 2022. "Idaho Lt. Gov. Janice McGeachin Wants Gov. Little to Intervene in Child Welfare Case." *Idaho Statesman*, March 15.

Little, Brad. 2021. "Repealing Executive Order No. 2021-13." Executive Order 2021-14, October 6. https://gov.idaho.gov/wp-content/uploads/2021/12/eo-2021-14_rev.pdf.

Malloy, Chuck. 2022. "Opinion: Give Taxpayers a Break, Janice, and Do Nothing." *Lewiston Tribune*, September 4.

McGeachin, Janice. 2020. "It's Up to Idahoans to Ameliorate Government's Heavy Hand." IDED News, May 13. https://www.idahoednews.org/voices/its-up-to -idahoans-to-ameliorate-governments-heavy-hand/.

Pfannenstiel, Kyle. 2021. "McGeachin's Office Used Misleading Number to Disparage COVID Vaccines." *Idaho Falls Post Register*, September 2.

Ridler, Keith. 2021a. "Lt. Gov. Janice McGeachin Announces Run for Idaho Governor." AP News, May 19. https://apnews.com/article/idaho-health-coronavirus-pandemic -government-and-politics-a074994845d53b1c93a01e2617be025d.

Ridler, Keith. 2021b. "Idaho Lieutenant Governor Keeps Focus on Vaccine Mandates." AP News, July 20. https://apnews.com/article/business-health-government-and-politics -coronavirus-pandemic-idaho-7378216f7c72faebf2acdfc28795e0c4.

Ridler, Keith. 2021c. "Idaho Governor Repeals Political Rival's Executive Order." AP News, October 6. https://www.kivitv.com/news/political/inside-the-statehouse/ idaho-governor-repeals-political-rivals-executive-order.

Rohrlich, Justin. 2020. "Idaho's Anti-Lockdown Lieutenant Governor Has Gone Rogue." *Daily Beast*, May 25. https://www.thedailybeast.com/idahos-lt-gov-janice -mcgeachin-has-gone-rogue-over-coronavirus.

Russell, Betsy. 2022. "Little Heads to Governors' Conference in Nashville, Keeps Duties in Snub to McGeachin." *Idaho Press*, May 24.

"Tracking Coronavirus in Idaho: Latest Map and Case Count." 2022. *New York Times*, September 20.

"We the People of Idaho Reaffirm our Commitment to Freedom." 2020. Washington Post, October 27 [video]. https://www.washingtonpost.com/video/politics/campaign -ads-2020/idaho-freedom-tv-we-the-people-of-idaho-reaffirm-our-commitment-to -freedom-campaign-2020/2020/10/30/732cf8e4-231a-48bf-bd22-3385fafc1165_video .html.

INDEX

Page numbers in *italics* refer to figures.

Chicago Studies in American Politics

A series edited by Susan Herbst, Lawrence R. Jacobs, Adam J. Berinsky, and Frances Lee; Benjamin I. Page, editor emeritus

The Social Citizen: Peer Networks and Political Behavior
by Betsy Sinclair

Follow the Leader? How Voters Respond to Politicians' Policies and Performance
by Gabriel S. Lenz

The Timeline of Presidential Elections: How Campaigns Do (and Do Not) Matter
by Robert S. Erikson and Christopher Wlezien

Electing Judges: The Surprising Effects of Campaigning on Judicial Legitimacy
by James L. Gibson

Disciplining the Poor: Neoliberal Paternalism and the Persistent Power of Race
by Joe Soss, Richard C. Fording, and Sanford F. Schram

*The Submerged State: How Invisible Government Policies
Undermine American Democracy*
by Suzanne Mettler

Selling Fear: Counterterrorism, the Media, and Public Opinion
by Brigitte L. Nacos, Yaeli Bloch-Elkon, and Robert Y. Shapiro

Why Parties? A Second Look
by John H. Aldrich

Obama's Race: The 2008 Election and the Dream of a Post-Racial America
by Michael Tesler and David O. Sears

News That Matters: Television and American Opinion, Updated Edition
by Shanto Iyengar and Donald R. Kinder

Filibustering: A Political History of Obstruction in the House and Senate
by Gregory Koger

Us Against Them: Ethnocentric Foundations of American Opinion
by Donald R. Kinder and Cindy D. Kam

*The Partisan Sort: How Liberals Became Democrats and
Conservatives Became Republicans*
by Matthew Levendusky

Democracy at Risk: How Terrorist Threats Affect the Public
by Jennifer L. Merolla and Elizabeth J. Zechmeister

www.ingramcontent.com/pod-product-compliance
Lightning Source LLC
Chambersburg PA
CBHW031556060326
40783CB00026B/4095